Approaches to moral
development.

DATE		

Approaches to Moral Development

New Research and Emerging Themes

Approaches to Moral Development

New Research and Emerging Themes

Edited by
Andrew Garrod

Teachers College, Columbia University
New York and London

Published by Teachers College Press, 1234 Amsterdam Avenue, New York, N.Y. 10027

Library of Congress Cataloging-in-Publication Data

Approaches to moral development: new research and emerging themes/
  edited by Andrew Garrod.
    p. cm.
  Includes bibliographical references and index.
  ISBN 0-8077-3247-8 (hard: alk. paper).—ISBN 0-8077-3246-X
(pbk.: alk. paper)
    1. Moral development.   I. Garrod. Andrew, 1937–
BF723.M54A66 1993
155.2'5—dc20   92-44918

0-8077-3247-8
0-8077-3246-X (pbk.)

Printed on acid-free paper
Manufactured in the United States of America
99 98 97 96 95 94 93 8 7 6 5 4 3 2 1

This book is dedicated to the memories of my mother and father.

Contents

Foreword

Although the proper moral development of its young is central to any society's welfare, the study of moral development occupied little more than a marginal position in academic life until well into this century. The scholarly lack of interest in moral development may have been just another case of intellectuals coming late to common concerns. But there also were some stubborn points of resistance in the university dogmas of the day. The behavioral sciences were uncomfortable with moral phenomena, considering them too subjective for serious study. The humanities were uncomfortable with the notion of development, considering it an idea with dangerously arbitrary meanings. Not until the 1960s did the logjam break, largely due to Lawrence Kohlberg's galvanizing research program. Kohlberg's great contribution was to show how moral development could be studied in a manner that was empirically sound at the same time as it was philosophically coherent. The results were informative. The present volume, while going beyond Kohlberg's own insights, follows in the expansive tradition that he fostered.

There is no question that moral development has made its way into the heart of academe by now. Studies flourish in psychology, philosophy, education, anthropology, sociology, and even biology. The only real question is perhaps the most basic one: What does "moral development" mean to all the diversity of scholars who have become interested in it? This is a question that would take a book in itself to address. It is clear from the start that there are multiple answers to this question. Rather than a single construct, the answer is a loose constellation of ideas that may have little or nothing to do with one another.

As an example, take the tripartite distinction between moral reflection, moral emotion, and moral conduct—the head, the heart, and the habit, in ancient, tried-but-true phraseology. Clearly, these three are all of interest to the study of moral development. But they are rarely examined together, and when they are, it is hard to find robust associations between them.

Part of the problem is method, part with the nature of the populations studied, and part with our visions of morality. Observations of conduct tell us little about intention, the key indicator of moral meaning. Instruments for studying moral reflection, such as interviews and narrative analysis, are not compelling for plumbing the depths of moral feeling or for predicting action. Very young children, who make the best subjects for experiments on moral affect and habit, make the worst subjects for studies of moral reflection. And so on, which creates a clutter of disconnected findings. Throughout the disarray, there is a sense that our visions of morality are not well joined. Are we in fact looking at one thing or at many? Should we expect to find connections between the head, the heart, and the habit or should we be content to understand them separately and to argue, implicitly or explicitly, about which has the greater moral import?

If the study of moral development were a mere academic exercise, we could rest with the latter enterprise and keep protecting our own turf. But moral development is front-page headlines today. The values and conduct of our young, of our political leaders, and of ourselves have become the cause of a cultural crisis that our society faces. There is some urgency to this issue. This is a time when our efforts and insights must be coordinated to maximal possible effect.

What appeals to me most about *Appoaches to Moral Development: New Research and Emerging Themes* is the way it reaches out to engage some of the questions about moral development that we now need to understand. There is work on the origins of morality in the home, on the fostering of morality in the schools, and on the directions of morality in young adulthood. There is work on moral thought and on moral feeling, and there are examinations of how young people make moral choices in the heat of real-life conflicts. The collection takes unexpected turns and opens new possibilities. It bridges the gap between our academic interests and our societal concerns.

I see this collection as a beginning of some new routes to exploration—routes that take us into the meaning of community, diversity, and the stories that young people tell about their own lives. My own belief is that these avenues could be profitably integrated into other worthwhile approaches that begin with diverging assumptions; the character development focus of places such as Boston University's Center for Advancement of Ethics and Character is but one example. What Martin Hoffman in Chapter 8 says of empathic capacity is also true of scholarship. We all have our biases, and these can have their uses—whether for empathy or for truth seeking. But in the long run, best results will be achieved by minimizing bias and encouraging impartiality. The "whole picture" of moral development is enormously complex and multifaceted. No doubt it will elude us for some time to come. When we finally capture it, it will be through piecing together the puzzle parts gained by many innovative enterprises such as this one.

William Damon
Brown University

Acknowledgments

This book was, in part, made possible by generous funding from the Presidential Venture Fund at Dartmouth College, which supported a two-day international conference on moral development and moral education at the college in 1988. To Gregory Norman, who was the coordinator of that conference, I am deeply grateful—for his patience, persistence, and organizational skills.

In helping me to edit and assemble the book, I owe very special thanks to Jay Davis and Kevin Lewis; their intelligence, good judgment, and editorial skills considerably improved the quality of the final manuscript. I am also grateful to Marcia Finley for her editorial suggestions, and to Timothy Hodsdon for his assistance with the manuscript in its early stages.

Finally, the staff of Teachers College Press has been enormously supportive throughout the preparation of this book. At critical points, Brian Ellerbeck and Cathy McClure have shown encouragement and good humor as well as confidence in the publication of these essays. Their support, and the support of the late Ron Galbraith, has been sustaining and invaluable. A final thank you to Nancy Berliner for her meticulous preparation of the manuscript and proofs for publication.

Introduction

Andrew Garrod

Dartmouth College

A year after the tragic death in 1987 of Lawrence Kohlberg, a seminal figure in the field of moral psychology and moral education, there seemed a need for scholars, researchers, and educators aligned with the developmental school to do some stock-taking of past thinking and programs and to explore future lines of research and practice that held promise. Out of this need came the conference "Old Challenges/New Directions in Moral Education: What Parents, Teachers, and Colleges Can Do," held at Dartmouth College, New Hampshire, in 1988. Three central foci of the conference were the burgeoning research on moral orientation, girls' development, and moral education. The chapters in this book, primarily based on presentations at the Dartmouth conference, reflect emphases within the developmental tradition, and present various approaches—theoretical and practical—to moral development and education. These approaches fall into three interrelated categories: (a) the process of *knowing* and the connection to moral issues, (b) the process of *reasoning* about moral choices, and (c) the process of *teaching* and how particular interventions may aid moral development. The lines are not, of course, clear cut, since some chapters explore two out of three processes identified (e.g., Langdale [chapter 2], Hoffman [chapter 8]).

Since this book is based on a developmental model, the contributions are presented as they refer to three age groups: (1) childhood, (2) adolescence, and (3) young adulthood. The first age group, childhood, which Kohlberg characterized as marked by both a punishment and obedience orientation and a concern for instrumental hedonism, is examined here for the earliest signs of moral understanding; for the connections between peer relationships, gender identity, and moral development; and for sex differences in moral orientation. The second age group, composed of adolescents now capable of abstract reasoning, is described by Kohlberg in terms of conventional morality and a shift from the concrete interests of individuals to the standards of one's group or society— from concern with the self to care for others and a subsequent legalism. Here the important role of the family as an environment for the adolescent's moral socialization is considered—a topic not discussed in Kohlberg's work. The major concern of the adolescent section is a focus on our need to broaden our understanding of what constitutes development; in particular, we concentrate on the development of adolescent girls, who have only recently begun to receive adequate attention in research. The final age group—young adulthood—which is customarily discussed in moral developmental literature in terms of autonomous moral reasoning (what Kohlberg calls stage 5 of his postconventional level) is examined here not only through the Kohlbergian lens but also through the lenses of empathy and moral development, epistemology and moral development, and mentoring and moral development.

Finally, since many recent studies of moral development have highlighted the topic of gender differences in ways of moral knowing and reasoning, three chapters deal with this issue, not only conceptually and practically but also with suggestions for interventions to assist the moral development of both girls and boys.

Part I: Childhood

Three of the chapters in Part I deal with different aspects of moral development among young children and development via parents, peers, and teachers. The fourth chapter focuses on the overarching goal of teachers: to be aware of, and develop, students' ways of knowing.

Sharon Lamb, in "The Beginnings of Morality," examines the interactions between four mothers and their young children (1–2 years old) within the general developmental theory of the Kohlbergian stage 1 orientation, "Fear of Punishment" and the later orientation "Development of Empathy." The mothers' quality of prohibitions of certain behavior is categorized, as are the reactions of the children. The intensity of the prohibition was found to be related to the mothers' judgment of the seriousness of the transgression if it entailed danger to self and harm to others, but not if it entailed destruction of property. In addition, Lamb found that the children's behavior was not always influenced by the intensity of the mothers' prohibitions. Lamb's discussions of these and other findings highlight the importance of focusing on the development of the natural emotions as a precursor to the later development of moral reasoning.

In her chapter, "Moral Development, Gender Identity, and Peer Relationships in Early and Middle Childhood," Sharry Langdale examines both the formation of gender identity in school-age children and how this identity leads to the formation of distinct moral orientations. She highlights the mounting evidence that children's relationships tend to be formed in same-gender peer groups. The formation of these gender-specific groups is linked to the different ways in which boys and girls conceive the "self." Within these groups, Langdale found that moral statements made within boys' groups tended to show an emerging orientation towards Fairness (or Justice) whereas in girls' groups, statements were made that reflected an orientation towards Care. Since gender-specific peer groups are a primary context of the development of moral orientations, and since adults who are care-givers for young children have presumably been themselves socialized in such peer groups, it is important that adults be aware of their own gender-biases and understand how these affect and mold the moral orientations of school-age children.

Garrod and Beal point out in "Voices of Care and Justice in Children's Responses to Fable Dilemmas" that while much research has focused on issues of justice in children's moral learning, much less is known about children's use of the care orientation in dealing with their moral problems. Responding to this gap, they report on a study conducted with 132 children, ages 5–12, from a range of socioeconomic backgrounds. As there is not yet a consistent method for coding moral orientation in real-life dilemmas, fables were used as the moral dilemmas, and the children were asked how they would solve the problems in these fables. In addressing these moral problems, the children were significantly more likely to assess a care orientation as the best solution than to offer it as a spontaneous solution. Although much of the literature indebted to Gilligan's theorizing indicates that it is girls who are more likely to follow a care orientation, Garrod and Beal found that not only did the children offer the same kind of reasoning regardless of the fable's content, there was also no difference between boys and girls at any grade level. In addition, there was a marginally significant relationship between moral orientation and class. Finally, the ability to explain the logic of both orientations to the fable problems was correlated with the children's use of abstract reasoning skills on beginning formal operational tasks.

In "Minding the Curriculum: Of Student Epistemology and Faculty Conspiracy," Robert Kegan draws on his belief that the common goal of all teachers is the development of the student. He suggests that this common goal can transcend differences in individual teaching styles or ideologies. He believes that the tensions that inevitably arise on faculties when different teachers have differing personalities are not insoluble. Instead, these tensions reflect a lack of awareness of one unifying goal at which all teachers aim: the ongoing development of their students' minds. In hopes of increasing this awareness, Kegan first establishes a continuum of teaching philosophies, ranging from a "back to the basics" philosophy to a "whole child" philosophy. The former stresses the acquisition and mastery of a set of cognitive skills, while the latter emphasizes the need for attention to a student's emotional and social development. By using hypothetical examples from high school literature classes, Kegan shows that committed and well-trained teachers, regardless of their placement on the philosophical continuum, give priority to the students' mental development.

Part II: Adolescence

Here some key aspects of adolescent development are reflected on by Reimer, Gilligan, and Lyons. Reimer, in his chapter "The Case of the Missing Family: Kohlberg and the Study of Adolescent Moral Development," indicates a gap in the Kohlbergian approach to moral socialization. Kohlberg's early work focused on individual moral development, and only in his later years did he study the school as an environment that influenced moral maturity. However, Reimer's interest lies with the family as an environment for moral socialization. He emphasizes the characteristics of the family that help to develop more maturity in adolescents, and underscores the need for affective support and freedom to discuss moral issues.

Carol Gilligan, in her chapter "Adolescent Development Reconsidered," advocates a reconsideration of the psychology of adolescence and adolescent development. She outlines what she sees to be the four fundamental reasons for changing our way of thinking about adolescence: (1) children are much more concerned with their connections to others than had been previously thought; (2) girls have not been sufficiently studied—a fact that invalidates any meaningful discussions of self, development, and relationship; (3) our concept of cognition relies too heavily on the Piagetian view that we live in a timeless world of abstract rules; and (4) psychologists have placed too much emphasis on separation, individuation, and autonomy when studying development. Gilligan underscores the need for teachers and students alike to engage in communal enterprises to address these biases in moral education.

In "Luck, Ethics, and Ways of Knowing: Observations on Adolescents' Deliberations in Making Moral Choices," Nona Lyons describes how life's unexpected situations or contingencies are a factor in people's ethical decision making. Her chapter looks at moral decisions from two perspectives—examining how moral conflict arises from one's relations to others, and exploring how life's chance events are a substantial part of the conflicts adolescents try to resolve. This way of thinking about moral decision making has not been seriously explored in adolescent moral development studies. These tend to argue that adolescents are usually motivated by idealistic notions of morality, which they may or may not be able to transfer to the realm of the unexpected "here and now," the position of the pack dealt to them by "Lady Luck." Thus Lyons argues that one important but little explored strand of adolescent development is the emerging ability to see, acknowledge, and deal with life's realities and contingencies.

Part III: Young Adulthood

This section contains chapters on four aspects of moral development in young adulthood: empathy and moral development (Hoffman), epistemology and moral development in college age women (Clinchy), moral development in college students (Rest), and the effect of mentoring communities on moral development (Parks).

Hoffman's chapter "Empathy, Social Cognition, and Moral Education," shows how four affective components are necessary parts of any comprehensive moral theory. These are empathic distress, sympathetic distress, guilt, and empathic anger. Such components are related to both the Care and the Justice orientation in moral decision making. An awareness of these affective states may also sensitize those who behave (actors) and those who comment (observers) in situations where the plight of certain victims might otherwise go unnoticed. This chapter has obvious implications for moral education and socialization.

In "Ways of Knowing and Ways of Being: Epistemological and Moral Development in Undergraduate Women," Blythe Clinchy claims that the predominant mode of knowledge among many undergraduate women can be identified as *connected knowing*. Such connected knowing is oriented more toward understanding than toward evaluation. It relies more on the concrete particularities of first-hand experience than on abstract principles or authoritative pronouncements. It involves feeling as well as reason and is rooted in personal relationship with the object of knowledge. Clinchy discusses some implications of connected knowing for moral judgment. For example, the obligation to understand a person's actions makes it difficult to judge the action if it is divorced from the complex considerations of the "actor" in the situation. This holistic view of actor–act–situation is a useful perspective from which to engage in moral education.

James Rest, in "Research on Moral Judgment in College Students," summarizes the evidence that shows how students' moral judgment advances dramatically in the college years. Within the college experience, he examines the success of moral education programs, the effects on moral development of students' areas of specialization, and aspects of the curricular and extracurricular experience that are related to desirable moral characteristics of graduates in later life. This focus on young adults in transition to the complexities of moral living will be of interest to parents, teachers, and all who are in care-giving roles related to this sensitive age group.

Sharon Parks, in the final chapter "Young Adults, Mentoring Communities, and the Conditions of Moral Choice," distinguishes young adulthood from both adolescence and a fully equilibrated adult stance, and stresses that young adulthood is a sensitive period in the formation of moral commitments. In such formations, she claims, there is not only an appropriate need for worthy mentors but also for the heretofore little recognized but necessary role of "mentoring communities." Such mentoring communities are a unique and necessary form of socialization for morally mature young adults. Parks points to the gap in the moral maturation of young adults who are deprived of such mentoring communities. This chapter is yet another pointer to the need for care, connectedness, and support in the moral socialization of young adults.

PART I

Childhood

CHAPTER 1

The Beginnings of Morality

Sharon Lamb

Bryn Mawr College

How we become moral human beings is one of the oldest philosophical questions. Throughout history, philosophers, priests, and psychologists have wondered whether civilization instills in each of us a sense of right and wrong or whether it takes away inborn benevolent inclinations—whether rational thinking or biological forces lead people, in spite of selfish wishes, toward moral behavior. Unfortunately, researchers have focused all too infrequently on the early years of life and the context in which the beginnings of moral awareness may unfold.

At What Age Morality? Traditional Psychological Views

Child development research in the past focused not on the child but on techniques of child rearing: how to raise "good" (well-behaved) children, not necessarily "good" (concerned and empathic) children. When the child did serve as subject, the main interest was in when and how a child internalizes parental controls so as to develop self-monitored "good" behavior. Such internalization was not thought to occur until around age four or five, and in this sense the early years had been neglected. Psychoanalytic theory, also concerned with internalization of parental controls, placed the beginning of moral awareness at around age five, when the Oedipal complex was resolved. Cognitive psychologists, following Piaget (1952), were convinced that before the age of seven, children were cognitively egocentric. Social psychologists like Lewin (1942) believed children under the age of eight to be incapable of considering the needs of others before the needs of self.

Moral theorists even more blatantly ignored the very young child. Kohlberg (1981) envisaged moral development as emerging parallel to the development of reason and did not discuss what might be discovered in the

9

practically preverbal child. Turiel (1980) also claimed that reasoning is at the core of an individual's moral functioning, and others (Stent, 1980) concluded that the prerequisites for morality are the ability to differentiate self and other, to infer feelings, and to recognize goals, intentions, and consequences of one's actions. These cognitive skills automatically point the researcher to the older child.

Recent Research on Early Childhood

Despite this traditional focus on the older child, more recent research has presented evidence of "moral" action, feeling, and thought in the preschool years and suggests that events during the second year of life may be essential to moral development. It is now recognized that very young children do exhibit prosocial behaviors. They help care for baby siblings (Dunn, Kendrick, & MacNamee, 1981), and they share with, help, nurture, and try to protect other children (Bar-Tal, Raviv, & Goldberg, 1982; Radke-Yarrow, Zahn-Waxler, & King, 1976; Rheingold & Emery, 1986; Rheingold & Hay, 1980). Empathy also seems to emerge in the second year. Between 12 and 20 months, children will respond to distress by orienting to another (Eisenberg-Berg, 1982). During the second year, toddlers cry less, show empathic distress in facial responses, begin to make tentative approaches to victims, and sometimes attempt to comfort others in distress (Hoffman, 1982). Children as young as 14 months have been observed to exhibit empathic responding (Dunn, 1988; Dunn & Kendrick, 1979). In a study of empathy in the preschool years (Zahn-Waxler & Radke-Yarrow, 1982), children of 18 months responded to an average of one third of all distresses. The greatest increase of altruism in response to a distress situation was found in children between the ages of 16 and 24 months. Positive initiations to others in distress began to appear at 12 months and included tentative pattings or touching of the person. These contacts became more differentiated and more frequent by 18 to 24 months.

Research on children's awareness of standards has focused primarily on the teaching of values and self-control, which, in turn, encourages children to live by accepted social rules. For over 2 decades, researchers have analyzed primarily maternal control techniques (Minton, Kagan, & Levine, 1971; Olim, Hess, & Shipman, 1967); however, some of the literature on standards focused specifically on the young child's increasing ability to inhibit his or her actions and to comply with parental desires (Erikson, 1963; Flavell, 1977; Gesell & Amatruda, 1945; Vaughn, Kopp, & Krakow, 1984). Kopp claims that during the second year, the integration of cognitive, social, and communicative abilities (Nelson, 1979), as well as the beginning of representational thinking (Bruner, 1972; Piaget, 1952) and recall memory (McCall, Parke, & Kavanaugh, 1977; Piaget, 1962), enable children to control themselves. Yet a study by Vaughn, Kopp, and Krakow (1984) sees 18-month-olds as restraining themselves only fleetingly in experimental tasks. Such research takes the limited view that self-control is merely a reflection of the desire for autonomy and is a result of the internalization of the caregiver.

Kagan (1981), on the other hand, suggests that children have a natural interest in standards and that children's self-control has internal motivation apart from caregivers' teachings. In Kagan's studies, children in the latter half of the second year displayed concern over an object or event that violated something that adults regard as normative and showed distress at a broken toy or a torn piece of clothing. Children's speech first referred to standards after 19 months, and children expressed distress after an examiner modeled an act that was too difficult for them to imitate. Kagan suggested that these children were aware of a standard of performance and were upset because they could not meet it. Largo and Howard (1979) showed that children over 15 months can judge whether a task is "too easy" for them. And when completing a difficult task, young children will sometimes smile whether or not an adult is present (Kagan, 1981; Stipek & McClintic, 1989).

In a longitudinal study of moral development in the second year, Lamb (1991a) observed that a peak in awareness of standards occurred between 17 and 18 months. Furthermore, maternal communications regarding behaviors indicative of an awareness of standards increased and decreased in a pattern suggesting that the mothers were following the children's changes. Similar to Kagan's (1981) study, interest in flawed objects and discrepant events occurred in the second year and emerged almost completely free from maternal input.

The Current Study

The studies cited show the emergence of prosocial behavior, empathy, and awareness of standards in the second year of life. They provide, however, little information about the social context in which the beginning moral sense arises. Factors such as parent-child conversation, family and cultural rules, elaboration of narratives, and direct teaching need to be examined to flesh out the real situations in which, once moral concern arises, it is dealt with and shaped. Researchers often do not take advantage of the rich opportunities afforded by home observation; instead, they may count merely total responses with too little regard for the fact that responses happen over time and are organized sequentially (Schaffer, 1979).

Using a case study approach, this research included frequent and longitudinal observations of four toddlers and their mothers at home. In addition to using data presented elsewhere (Lamb, 1991b) the data obtained address the following broader research questions: What is morality as it first appears? Are there any developmental patterns that characterize its emergence and unfolding? In what socially interacting contexts do moral concerns arise? What are the breaches of morality or distress situations that elicit emotional responses in children of this age? What sorts of transgressions do caregivers pay attention to and what does this say about their beliefs, values, and child-rearing goals? The naturalistic study of children's moral development is crucial to hypothesis building at this stage in the field. Observations in the home help us to put empirical findings in a context, to understand the process of the development of moral concern, and to examine the environmental contribution and response to changes in the child.

Subjects

Four children (Shane, Sophie, Hazel, and Sasha) and their mothers were observed for approximately 8 months. At the beginning of the study, the four children were between the ages of 13 and 14 months and had no siblings. Previous research had indicated that at this age, significant moral awareness had not yet emerged. To ensure this, each mother was asked whether she had observed her child restraining him- or herself before engaging in taboo activities or expressing concern when mother was distressed. The mothers and children were located through old membership lists of a center that provides pregnancy exercise and childbirth classes. The four families chosen were fairly homogeneous to control for a number of factors that might interfere with development because this was a very small, detailed, exploratory study. They were all well-educated, Caucasian, two-parent families of similar socioeconomic status. To control partially for the socializing influence of other caregivers, all the mothers were their child's full-time caregiver. Despite interaction with baby-sitters and fathers, the mothers were, at this point in the children's lives, the primary agents of socialization.

Data Collection Procedures

Observation sessions occurred every 3 to 4 weeks for approximately 2-1/2 hours. The time of each session was the same so that frequencies of behaviors could be easily compared among subjects during data analysis. Each child was seen either 12 or 13 times over the 8-1/2-month observation period, excluding the first "get acquainted" visit, which occurred to accustom both mother and child to the researcher. The researcher audiotaped a running commentary of the child's activity as she followed the child around the house. Transcripts of these commentaries were used to obtain categories of acts that may be related to moral awareness. The mothers also wore audiotape recorders so that all of their comments could be recorded and later analyzed. All interactions around morally related events were transcribed in full.

The Character of the Changes: Toddlers and Prohibitions

Several events that appeared to be related to awareness of standards were documented:

1. Gives proud looks or achievement smiles; comments about own achievement.
2. Shows awareness or interest in flawed, missing, or discrepant things or events, for example, by saying "uh oh," but not exclusively through verbal means.
3. Says "uh oh" or "oops" in reference to accidents, spills, or something being dropped.
4. Says "uh oh" with no particular reference.
5. Shows awareness of a violation and restrains self.
6. Shows awareness of a violation and doesn't restrain self.
7. Transgresses and then shows awareness.
8. Transgresses, mother points out violation, and child then shows awareness.
9. Points out/gives something potentially harmful to mother.
10. Labels an action as good or bad.
11. Labels something as "dirty," "yukky," or "garbage."
12. Questions mother/recites a rule regarding a standard.

Most of the morally related interchanges between mother and child involved either appreciation of new tasks learned, new competences exhibited, or prohibitions. Mothers' appreciation of achievement was present throughout the year and increased somewhat as the children were able to interact with the environment more. Mothers' and children's interactions around prohibitions were more varied. When children committed a transgression knowingly or unknowingly, the mothers responded by saying "no" with various degrees of forcefulness, giving reasons, and stating "house" rules. They also distracted their children, substituted one toy or activity for another, or simply removed the children or the object. There was no trend in mothers' responses over time, except that as the children became more verbal and understanding of their mothers' speech, the mothers talked more about what they were doing and why. There was, however, a change in the interaction around prohibitions that is more difficult to describe. The mother-child interaction during this period revealed what might be described as a three-phase developmental change. An initial phase is followed by a transitional phase at around 15 to 19 months (around the time of the peak in awareness of standards for the children) and is then followed by a later phase in which some of the conflict of the transition is resolved.

Initial Phase   Interaction in the early phase is about conflicting wants. For example, a child wants something and her mother doesn't want her to have it. She fusses, and mother takes the object away or substitutes another object for it. Depending on how intensely the child desires the object or desires to continue the act, the child will return to her former activity as if forgetting her mother's prohibition—if the child understands prohibitions at all. Even if the child does remember her mother's prohibition (and there are few signs of this), over time the force of the prohibition will wane and her own desires will take precedence. The child seems to understand she is to restrain herself, yet this understanding seems different from understanding a transgression. It is purely at the level of understanding an order.

> At 14 months, Hazel and her mother were washing dishes at the sink, and Hazel spilled water on the floor. Her mother said, "Look, Hazel, if you're going to spill, spill it only in the sink." Hazel spilled water in the sink, and mother said, "Good girl." A few minutes later, Hazel poured the water on the counter, and her mother said, "In the sink, in the sink," and Hazel poured some in the sink. A few minutes later, she poured some on the counter again, showing no sign of knowing that her mother disapproved. Her mother said more strongly than before, "Oh, Hazel, no. Pour it in the sink." Her mother showed her again how to pour it in the sink, and Hazel followed suit. But when Hazel returned to pouring the water on the counter and floor, her mother decided they should stop washing dishes together.
>   Sophie, at 13-1/2 months, pulled on her mother's microphone. Her mother said, "No," and pulled it away. Sophie screamed and reached for it. Her mother said, "No," and pulled it away again, and Sophie screamed. This went on and on until the mother redirected Sophie to a toy.

The emotion expressed by the child in this phase is frustration: She fusses when she doesn't get what she wants or when mother restrains her by hand or voice. The child will sometimes inhibit on command. She responds to her mother's voice alone often enough, but the restraint lasts only as long as the prohibition is remembered.

Aside from the frustration, however, there is a surprising lack of emotion. The child appears to have no emotional reaction to her mother's prohibitions except when the mother raises her voice, and at those times the child simply stares. This could be due in part to a limited "facial vocabulary" to express emotion. It could also suggest a lack of understanding and/or interest either in the standards themselves or in pleasing mother.

Transitional Phase During the transitional phase, standards become a focus, and a sense of willfulness appears. This is when children experiment with standards, and negotiations around standards can allow children to exercise their will.

One example of the child's experimentation during this phase is when he returns to the same transgression but references mother each time, as if to test whether she will react:

> Shane was holding his bottle upside down. His mother took it away from him, put it on the kitchen table, and said, "No, no." Shane stared at her. She waited a few minutes and gave it back to him, but when she went into the next room, he ran after her, stood in front of her, and held his bottle upside down.

During this phase, children also question whether an action is prohibited by making inferences about actions similar to those already prohibited:

> Hazel found a cigarette butt on the ground and started to put it in her mouth. Her mother said, "No, don't eat that. That's garbage." Her mother asked her to throw it in the garbage, and Hazel said no. Her mother then asked her what she was going to do with it, and Hazel replied, "Eat it." Her mother said, "No, you can't eat it," and gave Hazel a bagel as a substitute. Hazel asked, "Garbage?" Mother replied, "No. It's not garbage. It's good." Later on, Hazel picked a candy wrapper off the ground and brought it to her mother, saying, "Garbage."

Shane and Sophie show similar questioning around standards. Shane pointed to an object on his mother's dressing table, and she said, "No." He then proceeded to point to each item on the table and to ask, "No?" Sophie, at around 18 months, seemed to be asking the researcher whether she could play with a cassette cover. She held it up and referenced the researcher until the researcher said it was okay to play with it.

Children also seem to experiment with standards in a playful way during this phase. For example, Hazel acted out a transgression and responded to it immediately as if testing it out. Hazel put gravel on the researcher's coat and said, "No, no," while brushing the gravel off. This occurred a few minutes after her mother told her not to put gravel on her own coat.

At this phase, children appear to know what a transgression is, show little distress over committing it, and use an interaction around a transgression as an assertion of will, independence, and a newly realized "self." We see defiance. The emotionless repetition of violations that occurred in the early phase becomes more rare. At times, it seems as if the child has no restraint at all. At times, the mother's voice no longer has the effect of even temporarily restraining the child.

A blatant example came from Shane at 17 months:

> His mother had been telling him to stay away from the street as he was riding a little toy car around. He advanced slowly toward the street, and his mother said, "No, no." He looked up, smiled at her, and said, "Noooo." She stood in front of his car to prevent him from going into the street and explained why it was dangerous. She added, "You better not go in there or you'll make Mommy very mad." As soon as she stopped her vigilant watch, he headed toward the street, again saying, "No." His mother said, "Shane, no, no, no," went to him, and picked him up off his car. He then deliberately pushed the car right into the street.

Another behavior that emerges during these months is smiling while transgressing and teasing one's mother by transgressing. Children seem to derive pleasure from transgressing, and they wait with glee for a reaction from their mother. Sometimes, after a mother has prohibited an act, the child will stand in front of her and almost repeat it. The child appears to be teasing the mother, because the purpose of the behavior is not to perform the prohibited act but to get the mother's reaction.

> When Sophie was 17-1/2 months old, her mother had been allowing her to "fix" things in the house with transparent tape. After half an hour, Sophie crumpled up a long piece of tape, put it halfway into her mouth, and stood in front of her mother smiling. Her mother, not upset, said, "Sophie Alisa, no, no, no, no, no, no." Sophie then took it out and pretended to put it in her mouth again, holding it poised at her lips.

During this transitional phase, negative emotion is rare. Children may appear happy while challenging their mothers, but they are hardly ever distressed at the violation of a standard. They show interest simply in what a standard is and in what situations it can be applied.

Later Phase   The third phase is qualitatively different, marked by an understanding of standards in relation to other people. Children not only begin to understand their mothers' wishes with regard to standards, but they also show a desire to do what their mothers want them to do. We see them beginning to make reparations for wrongs done, to question their mothers regarding their wishes, to "tattle" on themselves and ask for praise when they've shown restraint, to hide wrongdoings from their mothers, and to show signs of inner conflict when mothers' wishes conflict with their own.

> Sophie began to "make reparations" rather early. At 18-1/2 months, she pointed excitedly to something torn out of a book and tried to fix it first by putting it back where it was and later by taping it. At 23 months, Sophie stood staring at some crayon marks that she had made on a coffee table. She then left the room and got a damp washcloth and started wiping at the crayon marks to get them off, saying, "Uh oh, uh oh, uh oh," over and over again. She looked quite concerned. As the researcher also tried to wipe them off, Sophie said, "No, no," to her and pretended to hit her. Sophie then brought in a paper towel and tried that. When the paper towel removed the marks, Sophie appeared quite happy.
>
> Shane (20-1/2 months) was fighting with a little girl over a rocking horse. He hit her, and she began to cry. When his distressed mother went to comfort the girl, Shane joined his mother and patted the girl on the head as if to make reparations or please his mother.

During this phase, children seem to question their mothers more frequently regarding what they mean, what pleases them, and what the parameters of a prohibition are. They seem to take their mothers' wishes more seriously.

> Hazel threw a book, and her mother said, "Did you throw a book?" Hazel replied, "Yes," and smiled. Mother then said, "Don't throw books." Hazel then asked, "Don't throw books?" Mother answered, "Yes, it might hurt people and hurt me." Hazel asked, "Hurt people and hurt me?" Mother answered, "Yes, hurt you." Hazel then went to play with her pretend dishes and sink.
>
> Hazel and her mother had a more extended discussion when Hazel was 22 months and her mother asked her not to blow bubbles in her milk. Hazel asked, "In the bathtub?" and her mother replied that she could blow bubbles with a straw she takes into the bathtub. "In the sink?" questioned Hazel, and her mother discussed with her that possibility.

Another indication of greater awareness of standards as acts that are negotiated or defined interpersonally is the children's tendency to confess when they have done something wrong or, for that matter, right:

> Sophie, at 21-1/2 months, pointed out to the researcher that she had drawn on the wall with crayon. Her mother responded by saying, "Yes. Who's the naughty girl who did that?" Hazel, at 22 months, reminded her mother

that she was being "good" after her mother had asked her not to take the pins out of a quilt she was sewing. Hazel touched a straight pin and announced to her mother, "I'm leaving this in."

Although the children do have difficulty restraining themselves from doing what they want, they seem to show a desire to do what their mother wants and to internalize her prohibitions. When they tease her, they will often give in. When she leaves the room, they will continue to restrain themselves:

Shane, at 21 months, had been fighting with his mother about putting crayons in his mouth. In the middle of the conflict, his mother left the room. Shane stared after her and lifted a crayon to his mouth. He did not, however, put it in his mouth. He instead put it back down and got up to find her.

When there is a conflict of wishes or desires during this phase, the child will often inhibit but with some fussing, as if internally torn between what he wants to do and what his mother wants him to do. This does not appear to be a product of fear of the consequences (if there were any consequences for transgressing, they were very mild for all the children). At 20-1/2 months, Shane had a full-blown confrontation with his mother about throwing crayons. She kept saying no, and he kept throwing them or wanting to throw them. He stared at her; he seemed to want to throw the crayon; he held the crayon poised in midair; then he compromised and sort of let it drop to the ground. He didn't place it on the ground, but he didn't exactly throw it either. Instead of a mere test of his mother, this act seemed to epitomize Shane's own conflict.

Also, during this third phase, children show more emotion with regard to standards. They are pleased to be doing what their mothers want. They seem anguished when they are forced to choose between what they want to do and what their mothers want them to do. Whereas in the first phase, children simply continue doing what they want with almost no emotion, and in the middle phase, they are still quite nonchalant although willful, in the third phase, children occasionally become distressed over transgressions.

It is possible to venture an answer to the question of what is happening around 17 or 18 months that explains the sudden increase in awareness of standards (Lamb, 1991a). First, it seems that children are more emotionally reactive in a way they were not previously. There is concern, distress, devilish glee, and defiance. These emotions were rarely seen before the transitional period in relation to any act, let alone morally related acts. Second, children seem to show a growing curiosity about standards or possibly about the fact that there are rights and wrongs. Third, there seems to be a personal invest- ment or responsibility in their acts. They are beginning to be distressed when they break things or do something like throwing a large object down the toilet. One wonders if there is some beginning awareness (pride and fear, perhaps) that it is the self who is committing these transgressions. This sense of self, which may in part be a result of new competences in experiencing and/or expressing emotions, may also be central to the beginnings of an awareness of standards and even empathy.

Development of Empathy

The mothers reported that early in the second year, the children responded in several ways to their mothers' distress, crying, sadness, and yelling: They would either stare, become upset, or laugh. These behavioral responses can be interpreted in a number of ways. The children may have stared because they were surprised or curious. They may have become upset because they were anxious when they saw their mothers behaving that way. They may have laughed because they thought their mothers looked funny when crying or yelling or because they were unsure of what their mothers' emotions meant and needed to find out if everything was all right. If Mom laughed back, everything must be all right. Thus, it is difficult to conclude that these responses signify the beginning of empathy.

At a later age, children's responses are more likely indications of empathy. Shane, for example, gave his crying mother a big hug and said, "Mommy." He wasn't upset at the time, which could mean that his hug was not for his own comfort but for hers. Shane also gave his mother a kiss and acted "loving," in his mother's words. Another time, he stroked her head and said, "Aw, Mommy." Yet another time, he put his arm around her, said, "Mommy," and made believe he was crying, too.

Sasha may have been showing some sympathy when he smiled at his crying mother and said, "Hi." His mother thought, at the time, that he was trying to cheer her up. Later in the year when she was crying, he went up to her and said, "Momma, hurt," and kissed her where she hurt herself "to make it better."

Sophie's first sign of "sympathy" was patting her crying mother. Later, when her mother hurt herself, Sophie wanted to put a bandage on her mother's finger. At another time, her parents were arguing and were very upset, and Sophie tried to get them to laugh. And later in the study, when her mother was crying, Sophie took her mother's face in her hands and said gently, "Hi, Mommy."

Hazel continued to get upset along *with* her mother later in the study, but she also wanted to give her mother "big hugs." She also expressed concern for her mother when her mother approached the stairs because her mother had once had a bad fall on the stairs. Later in the study, Hazel expressed her concern over babies' crying, often asking, "Is the baby better yet?" When her friend Max was sick, Hazel asked her mother, "Is Max's mother very sad?"

Although it is difficult to say conclusively that these children are showing empathy, they do become more emotionally responsive to the pain of other people. It is also unclear whether children's distress at the pain of another is an index of empathy or whether it precludes empathy because it means they are thinking of their own discomfort rather than the other's discomfort.

The preceding examples are all mothers' descriptions of empathic responding in their children. The researcher's observations yield surprisingly few incidents of empathy or even opportunities for empathy. When there are opportunities for empathy, the children's reactions are similar to what the mothers observed.

Throughout the study, but especially during the early months, there were missed opportunities for empathy. When Hazel was 16 months old, her mother hit her chin on Hazel's head and said, "ooh," in a moment of brief but seemingly intense pain. Hazel didn't appear to notice this event. Shane (14-1/2 months) stepped on a little boy who was visiting him. The little boy started to cry, but Shane didn't even turn around to look at him.

At other times, the children smiled when their mothers reacted to physical pain. At 14 months, Shane was pulling his mother's hair, and she said, "Ow, ow, ow." He stopped but kept smiling. Sophie at 15 months hit her mother on the cheek with a branch. Her mother said, "Ouch," and Sophie squealed with delight but didn't repeat the act.

Other incidents were observed in which the children became upset when their mothers were hurt. Sasha at 19 months was hitting his mother, who said, "Sasha, don't hit me. It's not nice to hit people with a hammer." He said, "Mommy, hammer," and became slightly distressed, whimpering a little. At 16 months, Hazel and her mother were at a playground when Hazel's mother hit her head very hard on the jungle gym, but Hazel didn't appear to notice. After reeling a bit, her mother laughed and said, "Mommy got a bump. It hurts. Give Mommy a kiss?" Hazel listened to her mother and then burst into tears and hugged her, holding on to her mother's legs.

Another early response to someone else's pain, if the child had caused it, was to repeat the incident. Shane at 15 months pinched the researcher, who said, "Ouch. That hurts." He then pinched her again.

It is difficult to pinpoint the first time a child expresses concern, because of the multiple possible interpretations of any behavior and because these incidents are so rare in the observations.

Sasha was 22-1/2 months old when his mother burned something in the oven and cried out, "Oh no, oh no, oh no." Sasha looked at her, quite concerned, and asked, "Mama hurt?" He repeated this question through several additional cooking accidents. He expressed concern but perhaps not empathy.

Shane was 17 months when he overheard the researcher talking about a pain in her chest. He came over, stared at the part of her chest she was touching, and patted her stomach. Although his facial expression was fairly blank, he went and got a toy truck and handed it to the researcher.

Sophie was 17-1/2 months when she hit her mother with a magnifying glass. Her mother said, "Ooh, you hurt me." Sophie became very serious and put the magnifying glass away. She then climbed on her mother's lap and allowed her mother to put her socks and shoes on. (Her mother had been attempting to get Sophie to allow her to do this all morning.) As her mother put the socks and shoes on, Sophie blew kisses into the air. Perhaps these were apologetic kisses.

Hazel at 18 months was looking at a toy mouse with her mother. The mouse was missing an eye and was partially torn. Her mother said, "This is a sad mouse," and Hazel repeated "sad mouse" twice with much expression in her voice.

These incidents show a certain responsiveness to the feelings of another. There seems to be an understanding of or an attempt to understand the emotion of another, and quite possibly there is a concomitant emotion on the part of the child.

Sometimes children seem to show particular responsiveness to a story.

Shane at 21-1/2 months was listening to his mother read a story about a bunny whose foot hurt. His mother read the story with much vocal expression, and Shane began to whine, "Mommy, Mommy." He started to cry very lightly as his mother read on. She read quickly to reach the part where the bunny gets better, and at this point Shane stopped crying.

These incidents make one wonder whether the ability to reexperience one's own painful emotions is linked to the ability to express empathy. When we define empathy as reexperiencing our own painful emotions at the sights and sounds of another person in pain, we also make it harder to study. We could then ask whether a person also needs to be concerned about the other person and to make some gesture toward comforting. If not, is empathy mere emotional contagion? The difficulty in studying empathy would then be differentiating between personal pain and personal pain derived from and augmented by concern for another.

The researcher observed two incidents in which a mother learned or talked about something tragic in her life while her child watched. Each child responded by becoming quiet for an extended period of time, but it is hard to know whether this response was purposeful.

There is some "training" for empathy going on during the second year.

Although the mothers did not describe the internal states or emotions of others very often, they did ask the children for behavior that shows some understanding of another's feelings. The mothers ask their children to give kisses to someone who is hurt, to express sadness over a torn doll, and to make reparations for hurt they may have caused.

If we must be cautious in labeling the spontaneous acts of sympathy as empathically motivated, we can at least comment on the growing responsiveness to others' emotions. Especially after the 17- to 18-month peak, these children appear to be much more in tune with and interested in the emotions of their mothers. Possibly they are able to infer emotions from their mothers' behavior.

Content and Quality of Mothers' Prohibitions

The most lengthy and emotionally laden interchanges between mothers and children of this age involve prohibitions around conflicting desires. Although other research suggests a natural development of interest in that which is moral, an examination of the kinds of prohibitions that mothers make tells us about the children's first experiences with right and wrong and about the way mothers attempt to socialize their children to join the "moral" world around them.

Over the 8 or 9 months of the study, we noted a total of 411 prohibitions: about eight prohibitions a session, or four prohibitions an hour. The mothers differed in frequency of prohibitions. Of the 411 prohibitions observed, 37 percent were made by Sophie's mother, 29 percent by Shane's mother, 23 percent by Hazel's mother, and 11 percent by Sasha's mother. One cannot conclude that Sophie's mother was more concerned or more frustrated than the other mothers; it may have been Sophie's adventurous, challenging, or active behaviors that warranted so many prohibitions. We also cannot conclude that Sasha's mother had a more laissez-faire attitude (saw fewer acts she thought in need of prohibition), because perhaps Sasha acted in a way that demanded fewer prohibitions. These percentages merely help us to compare differences in the types of prohibitions made by each mother.

After the study was over and the mothers were told what the study was about, they were asked which prohibitions they considered to be the most important. All the mothers agreed that the prohibitions regarding safety were the most important. Prohibitions against harming others were also seen as important.

Most of the 411 prohibitions, however, did not belong to these categories. These prohibitions were examined to see whether they fell into any reasonable categories. Many of the prohibitions seemed to be about not making a mess, not destroying or hurting things (as opposed to people), and not doing something that was quasidangerous (such as putting a ball in one's mouth) or unsavory (like playing with garbage). Prohibitions were categorized according to the reasons that mothers stated at the time they made the prohibitions and according to inference on the part of the coder (for example, when a mother told a child not to touch hot coffee, her concern was for the child's safety first and not that he might spill it and make a mess). (See Table 1.1.)

Prohibitions made regarding the children's safety were predictable. The mothers did not want their children to go out in the street, touch hot things, play on high pieces of furniture, or play with wall sockets. In addition, mothers prohibited their children from playing with scissors, standing too close to the color TV, and running around after a bath when they might slip and fall.

Prohibitions against harming others were made most often in response to the child's hitting or throwing something at someone. Prohibitions were also made against acts that seemed not to be intentionally aggressive on the part of the children, such as stepping on another child or pinching the mothers' cheeks in fun.

The prohibitions regarding the consideration of others had to do with respect for another person's rights and property as well as manners and customs. Children were prohibited from taking food off other people's plates, from waking sleeping relatives, from screaming in people's ears, from teasing other children, and from playing with another child's toy when the other child wanted it.

The mothers also tried to prohibit their children from spilling things, playing with toys that make messes (such as paints), from dropping a whole deck of cards on the floor, from putting dirty things on their clothes, and from dropping bits of food on the floor.

A high percentage of the prohibitions were motivated by a concern for property. The mothers asked or told their children not to play with things or bang things that might break; not to draw on furniture; not to overwater plants;

Table 1.1. Types of Prohibitions Mothers Made

Prohibition Category	Number	Percentage of Total
1. Personal danger	34	8
2. Harm to others	20	5
3. Inconsiderate of others	32	8
4. Making a mess	45	11
5. Destruction of property	103	25
6. Quasidangerous/unsavory	105	26
7. Other	72	18

not to play with pens, because the ink might get on things; not to tear books, magazines, and photos; not to get stuffed animals dirty; not to flush large things down the toilet; and not to throw things, because they might break something in the house.

A significant percentage of the prohibitions seemed motivated by the mothers' concern that their children not do things that have a small potential for being dangerous or at least unsavory. The children were told not to put dirty things in their mouths or pick up garbage. Putting crayons and other small objects in the mouth was also forbidden. The mothers prohibited their children from walking in dog droppings, walking while drinking, drinking soapy water, taking their hats off outside, and playing near dirt or garbage. In fact, a major concern of the mothers was dirt—that the child would play in it or would eat something dirty. This probably reflects what Europeans have claimed is Americans' obsession with cleanliness.

It is interesting to note that the categories the mothers named as most important were the categories about which they made the fewest prohibitions (the first three on Table 1.1). The most obvious explanation is that the children transgressed less often in these ways. Even so, we are still left to question whether the children transgressed less in these ways because of how mothers responded to these transgressions or because of a natural disinclination to do dangerous things or to hurt other people. That is, do children learn quickly not to do these transgressions or is the children's own incipient judgment strongest for transgressions involving major danger, harm, or lack of consideration for others?

An examination of the intensity ratings can tell us something about whether mothers are responding differently to the first two or three categories as compared with the other categories. As the coder listened to the tape recordings of the mothers, when there was a prohibition or a conflict about a prohibition, she wrote down what was said verbatim, described the tone with which the comments were made (for example, matter-of-fact, angry, or worried), and rated the intensity of the comment on a scale of 1 to 5. A rating of 1 was given to prohibitions that were made so matter-of-factly that it seemed the mothers had no emotional investment in whether the child minded or not. A rating of 5 was reserved for times when the mothers were quite insistent and angry. Intensity ratings were made on the basis of tone, volume, and persistence.

The average intensity ratings are shown in Table 1.2. The average of all mothers' average intensity ratings for each prohibition was calculated because the mothers differed in the frequency with which they made types of prohibitions. The mothers made prohibitions less intensely when their children were being inconsiderate of others, making a mess, or doing something quasidangerous or unsavory. The intensity ratings for prohibitions made over harm to others, the child's personal safety, and destruction of property were higher. In

Table 1.2. Intensity Ratings for the Six Prohibition Categories

Prohibition Category	Rating
1. Harm to others	2.64
2. Personal danger	2.42
3. Destruction of property	2.40
4. Inconsiderate of others	2.24
5. Making a mess	2.20
6. Quasidangerous/unsavory	2.12

general, mothers responded more intensely to transgressions that they rated more important and that were also shown to be transgressions for which they were less likely to make prohibitions. Because the mothers responded with such intensity, their children may have used more restraint in these areas. It is interesting to note, however, that even though mothers responded with high intensity to the destruction of property, children continued to transgress quite frequently in this area. This suggests that the children may be using *some* personal judgment with regard to restraint in the first two areas and not merely relying on mother's judgment as expressed by the intensity of her prohibition.

When it came to differences in frequency of prohibition among mothers by category, all four mothers in general maintained their respective shares of prohibitions for the categories "destroys property" and "does quasidangerous or unsavory things." Shane's mother prohibited for "personal danger" and "no harm to others" slightly more than the other categories and undervalued being considerate to others, relative to the other mothers. Sasha's mother also prohibited more frequently for "personal danger" and "no harm to others" over the other categories, with particular emphasis on no harm to others. It is interesting to note that these were the mothers of the two boys, while the mothers of the two girls undervalued these categories in comparison with other categories. The mothers could have been responding to stereotypes of boys as more rambunctious and less empathic and as in need of greater restraint in these areas. On the other hand, perhaps these boys were less careful to restrain themselves in these areas.

Another question considered was whether the mothers changed over time in the kinds of prohibitions they made. We compared these changes with the changes in awareness of standards that happens between 17 and 18 months. Each mother did change in the kinds of prohibitions she made over time; however, there were no patterns among the changes, save for one interesting similarity. Sophie's, Hazel's, and Shane's mothers all showed an increase in prohibitions against harming a person within a couple of months before the children's peak in awareness. Sasha's mother, on the other hand, showed an increase in this type of prohibition after Sasha's peak in awareness of standards. This commonality could suggest an aggressive surge on the part of three children right before the 17- to 18-month transition. It could also indicate that when children become aware of standards and/or begin to have empathy, they tend to hurt other people less (that is, they show restraint in this area). As a result, their mothers needed to prohibit less in this area after the peak. Another commonality was revealed among Shane's, Sasha's, and Sophie's mothers, who increased their prohibitions against the destruction of property before and up to the children's peak in awareness of standards. As in the case of prohibitions against harming a person, perhaps the children experienced some aggressive surge right before awareness blossomed, and after becoming more aware, they were able to restrain themselves better.

It is also interesting to see in which aspects of the moral sphere the children expressed the most interest and emotional involvement during their second year. These aspects were somewhat different from the interests and involvements of their mothers. The children were most interested in interacting with their mothers in playful or teasing ways around transgressions, and no particular content category stands out. But the events toward which the children showed the most curiosity, emotional intensity, and distress were discrepant events, broken and flawed objects, spills, torn things, and empty containers. This self-initiated concern is with them throughout much of the second year and may involve a standard of "rightness," the way things ought to be, akin to children's love of order.

Discussion

The middle of the second year of life appears to be a high point in the beginnings of morality. An awareness of standards may emerge at about 17 months, and empathy appears more regularly after about 18 months. Qualitative data suggest a more emotional, self-invested comprehension of morally related acts after this time, but we must use caution when generalizing from so small a sample.

An examination of prohibitions revealed that mothers more frequently prohibited destruction of property or unsavory activities, while prohibiting with more intensity harming others and staying out of danger. The prohibitions for these latter two categories waned after the peak, which may reflect greater restraint on the part of the children in these areas and a possible natural understanding of the greater import of these two prohibitions for surviving in the world.

These qualitative data allow us to consider the 18-month-old in the same light in which theorists have considered adolescents. They note adolescents' intense concern with moral issues, the passion with which they reason about moral dilemmas, and their deep commitment to principles (Erikson, 1958, 1964, 1968; Kohlberg, 1981; Kohlberg & Gilligan, 1971). They suggest that adolescence is a critical time in the development of morality and that this is because adolescents are suddenly able to reason at an abstract level (Kagan, 1984; Piaget, 1952). Adolescence has also been seen as a time of emotional instability (Blos, 1967; Freud, 1958; Mahler, Pine, & Bergman, 1975; Tanner, 1972).

We can look at what happens to the toddler in the middle of the second year in much the same way, noting the toddler's rebelliousness, need for confrontation with parents around transgressions, emotional instability, and need to assert the newly found sense of self.

Whether emotional instability leads to a more intense interest in moral concern is a question that researchers might address in the future. Teenagers and toddlers may simply feel more intensely in response to the sound of someone in distress, to the failure of meeting a standard of performance, or to the sight of a flawed object. What makes people feel anything at all in response to these things? Are these natural emotions, and does the child first experience such emotions in the second year? Unfortunately, methods need to become more subtle to even begin to address this question and, indeed, the general question of the extent to which emotional development is tied to emerging moral awareness. We need to examine more closely the development of morality in its interacting context, for it is within these early relationships that the emotional urges beneath our desire to help, to do well, and to do good are received and, we hope, nurtured.

References

Bar-Tal, D., Raviv, A., & Goldberg, M. (1982). Helping behavior among preschool children: An observational study. *Child Development, 53*, 396–402.

Blos, P. (1967). The second individuation process of adolescence. *The Psychoanalytic Study of the Child, 22*, 162–186.

Bruner, J. S. (1972). The nature and uses of immaturity. *American Psychologist, 27*, 1–22.

Dunn, J. (1988). The beginnings of morality: Developments in the second year. In J. Kagan & S. Lamb (Eds.), *The emergence of morality in young children* (pp. 91–112). Chicago: University of Chicago Press.

Dunn, J., & Kendrick, C. (1979). Interaction between young siblings in the context of family relationships. In M. Lewis & L. A. Rosenblum (Eds.), *The child and its family* (pp. 143–168). New York: Plenum Press.

Dunn, J., Kendrick, C., & MacNamee, R. (1981). The reaction of first-born children to the birth of a sibling: Mothers' reports. *Journal of Child Psychology and Psychiatry, 22,* 1–18.

Eisenberg-Berg, N. (1982). *The development of prosocial behavior.* New York: Academic Press.

Erikson, E. (1958). *Young man Luther.* New York: Norton.

Erikson, E. (1963). *Childhood and society.* New York: Norton.

Erikson, E. (1964). *Insight and responsibility.* New York: Norton.

Erikson, E. (1968). *Identity, youth, and crisis.* New York: Norton.

Flavell, J. H. (1977). *Cognitive development.* Englewood Cliffs, NJ: Prentice-Hall.

Freud, A. (1958). Adolescence. *The Psychoanalytic Study of the Child, 16,* 255–278.

Gesell, A. L., & Amatruda, C. S. (1945). *The embryology of behavior: The beginnings of the human mind.* New York: Harper.

Hoffman, M. (1982). The development of prosocial motivation: Empathy and guilt. In N. Eisenberg-Berg (Ed.), *The development of prosocial behavior.* New York: Academic Press.

Kagan, J. (1981). *The second year: The emergence of self-awareness.* Cambridge: Harvard University Press.

Kagan, J. (1984). *The nature of the child.* New York: Basic Books.

Kohlberg, L. (1981). *Essays on moral development* (Vol I). San Francisco: Harper and Row.

Kohlberg, L., & Gilligan, C. (1971). The adolescent as a moral philosopher. *Daedalus, 100,* 1051–1086.

Kopp, C. B. (1982). Antecedents of self-regulation: A developmental perspective. *Developmental Psychology, 18,* 199–214.

Lamb, S. (1991a). First moral sense. In W. Kurtines & J. Gewirtz (Eds.), *Handbook of moral behavior and development* (pp. 171–189). Hillsdale, NJ: Erlbaum.

Lamb, S. (1991b). Internal state words: Their relation to moral development and maternal communications about moral development. *First Language, 2,* 391–406.

Largo, R. H., & Howard, J. A. (1979). Developmental progression in play behavior of children between 9 and 30 months. *Developmental Medicine and Child, 1/2,* 299–310.

Lewin, K. (1942). Changes in social sensitivity in children and adults. *Childhood, 19,* 53–57.

Mahler, M. S., Pine, F., & Bergman, A. (1975). *The psychological birth of the human infant.* New York: Basic Books.

McCall, R. B., Parke, R. D., & Kavanaugh, R. D. (1977). Imitation of live and televised models by children one to three years of age. *Monographs of the Society for Research in Child Development, 42,* 3.

Minton, C., Kagan, J., & Levine, J. A. (1971). Maternal control and obedience in the two-year-old. *Child Development, 42,* 1873–1894.

Nelson, K. (1979). The role of language in infant development. In M. Bornstein & W. Kessen (Eds.), *Psychological development from infancy: Image to intention.* Hillsdale, NJ: Erlbaum.

Olim, E. G., Hess, R. D., & Shipman, V. C. (1967). Role of mothers' language styles in mediating their preschool children's cognitive development. *School Review, 75,* 414–424.

Piaget, J. (1952). *The origins of intelligence in children*. New York: International University Press.

Piaget, J. (1962). *Play, dreams, and imitations in childhood*. New York: Norton.

Radke-Yarrow, M., Zahn-Waxler, C., & King, R. (1976). Dimensions and correlates of prosocial behavior in young children. *Child Development, 47*, 118–125.

Rheingold, H. L., & Emery, G. N. (1986). The nurturant acts of very young children. In D. Olweus, J. Block, & M. Radke-Yarrow (Eds.), *The development of anti- and prosocial behavior: Research, theories, and issues* (pp. 75–96). Orlando, FL: Academic Press.

Rheingold, H. L., & Hay, D. F. (1980). Prosocial behavior of the very young. In G. S. Stent (Ed.), *Morality as a biological phenomenon: The presuppositions of sociobiological research* (pp. 93–108). Berkeley: University of California Press.

Schaffer, H. R. (1979). Acquiring the concept of the dialogue. In M. H. Bomstein & W. Kessen (Eds.), *Psychological development from infancy*. New York: Erlbaum.

Stent, G. S. (Ed.). (1980). *Morality as a biological phenomenon: The presuppositions of sociobiological research*. Berkeley: University of California Press.

Stipek, D., & McClintic, S. (1989, April). *Factors affecting toddlers' reactions to completing tasks*. Paper presented at the meeting of the Society for Research in Child Development, Kansas City, MO.

Tanner, J. M. (1972). Sequence, tempo, and individual variation in the growth and development of boys and girls aged twelve to sixteen. In J. Kagan & R. Coles (Eds.), *Twelve to sixteen* (pp. 1–24). New York: Norton.

Turiel, E. (1980). The development of moral concepts. In G. S. Stent (Ed.), *Morality as a biological phenomenon: The presuppositions of sociobiological research* (pp. 109–123). Berkeley: University of California Press.

Vaughn, B. E., Kopp, C. E., & Krakow, J. B. (1984). The emergence and consolidation of self-control from eighteen to thirty months of age. *Child Development, 55*, 990–1004.

Zahn-Waxler, C., & Radke-Yarrow, M. (1982). The development of altruism: Alternative research strategies. In N. Eisenberg-Berg (Ed.), *The development of prosocial behavior* (pp. 109–138). New York: Academic Press.

CHAPTER 2

Moral Development, Gender Identity, and Peer Relationships in Early and Middle Childhood

Sharry Langdale

Wheelock College

If some mad sociologist should ever settle a thousand little boys in a compound and give them dolls to play with and give footballs to a thousand girls in another compound, I feel certain that within a few days a small minority of the girls would be kicking and throwing the footballs around, while the majority would be cuddling their footballs and scolding them for being naughty. And I'd bet . . . that 60% of the boys would have dismembered their dolls to use the limbs and torsos for batting the heads about the compound; and the 10% who went in for cuddling would have had their dolls stolen for dismemberment by the majority. (Middleton, 1980, p. 26)

Whether we view this scenario as amusing speculation, a memory of things past, or a dangerous perpetuation of gender stereotypes, our response is likely to be colored by ambivalence. Our ambivalence comes from the realization that the scenario reflects our everyday observations and the results of systematic study of boys' and girls' behaviors, while it also belies the ideology in contemporary society that seeks to eliminate gender differences. In this chapter, I will draw from the psychological literature on moral and cognitive development, gender identity, and gender differences in children's interactions with same-sex peers to argue that, from a developmental perspective, this ideology is misguided. I will focus on connections between key ideas in the literature to illuminate the developmental importance of such gender-related behaviors that may help us to gain insights into our own concerns and understand what we observe. I will point to specific conceptual links between two different moral orientations (justice and care) and typical developmental characteristics and behaviors in children in early (ages 2 to 6) and middle (ages 6 to 11) childhood. This analysis will reveal that same-sex relationships in early and middle childhood are important contexts for the development of these two moral orientations and the social skills inherent in each. In light of the male/justice bias that has permeated our society and our psychology (Gilligan, 1982; Miller, 1976), I then discuss the practical implications of the developmental importance of care orientation behaviors. Traditionally, such behaviors have sometimes been viewed as having some intrinsic value that does not significantly contribute to development. More often, they have been viewed as an impediment to girls' growth.

Theoretical Perspectives on Moral Development

The Justice Orientation

Historically, the study of moral development has been based on the a priori assumption that the whole of the moral domain is encompassed by the concept of justice: ideas of fairness, equality, reciprocity, the rights of individuals, and the rules and roles that regulate and serve as guidelines to human behavior. This equation of morality with justice has a long tradition in Western philosophy and permeates the psychological literature (Damon, 1977; Eisenberg-Berg, 1979; Freud, 1925/1961b; Gibbs & Wideman, 1982; Haan, 1977; Kohlberg, 1969, 1971; Rest, 1979). The justice orientation was first introduced in the moral development literature by Piaget (1965) in *The Moral Judgment of the Child* (1932/1965) and has been most extensively represented in Lawrence Kohlberg's theory and research.

Piaget studied the practice and consciousness of rules in boys playing marbles. He questioned boys about the rules of this game and about rules in general (e.g., Where do rules come from? Could you invent a rule?) and compared their responses with observations of what the boys actually did while playing the game. From this research, Piaget generated a model of moral development from early through middle childhood focused on the child's changing understanding of rules. He characterized the concept of justice in early childhood as heteronomous morality, whereby the child believes that rules are immutable and externally imposed by powerful adult authorities and require unilateral respect. Yet during this time, the child's behavior is frequently marked by an apparent disregard for rules. A child who races past you shrieking five minutes after your explaining that the school rules are to "walk rather than run" and "use your 'inside' voice" demonstrates this discrepancy between the consciousness of rules and the practice of rules. Piaget uses the term *autonomous morality* to characterize the understanding of rules and justice that usually emerges around age eleven. By this age, children become aware that rules are a necessary condition for cooperating or, as an 11-year-old boy in Piaget's study put it,

"So as not to be always quarreling, you must have rules" (p. 66). Autonomous morality requires mutual respect and means anyone can create rules. If everyone agrees, the rule is fair; if you uphold it, you are good.

Piaget recognized that the inequality inherent in the adult/child relationship inevitably limits "mutual respect" and the joint construction of rules in that relationship. Thus, he proposed that changes in children's concept of justice result primarily from their interactions with peers rather than with adults. The child and his or her peers are equals; their interactions open up possibilities for constructing rules, assuming roles, and imposing sanctions for violations in ways not possible in adult/child relationships. Some examples of this are observations of peers in middle childhood forming clubs and devoting more energy to defining rules and roles than to fulfilling the club's ostensible purpose.

Like Piaget, Kohlberg equated the moral domain with the concept of justice and selected a sample of males for his theory-building research. Rather than focusing on peer groups and children's games, Kohlberg saw the relationship between the self and society's rules, roles, and expectations as primary to moral development. He identified changes in people's understanding of justice by studying their responses to hypothetical dilemmas. (The Heinz dilemma, which asks whether a man should steal an otherwise unavailable drug to save his dying wife's life, has become one of the most widely used instruments in moral development research.) Kohlberg used his longitudinal study of males to generate a six-stage, three-level model (preconventional, conventional, and postconventional) of justice reasoning. With respect to children, research based on Kohlberg's model indicates that through middle childhood, most children reason at the preconventional level (stages 1 and 2), where their logic for following rules centers on avoiding punishment or gaining personal benefit. The conventional level, with an emphasis on interpersonal considerations (stage 3) or on law and order in society (stage 4), does not appear until the end of childhood or in adolescence (Kohlberg, 1976).

Both Piaget and Kohlberg encountered problems when they applied their developmental models to girls and women. Piaget's first problem was his discovery that boys and girls engaged in different kinds of activities when they played with one another; marbles was not a game that girls typically played. Instead, he found them playing less formal, less competitive, turn-taking games like hopscotch or jump rope. Piaget's second problem came with his discovery that in games that the girls did play, they did not formulate extensive rules. Piaget (1932/1965) describes this discovery as follows:

> The most superficial observation is sufficient to show that in the main the legal sense is far less developed in little girls than in boys. We did not succeed in finding a single collective game played by girls in which there were as many rules, and, above all, as fine and consistent an organization and codification of the rules as in the games of marbles . . . [as played by boys]. (p. 77)

The "problem" of a discrepancy between Kohlberg's developmental model and girls' and women's perceptions of morality appears empirically in the tendency for the moral reasoning scores of females to gravitate toward stage 3, where what is right is defined in the context of interpersonal relationships (Bar-Yam, Kohlberg, & Naame, 1980; Bussey & Maughan, 1982; Fishkin, Keniston, & MacKinnon, 1973; Gilligan, Kohlberg, Lerner, & Belenky, 1971; Haan, Smith, & Block, 1968; Haan, Langer, & Kohlberg, 1976; Holstein, 1976; Hudgins & Prentice, 1973; Kramer, 1968; Kuhn, Langer, Kohlberg, & Haan, 1977; Langdale, 1986; Parikh, 1980; Saltzstein, Diamond, & Belenky, 1972). The following excerpt from Holstein's (1976) longitudinal study of the development of the justice orientation in adolescents and their parents characterizes this problem as an inadequate representation of the development of girls' and women's moral reasoning:

> One of the hallmarks of stage 3 reasoning is a stress on compassion, sympathy, or love as a reason for moral action. Another hallmark of stage 3 is a concern for the approval of others, especially those in the primary group. This latter emphasis "catches" children's reasoning. But at the same time the stage 3 emphasis on sympathy, so stereotypically part of the female role, is characteristic of much adult female moral reasoning in the present study. Many of the women are either predominantly stage 3 or if stage 4, show so much stage 3 reasoning that their stage score is a mixed one. . . . [This] results in adult female reasoning being categorized with children's. (pp. 60–61)

However, like Piaget, Kohlberg (Kohlberg & Kramer, 1969) interpreted this discrepancy as stemming from girls' and women's moral development rather than as being a problem with male-based theory.

The Care Orientation and Contrasts Between Justice and Care

In the now classic article "In a Different Voice," Carol Gilligan (1977) identified the omission of females from Piaget's and Kohlberg's studies and theories as the source of the discrepancies they subsequently found. On the basis of her study of women deciding whether to terminate an unwanted pregnancy, Gilligan proposed expanding the parameters of the moral domain to include the moral orientation she referred to as the "voice of care." In contrast to the justice orientation, the emphasis in the voice of care is on themes of attachment, connection, interdependence, and the responsiveness of human beings to one another. Lyons (1983) elaborated on Gilligan's insights to develop a model of the distinctions between these two moral orientations and focused on different conceptions of self and of what constitutes a moral problem, different kinds of considerations taken into account in seeking a resolution to a moral problem, and different criteria used for evaluating one's moral decisions (see Figure 2.1). I

Figure 2.1. Concepts of Self and of Morality in Relation to Considerations Made in Real-Life Moral Choices

A Morality of Justice

Individuals defined as Separate/Objective in Relation to Others: see others as one would like to be seen by them in objectivity;	*tend to use a morality of justice as fairness that rests on an understanding of **Relationships as Reciprocity** between separate individuals, grounded in the duty and obligation of their roles;*	*moral problems are generally construed as* issues, especially decisions, of conflicting claims between self and others (including society); resolved by invoking impartial rules, principles, or standards, *considering:* (1) one's role-related obligations, duty, or commitments; or (2) standards, rules, or principles for self, others, or society, including reciprocity, that is, fairness—how one should treat another considering how one would like to be treated if in their place;	*and evaluated considering:* (1) how decisions are thought about and justified; or (2) whether values, principles, or standards are (were) maintained, especially fairness.

A Morality of Response and Care

Individuals defined as Connected in Relation to Others: see others in their own situations and contexts;	*tend to use a morality of care that rests on an understanding of **Relationships as Response to Another** in their terms;*	*moral problems are generally construed as* issues of relationships or of response, that is, how to respond to others in their particular terms; resolved through the activity of care; *considering:* (1) maintaining relationships and response, that is, the connections of interdependent individuals to one another; or (2) promoting the welfare of others or preventing their harm or relieving the burdens, hurt, or suffering (physical or psychological) of others;	*and evaluated considering:* (1) what happened/will happen or how things worked out; or (2) whether relationships were/are maintained or restored.

Source: Lyons., N. Two perspectives: On self, relationships, and morality. *Harvard Educational Review,* 53, 125–145, 1985. Adapted by permission.

now summarize the nature of these two voices and illustrate the distinctions between them with examples of how they appear in interview data.

Conceptions of self, other, and relationships form the core of social understanding. The centrality of these conceptions and the extent to which they provide coherence in our lives are reflected in the language we use to describe our interactions with others. Figure 2.2 illuminates the distinction between the social world of the "separate" self (the justice orientation) and that of the "con-

Figure 2.2. The "Connected Self" and the "Separate Self" in the Social World of Children

Self	Relationship	Other
	The "Connected Self" (A 6-year-old female)	
Me too [thinks about it].	We agree what we should do.	She thinks about it.
	We should play super-friends, then house.	
	We like superfriends better.	
	We just go think about it, we disagree, so we think about it.	
	We would go in another room.	
	We don't have a real fight.	
	We think it over.	
	The "Separate Self" (A 6-year-old male)	
I wanted to stay outside.	We argued about that.	He wanted to go in.
I wanted to stay out.	We argued.	He wanted to stay in.
I wanted to stay out.	Then we were playing.	Neil stopped arguing.
I went in anyway.		He would do what he wants.
[I felt] good.		
I'd go play by myself.		
I would argue with him.		
I would do what I want.		

nected" self (the care orientation) as it appears in the real-life dilemmas of two 6-year-olds, one male and one female. When asked about a real-life moral dilemma (i.e., a time when they had trouble figuring out what was the right thing to do), both children discussed the common childhood dilemma that arises when they and their friend want to play different games. In Figure 2.2, statements from their responses are placed into self, other, and relationship categories on the basis of the use of the pronouns "I," "s/he," and "we" to illustrate the difference in what is central to the two social worlds—that is, the individual to the separate self and the relationship to the connected self.

Even a cursory look at Figure 2.2 suggests the distinction between the separate self conception and the connected self conception identified in Lyons' model. The image of the connected self is conveyed in the frequency of the 6-year-old girl's statements about her relationship with her friend that are marked by her use of the pronoun "we." The image of the separate self is conveyed in the 6-year-old boy's greater number of statements about self or other, marked by his use of the personal pronouns "I" and "he." Substantively, the boy's statements reflect the justice-associated concern with fairness ("I would do what I want" and "He would do what he wants"), while the girl's statements reflect the care-associated concern with maintaining relationships ("We agree what we should do" and "We like superfriends better").

Theoretically, of course, these different voices are not simply a matter of pronoun usage; they represent something much deeper than word choice. Sociomoral understanding is rooted in our perceptions and experiences of social reality. In this sense, the two voices are different frameworks for social understanding, and key terms seem to take on different meanings. Thus, although both voices are grounded in our experience of social reality, they impose on that reality a different framework for organizing and interpreting experiences that may permeate all kinds of human activities. The following accounts of moral dilemmas from research interviews with two 12-year-olds reveal the logic of each orientation and show how the two orientations act as organizing principles, guiding both the formulation and the resolution of moral problems.

The Real-Life Moral Dilemmas of Two 12-Year-Olds

Asked to describe a situation of moral conflict in which he had to make a decision but wasn't sure what was the right thing to do, Jake relates the common middle childhood dilemma of whether to tell on a friend who has done something wrong—in this case, violated a school rule. In Jake's words, "Me and Sam were fooling around in the school yard after school with firecrackers. And the principal came and just I got caught." Jake casts both what he wanted to do and why he couldn't do it in terms of the justice orientation focus on fairness:

I definitely wanted to tell on him [Sam], but I couldn't. You see, I got in a lot of trouble, and I thought he was doing it with me so he should, too. But you don't tell on your friends if you've done something wrong and he doesn't get caught. Because that's not fair to him. I mean, you were doing just as much something wrong as he was. If he got caught, he probably wouldn't tell on you either.

To Jake, it initially seems unfair to be in trouble by himself when his friend was equally guilty. But this concern gives way as he resolves his dilemma by imposing a rule: "You don't tell on your friends." His decision then turns on his knowledge that if the situation were reversed, Sam would reciprocate by also upholding their rule. By favoring neither Jake nor his friend Sam and thus by being more impartial and objective, Jake's rule ensures equality in their relationship with one another.

In her interview, 12-year-old Beth also discussed a dilemma about whether to tell on a friend who had done something wrong. In her case, the problem arose when a friend stole some colored pens "that he really wanted and couldn't find" from another friend "who bought them and really wanted them, too." Casting her dilemma in terms of a choice in which "you've got to decide which is better, to send one person to get in trouble or to make the other person happy by getting their pens back for them," Beth expresses her concern for each friend and her awareness of the particular situations of each, as well as concern for her relationship with each. What makes it difficult for her to report the theft, she says, is "what happens to the other person that you tell on." She reiterates her concern for others and portrays the problem of telling on a friend as one of exclusion, where helping one friend means hurting the other. Her desire to avoid being known as "the school tattletale" initially suggests to Beth that she shouldn't tell and indicates she is also attentive to her own needs. Then her description of how she came to the decision that "it is really right and better to tell" reveals her search for an inclusive solution that will respond to her perception of the needs of both herself and her friends and reveals the care orientation imperative to maintain relationships and to avoid or minimize hurt:

The first thing you say is, "Well, I don't want to be known as the school tattletale. I won't tell." But later you start thinking, well, it's really right and better if I tell and it'll probably make more people happy. You usually have to think and tell because like your first thing, well, I saw my friend doing this, but you know no one will ever know I saw or anything, so if I don't tell, no one will know and nobody will hold it against me. But then, like, you start sitting there thinking about it and you think that somebody will always know—you'll always know that you never told. And you know,

it makes me feel really bad because my friend is sitting there, "Has any-
body seen my pens? Where are they?" And you know. So then I usually tell
because I don't think it's right for her to sit there, you know, "Where are
they? Help! I need my pens for my next class. Help! They're not here,
where are they?" And I think if you know that, it is better to tell. . . . [So
I would] tell and then put in a good word for them [the friend who stole],
like this is the first thing that he has ever taken and I know him and he is
a very nice person.

Thus, while Jake reaches his fair solution through his knowledge of rules
and reciprocity, Beth reaches her inclusive solution through her knowledge of
and response to her friends' and her own needs.

If we think of how often we say to children, "How would you feel if you
were Jack or Mary or Sue?" it is easy to speculate on how Jake came to believe
that "if he [Sam] got caught, he probably wouldn't tell on you either." But how
did Beth come to know what she knows? Of this, we know far less. Although
it is reasonable to assume that the voice of care has been articulated primarily
by women for a long time, its recognition as a developmentally important
framework for social understanding is new. Compared with the voice of justice, it is unfamiliar and undervalued. Historically, the psychological schemes
through which we have come to know and understand ourselves and the institutions of American democracy have presumed the primacy of the voice of
justice. As a consequence, the voice of justice is deeply ingrained in our conscious and unconscious awareness; we are educated to think in this voice.
When this imbalance influences how we listen, what we hear, and how we
interpret what we hear, we unwittingly perpetuate the male/justice bias. However, the effects of this bias are not powerful enough to silence the voice of
care in females. For example, in a study of moral dilemma effects, Langdale
(1983) found that an emphasis on the justice orientation in a hypothetical
dilemma decreases but does not eliminate the use of care reasoning by
females. And Gilligan and Attanucci (1988) found that moral reasoning
focused within the care orientation is an almost exclusively female phenomenon, whereas moral reasoning focused within the justice orientation is
used by both females and males.

The systematic research required to address important questions about the
use of the care orientation in early and middle childhood, where it appears in
everyday behaviors, and how it changes, largely remains to be done. It is
toward that end, in a spirit of raising questions, that we turn to the literature
on children's cognitive development and peer relationships for clues about the
roots and development of both of these moral orientations in early and middle
childhood.

Developmental Characteristics of Children's Thinking and Perceiving

Piaget's theory of cognitive development has led contemporary developmental psychologists to characterize early childhood as the time when children are "engrossed in a world of fantasy." At about age two, children develop the capacity for symbolic thought. They gain the ability to form mental representations and to act on things mentally rather than solely through their actions. This dramatic developmental achievement, which enables the child to use words and ideas to think and learn, underlies the tremendous imaginative abilities that permeate nearly every aspect of preschoolers' thinking, language, and behavior and make pretend play a very important part of the young child's life.

With the acquisition of symbolic thought, young children become aware of categories in the sense that they realize that words apply to more than one thing. As they begin to formulate concepts about themselves, they also become aware of gender as a category that in part defines who they are, and they begin to make moral distinctions, freely applying labels of right/wrong and good/bad in ways that reflect their engrossment in the world of fantasy.

At the same time, children's thinking in early childhood shows a tendency toward egocentrism, and they assume that what they see, think, and feel, others do, too. They also have difficulty distinguishing between fantasy and reality. They really believe that the monster in their dream is under the bed, that stuffed animals and imaginary friends are real, that they can change their gender by changing their clothes, and that if they accidentally fall down while walking in a forbidden place, they are being punished.

Because of these characteristics and other limitations in their cognitive abilities, young children do not really grasp concepts or categories as abstractions. Thus, at the same time that the capacity for symbolic thought makes it possible for a child to begin to formulate concepts, the concepts they construct—including concepts of themselves, gender, morality, and relationship—are unrealistic; they are not tied to objective reality or the actualities of the world. They can readily both cite and break a rule because they neither understand the purpose of rules nor see a logical connection between the rules and their behavior.

In contrast, we can capture the essence of cognitive development in middle childhood by saying that the school-age child becomes "engrossed in a world of reality." Children's thinking becomes more logical, coherent, and flexible and is characterized by *decentration* (the ability to see more than one relevant aspect of an object or event at a time). This movement away from egocentrism allows the school-age child to become aware that others maintain a different perspective. As they become better able to distinguish between fantasy and reality, school-age children give up magical explanations for what they see and experience, offering more realistic explanations and propositions instead.

These and other changes in the child's cognitive abilities all enhance concept formation in middle childhood. And, in fact, "true" concept formation does not really occur before this time. Thus, as a consequence of changes in the child's cognitive abilities, one of the major developmental tasks of middle childhood is to refine and elaborate the fantasy-imbued concepts of self, gender, morality, and relationships that children begin to construct in early childhood.

Children's Relationships With Peers

The idea that children's peer relationships serve distinctive and unique developmental functions is a prominent theme throughout the literature on these relationships (Z. Rubin, 1980; Youniss, 1980). These distinctive functions include developing a wide range of skills and techniques for establishing and managing social interactions, fostering a sense of group belonging outside of the family, and facilitating social comparison, which is central to the development of a self-concept. Learning about and evaluating ourselves through comparison with others who are like us—that is, peers—makes such comparison meaningful.

Early childhood, when children develop physical skills and exercise their new cognitive abilities to fantasize and engage in pretend play, is the time when peers first become important as an extension of the child's social world beyond the immediate family. Dramatic play with peers helps the child to clarify his or her own experiences, provides a defense against powerlessness, and gives the child experiences that heighten his or her awareness of others by requiring him or her to respond to the imagination of another person. Although adults are often not directly involved, most of the preschooler's interactions with peers take place with an adult present.

In middle childhood, children spend increasing amounts of time with peers outside of as well as in child care settings and school, and there is a dramatic reduction and often absence of direct adult supervision. As thinking becomes more tied to objective reality, peers provide a context for transmitting and constructing social knowledge without the element of adult approval or disapproval. As the different information and experience that each child brings to the group is pooled into a phenomenological account, school-age children gain a broader base for refining and elaborating sociomoral concepts and cooperate to generate new insights—for example, about what fathers and mothers are "really" like, what parents are "supposed" to do, and what friendship "really" means.

Of course, anyone who has spent time with children is aware that in both of these developmental periods, another prominent feature of children's peer relationships is their preference for same-sex peers.

The Phenomenon of Same-Sex Preference

Virtually every study of children's interactions with peers provides evidence that children prefer to interact with children of their own gender. This preference for same-sex peers appears to be universal (Omark, Omark, & Edelman, 1975) and to persist throughout the life cycle. It begins early; even before the age of three, children have been found to get along better with unfamiliar children of the same sex than of the other sex (Jacklin & Maccoby, 1978). By late childhood, sex segregation is almost complete (Hallinan, 1979). In adulthood, there is evidence that relatively few adults have close other-sex friends (Booth & Hess, 1974) and that lover and spouse relationships are neither synonymous with friendship (Grunebaum, 1976) nor a substitute for same-sex friends (L. Rubin, 1985).

The phenomenon of same-sex preference in children's spontaneous activities appears to be real, pervasive, persistent, and sufficiently complex to preclude attributing its existence to any single factor. Among behavioral scientists, the favored explanation is that adult socializers direct children to others of the same sex and to different sex-typed activities (Z. Rubin, 1980). Although it is reasonable to assume that cultural influences inevitably play a role in encouraging or discouraging what amounts to segregation by sex, there is also empirical evidence that same-sex preference is not simply the result of socialization (Serbin, Tonick, & Sternglanz, 1977). Furthermore, evidence also indicates that same-sex preference does not require a conceptual understanding of gender; even young children respond to the greater compatibility of behavioral styles among children of the same sex (e.g., boys' greater proclivity for rough-and-tumble play). Because perception of similarity has been found to be a powerful force in choices of associates at all ages, gender may register as a more powerful determinant of who plays with whom than age, race, social class, intelligence, or any other demographic factor. In summary, studies of the universality, early appearance, and persistence of same-sex preference throughout the life cycle suggest that along with socialization, same-sex preference may also be rooted in some core developmental need aimed at clarifying gender as an organizing factor of personality and self-concept and/or influenced by biological predispositions.

Same-Sex Preference and Gender Identity Development in Early Childhood

Kohlberg (1966) offers a theoretical explanation for the phenomenon of same-sex preference as well as for its appearance in early childhood that is important from a developmental perspective for two reasons. First, it indicates that the young child's preference for same-sex peers is developmentally essential and predictable; second, it suggests that children's same-sex peer relationships may be developmentally important in ways that distinguish them from cross-sex peer relationships.

Noting that as a universal category of human experience, "Gender identity is perhaps the most stable of all social identities" (p. 92), Kohlberg (1966) also proposes that the category of gender is a central organizing component of self-concept, which is in a formative stage in early childhood. As noted earlier, although young children don't really understand concepts as abstractions, with the acquisition of the capacity for symbolic thought, they do become aware of the category of gender. With this capacity, children begin to construct their ideas about gender. Their first ideas have to do with gender identity—the psychological awareness that one is male or female. At about age two, most children can correctly identify their own gender, and there is a rapid increase in gender labeling between the ages of two and three. Children of this age also have some understanding that words like "man" and "woman" are gender words but do not understand male and female as concepts (e.g., that the category of male includes both man and boy), nor do they yet understand that gender is a stable characteristic. In Kohlberg's terms, they have not yet acquired "gender constancy." Although gender identity occurs early and remains a central core of personality, Kohlberg found that gender constancy begins to appear at about age five, when children begin to recognize that even if a girl plays football or a boy has long hair, gender remains unalterable. Although subsequent studies reveal that the age at which children acquire gender constancy varies, research does confirm that these ideas emerge sequentially and occur cross-culturally (Munroe, Shimin, & Munroe, 1984; Slaby & Frey, 1975).

Psychologically, this developmental process can be thought of as the child first saying, "I'm a boy/girl" (gender identity), and then saying, "If I am going to be a boy/girl forever (gender constancy), what does that mean?" The child then seeks answers by closely observing and associating with same-sex persons to discover generalities about behaviors, values, and attitudes of others of their gender. Because adults are less useful for social comparison, association with same-sex children provides a more meaningful context for seeking answers to their question.

Consistent with Piaget's theory, Kohlberg (1966) proposes that children's answers to these questions do not come from simply imitating what adults say and do. Instead, children play an active role in the ideas they construct. They translate and interpret what they observe and experience, and their ideas reflect their level of cognitive development. This explains why their ideas about the characteristics of their gender are often very different from those of adults. For example, they tend to judge what fits in which gender category on the basis of physical characteristics such as strength, depth of voice, or clothes, and they conclude, for example, that men are smarter because they have bigger heads or that women are nicer because they have smoother skin (Ullian, 1981). Because young children's concepts are vague and young children do not yet grasp the idea of "role," their association with same-sex peers concretely confirms their gender identity.

The Developmental Functions of Same-Sex Peers in Middle Childhood

We need only go to the neighborhood playground or school lunchroom to see the pervasiveness of same-sex preference in middle childhood. On the surface, this may seem puzzling because neither schools nor homes are typically sex segregated. Because gender constancy appears to be attained in early childhood, we might expect that children's strong need to demonstrate and retain their gender identity would diminish. But there are also reasons why relationships with same-sex peers continue to serve developmental functions in middle childhood. For one thing, because of children's increased cognitive ability to see the uniqueness of their own perspective and simultaneously become more aware of others' perspectives, school-age children become very aware of difference. Social comparison intensifies, and experimenting with who is "in" and who is "out" by forming alliances with peers becomes a major activity. Gender is one obvious and psychologically important basis for alliances; to wit, the classic "boys against the girls." But the purpose of associating with one's own gender in middle childhood goes beyond forming group alliances. Although children attain gender constancy in early childhood, young children's answers to the question "What does being a boy/girl mean?" are limited by their cognitive abilities, and their initial concepts are inaccurate in terms of the actualities of themselves and the world. With their new cognitive ability to distinguish between fantasy and reality, school-age children also seek same-sex peers to define more clearly gender role and the psychological meaning of gender and to practice boy or girl behavior.

Learning about relationships is inherently a part of this process. This means that within these groups, school-age children are not only developing a concept of gender that is more closely tied to objective reality but are also developing more realistic concepts of themselves, social relationships, and morality. These revised ideas—now true concepts for the first time—and their associated characteristic patterns of interaction appear to have far-reaching effects. Satisfactory social relationships in middle childhood have an impact on not only development in other areas, including academic achievement and self-esteem, during this period (Best, 1983), but also on healthy development in subsequent periods (Spivak, Marcus, & Swift, 1986).

Evidence of a Link Between
Same-Sex Peer Relations and Moral Orientation

Kohlberg never linked his theoretical ideas about the development of gender identity and constancy to his theory of moral development, and I have found no efforts on the part of others to do so. Instead, Kohlberg and his colleagues focused on the school as an institution and on translating his moral development theory into practice (Hersh, Paolitto, & Reimer, 1979). Numerous studies support Piaget's notion that relationships with peers provide an important context for the development of children's concepts of justice and the social skills associated with that moral orientation. Damon's (1977) studies of changes in children's understanding of what he calls "positive justice" are a notable example of this work. However, there do not appear to be any studies that compare justice reasoning in same-sex and cross-sex peer relationships or any studies that examine whether and how the development of the care orientation might be fostered in peer relationships.

The hypothesis that there may be a link between the two different moral orientations of justice and care and boys' and girls' same-sex peer relationships is, however, supported by another persistent pattern in studies of children's interactions with peers: recurring findings that there are consistent and marked differences in the nature and quality of the social interactions that occur within same-sex groups. An examination of these differences reveals parallels to the themes and preoccupations that distinguish the two moral voices.

The Link in Early Childhood

To illustrate this parallel in early childhood, I draw on a major study of sex-role development by Pitcher and Schultz (1983) as presented in their book, *Boys and Girls at Play: The Development of Sex Roles*. To analyze their observational records of the free play of 255 preschool children, Pitcher and Schultz categorized children's interactions as either affiliative/positive behaviors (defined as facilitating, cooperative acts that elicit approval of another child and that seem designed to initiate or maintain contact with another child) or nonaffiliative/negative behaviors (defined as occurring when a child physically and/or verbally acts in a way that hurts or clearly conflicts with the interests of another child).

The significant quantitative gender difference they found is that there is a dramatic increase in same-sex affiliative/positive interactions in girls at age three, which remains relatively stable through ages four and five. In contrast, no increase in positive contacts was found for boys at age three, with a significant increase in this type of interaction coming for boys at age four and continuing to increase at age five.

In light of what may be regarded as the universal gender difference finding that females engage in more affiliative behavior than males do, these findings are not unexpected, although their appearance at such an early age is noteworthy. These results suggest a logical connection between affiliative/positive interactions in preschool girls' same-sex peer relationships and the care orientation focus on maintaining and restoring relationships. However, to avoid the misleading implication that affiliation and relationships are not significant to males and to shed light on the behavioral meaning of affiliation in relation to the care orientation in females, we need to examine this association more closely. Fortunately, Pitcher and Schultz's (1983) analyses of subcategories of affiliative/positive behaviors allow us to extend our thinking. The subcategory of interest is nurturant behavior.

The Care Orientation and Preschoolers' Nurturant Behaviors

The activity-centered nature of what affiliation means as a marker of the care orientation in preschool girls is clearly evident in their extensive use of nurturant behaviors to initiate and sustain interactions. The differences in the frequency of boys' and girls' engagement in nurturant behavior are also dramatic: Girls engaged in more nurturant behaviors than boys at all ages, and their use of nurturant behaviors progressively increased with age. In contrast, Pitcher and Schultz (1983) report that "Nurturance is almost absent in boy/boy dyads" (p. 35).

The tie between nurturant behaviors and the care orientation concern with responding to the needs of others is revealed in Pitcher and Schultz's (1983) report on the quality of girls' nurturant behavior. In the "housekeeping" corner, where much of the nurturant behavior of the girls they studied took place, the girls spent large amounts of time as "mothers"

> . . . dispensing coffee, tea, dessert, vegetables, and baked goods to one another . . . they protect babies, bathe and diaper them, and care for their injuries and illnesses. There are many instances of kissing, hugging, patting, stroking, and endearing remarks to other girls who assume baby roles. "How are you doing sister?" says one girl to another as she pats her head. (pp. 62–63)

As girls' physical skills become more refined, girls' nurturant behaviors extend into many areas. They help each other and boys with such tasks as putting on painting smocks and coats. They show an increasing ability to anticipate others' needs. For example, putting water at the foot of her baby's bed, one 5-year-old girl announces, "'This is in case you want some later,'" and, returning for a check before leaving the house, she says, "'I have to see if baby's settled'" (Pitcher & Schultz, 1983, p. 63). Their interactions are permeated with offers of special words of comfort, and "they are particularly attentive to the sick or wounded; and become deeply involved in cutting gauze, bandaging legs, providing medicine, and arranging for hospitals and operations" (p. 63).

In contrast, although boys also spend time in the housekeeping corner, they do not spend their time there engaging in nurturant behaviors involving the provision of food and care. Instead, Pitcher and Schultz (1983) found that:

> Boys are sometimes the recipients of food but rarely the providers. Although boys sometimes manipulate pots and pans at the stove, it is the mechanics of cooking and stirring that occupies them, not serving food to others. . . . Boys' involvement with food and drink is likely to be silly or inappropriate; "Hey, give me a little beer to drink". . . . They are the jovial recipients as they grab plastic food, then giggle and throw it around. (pp. 63–64)

These differences in the quality as well as the quantity of nurturant behaviors provide us with several important insights relating to the care orientation in girls. Most broadly, they identify same-sex relationships as an important context in which girls develop the central care orientation preoccupations with anticipating others' needs and a concern for the welfare of others. More specifically, we can conjecture that through practicing these nurturant behaviors, girls become increasingly knowledgeable about the subtleties of human relationships, and that while acting on these preoccupations, they are simultaneously acquiring the skills to deal with these details and to anticipate people's needs and reactions. Consistent with girls' level of cognitive development, the behavioral manifestations of these ideas and skills in early childhood are, of course, very concrete; often have an unrealistic quality; and may be exaggerated to help make them cognitively more clear. The conspicuous absence of boys' preoccupation with the care orientation themes evident in girls' nurturant behaviors is equally noteworthy because it implies the absence of opportunities to develop the social knowledge and skills acquired through this behavior in their same-sex relationships. And finally, these observations are an important reminder of the dangers of oversimplifying our interpretations of gender difference findings. For even when boys and girls in Pitcher and Schultz's (1983) study played in the same physical contexts and with the same toys, their interactions appear to have a different psychological meaning. Like Middleton's speculation, this underscores the need to look beyond superficial socialization factors such as toy preferences to understand gender differences.

The Justice Orientation and Preschoolers'
Rough-and-Tumble Play and Negative Contacts

A parallel between the justice orientation and boys' same-sex relationships in early childhood is, however, also evident in Pitcher and Schultz's (1983) cluster of affiliative/positive contact behaviors—specifically in the subcategory most predominant in the boys' same-sex behavior, rough-and-tumble play. As Pitcher and Schultz report, the boys "wrestle, playfully shoot water at one another . . . put clay in one another's hair, play puppet fighting, tickle and pretend to shoot one another, fall dead and roll on the floor" (p. 59). Such activities appear to enable boys to create psychological moments of separation by making the distinction between self and other concretely clear (e.g., "You have clay in your hair, I don't"; "When I'm holding you down, I can get away and you can't"; "You're dead and I'm alive"). This view of the self as separate from others is the self-concept assumed within the justice perspective. At the same time, the quality of this play in boys, which leads Pitcher and Schultz to classify it as positive rather than negative, speaks to boys' search and need for relationships with other boys. In contrast, when girls engaged in rough-and-tumble play, they tended to jostle *with* rather than *against* one another through such activities as gently poking one another as they jumped on mattresses or giggling and chanting as they danced around in circles. This suggests a view of the self as connected with others—the self-concept assumed from the care perspective.

The connection between the justice orientation and boys' same-sex peer interactions in early childhood is even more directly evident in Pitcher and Schultz's (1983) analysis of gender differences in nonaffiliative/negative contacts. With respect to the frequency of such contacts, at every age, the boys had more negative contacts than did girls. The pattern of change was that 3-year-old boys most often engaged in initiation of such contacts, 4-year-olds engaged in both initiation and response, and 5-year-olds most often engaged in response. The justice orientation concerns with rules, roles, rights, and autonomy is apparent in Pitcher and Schultz's descriptive summary of the nature and quality of these nonaffiliative/negative behaviors in boys:

> Among boys, assaulting and molesting behaviors often involve appropriation or retention of property; this is also true in boys' disagreeing with or reprimanding one another. They are concerned about other boys' infringements on territorial or property rights; their house, their car, their garage. They are attentive to equitable ["fair"] divisions of property: "You have too much more than me." They argue over such matters as methods of building, differences of opinion, and issues of control—who will be first, who will be the driver. Directives refer to rights and rules, not to what is socially desirable. . . . Whereas boys tend to use rules or reprimands instrumentally for their own purposes, girls seem more interested in preserving social order for its own sake. (pp. 56–57)

Pitcher and Schultz (1983) refer to the period when such conflict and negative contact reach their zenith in boys (age four) as their "vying for power" in relationships with one another. These power struggles resolve into hierarchical structures in boys' same-sex relationships at about age five, when they band together and their same-sex relationships become more stable and consolidated. Pitcher and Schultz propose that this hierarchical structure controls the expression of aggression either by minimizing conflicts and battles over power because power positions are prescribed by rules and roles within the hierarchy (e.g., the "worker" in the construction project in the block corner is governed by the "boss"), or by at least organizing aggression within groups.

In summary, the developmental portrait of early childhood that emerges from the foregoing analysis is highlighted by evidence that the dynamics at work underlying development are different for young boys and young girls in part because from the beginning, same-sex peer relationships are not the same phenomenon. Young girls and boys appear to socialize each other in ways that reflect the distinctive themes of the two different moral orientations. Thus, they emerge from this developmental period, when they begin to construct concepts of themselves, gender, relationships, and morality, with markedly different concepts. What happens to all this in middle childhood?

Evidence of a Link Between Same-Sex Peer Relations and Moral Orientations in Middle Childhood

Earlier, we noted that forming alliances becomes a major preoccupation in middle childhood and that one very common group against group form of this is boys against the girls. However, alliances within same-sex groups also occupy much of children's time and energy. The differences in the form and content of school-age boys' and girls' same-sex "who's in" and "who's out" experiments reflect more general, striking, and widely documented differences in patterns of social interaction within boys' and girls' groups in middle childhood (Eder & Hallinan, 1978; Lever, 1978; Maltz & Borker, 1983; Piaget, 1932/1965; Thorne, 1986; Waldrop & Halverson, 1975). The following composite summary of these patterns shows a continuation and refinement of the patterns drawn from Pitcher & Schultz's (1983) study of early childhood that was just discussed.

The old adage, "Boys form clubs to include other boys," may be rooted in the fact that boys tend to form larger groups than do girls. Within these groups, who's in and who's out experiments occur in the context of the hierarchy within the group—for example, who gets to be president of the club and who has to be the worker. The vying for power in boys in early childhood becomes a vying for position. The powers of logical persuasion and more realistic assessment of their own and others' abilities, facilitated by cognitive changes, become important in their communications and replace the threats, tears, and physical persuasion of preschoolers. Boys view their group as a collective entity, emphasize group loyalty and solidarity, and use the group in their quest for recognition and self-esteem while they jockey for position within the group. Behaviorally, this appears in their use of language to assert social position, attract an audience, and distract others when other speakers have the attention of an audience. Such techniques are often exhibited by the class clown and are used to gain support from other boys to enhance his position in the group. In their group interactions, boys prefer to play formal competitive games in teams. Teams provide a structure for hierarchy between groups in the conflict of group against group as well as within group (e.g., who bats first or gets to pitch and who gets stuck out in right field). In these games, cooperation is formalized: Getting along is spelled out by rules and roles.

In contrast, the parallel adage for girls—"girls form clubs to exclude other girls"—reflects girls' tendency to form smaller groups. When girls do play formal games, their games tend to involve close contact with a single child performing at one time (e.g., jump rope or hopscotch). (Recall that this is the same difference that Piaget observed in Switzerland 60 years ago.) Girls tend to view their group as a network of intimate relationships rather than as a hierarchy. The classic configuration is a group of three in which who's in and who's out experiments occur as ongoing informal games of inclusion and exclusion. Two girls at any given moment are pitted as a pair against the third, with the pairs within the threesome changing frequently (e.g., between the time that school starts in the morning and lunchtime). Through these activities, much of girls' time is spent in making, breaking, mending, and remaking relationships. It is not surprising that girls appear to be more aware of the fragility of relationships and of the ways in which one friendship may threaten another. To illustrate in the words of 11-year-old Sarah, as quoted in Z. Rubin (1980): "Joan's now trying to hang around the older kids so as to be admitted into their gang so she has no time to be with Liz who therefore tries to be friends with Christine which doesn't please Sally" (p. 108).

Behaviorally, this awareness is evident in girls' use of language to create, fix, and maintain relationships by clarifying the speech of others, explaining others' actions, criticizing in respectable ways, and expressing directives and disagreements in ways that merge speaker and hearer (e.g., "let's" or "we gotta") (Goodwin, 1980). They also use language to threaten and break up relationships. They know how saying certain things will affect particular people and they know the response they are likely to get, and they use this knowledge not only to help but also to hurt.

Because these distinctions between boys' and girls' same-sex interactions in middle childhood represent a continuation of the distinctions in early childhood that were identified in Pitcher and Schultz's (1983) study, we can conjecture that same-sex groups continue to be a primary context within which school-age children develop ideas about and practice social skills associated with the two orientations. At the same time, within each orientation, children's ideas shift from the world of fantasy to the world of reality. Boys, focused on the justice orientation, acquire the ability to understand the concepts of rules and roles and use that knowledge to manage their hierarchies. For girls, the danger lies not in being at the bottom of a hierarchy but rather in being excluded from the network. Their knowledge of relationships gives them both the power to prevent this for themselves and to impose it on others. Furthermore, their nurturing fantasies of imagined needs in early childhood are replaced with a more reality-based knowledge of psychological needs and of their function in human interaction, and with more effective skills in using this knowledge to manage real relationships.

The Male/Justice Bias and the Issue of Interpretation

The pervasiveness and consistency of these differences within same-sex relationships and across these two developmental periods clearly indicate that boys and girls grow up with different models of social relations. Accepting that, we can surmise that what each gender is doing and learning is also developmentally important. However, this is not the interpretation we find in the literature. As noted earlier, what we find instead in the moral development literature is a tendency to attach developmental significance to boys' perceptions and behaviors and to overlook the potential developmental significance of those of girls or to see them as a developmental handicap. Two representative examples will illustrate that this mode of interpretation is also evident in the literature on children's interactions with same-sex peers and is another manifestation of the male/justice bias that is in need of change.

An Early Childhood Example

In Pitcher and Schultz's (1983) study, after noting that "a commonly accepted mark of maturity involves behaviors that are more positive than negative" (p. 19), they interpret their findings that girls seem to form same-sex alliances at age three and that positive contacts among girls increased to a higher level, maintained through age five with relatively few negative contacts, as follows: "The much greater number of same-sex positive contacts observed among 3-year-old girls compared to 3-year-old boys suggest that girls mature earlier than boys in acquiring social skills and establishing positive relationships" (p. 27).

However, in their interpretation of the boys' patterns of negative contacts, they seem to lose sight of the implications and potential developmental significance of the social maturity they observed in 3-year-old girls:

We speculate that the greater amount of conflict present among the boys resolves into same-sex relations that are more highly developed than those of girls . . . [and] as the boys group becomes more united at age 5 . . . not only is the consolidated structure of the same-sex group apparently self-regulated in boys, suggesting a hierarchy, [but] the adjustment in same-sex interaction is consistently less among the girls. (pp. 32–33)

Thus, the experience of boys is taken as the model for what is developmentally advantageous. In spite of evidence that girls have an ability to engage in positive interactions with one another as early as age three, evidence that girls' nurturing behaviors expand during early childhood, and the sense that girls' modes of interactions contain some intrinsic value, girls' behaviors are in the end construed as a developmental handicap.

A Middle Childhood Example

A parallel example appears in Janet Lever's (1978) influential study of games and play in middle childhood, "Sex differences in the complexity of children's play and games." Lever operationalizes the concept of complexity by examining behaviors such as role differentiation; explicitness of goals; number and specificity of rules that are known to all players, are constant from one game to another, and carry sanctions for violations; team formation; and the size of group play (the larger the group, the more complex). Given this concept of complexity in light of the characteristics of typical boys' interactions described earlier, we can readily predict what Lever found: Boys' play is more complex in these ways than that of girls. Instead of displaying the characteristics Lever identified as markers of complexity, the girls typically played similar roles in smaller groups in games that less often required the formation of teams, did not have explicit common group goals, and had fewer rules governing their behavior. The interdependence girls displayed typically took the form of interdependence in action (rather than of roles prescribing performance) between members of a single group in a cooperative (rather than a competitive) context.

On closer examination, the male/justice bias in Lever's (1978) concept of complexity becomes apparent. What she and others identify in girls' interactions seem to be situations that require them to constantly monitor everything that is happening and make moment-by-moment judgments and adjustments in their behavior. Is this less complex? If we consider that functioning in situations in which rules and positions are not clear offers challenges not present in situations in which they are clear, and that shared explicit goals may be easier to accommodate than implicit goals, it would be more accurate to propose that the play and games of boys and girls are complex in different ways.

However, this possibility is not reflected in Lever's (1978) interpretation of the developmental significance and potential long-range consequences of what she sees as greater complexity in boys' play and games. Describing girls' play as a "mimic" of primary human relationships or as engagement in conversation rather than playing "anything at all," Lever does note that "there are probably benefits for their affective and verbal development" (p. 481). But the potential developmental significance of girls' interactions in terms of the knowledge about human relationships and social skills that they acquire and their functional adaptive value to subsequent development remains unacknowledged. Instead, Lever notes, "Boys' games provide a valuable learning environment" for developing a variety of social skills, including "the ability to deal with diversity in memberships where each person is performing a special task, the ability to coordinate actions and maintain cohesiveness among group members; the ability to cope with a set of impersonal rules, and the ability to work for collective as well as personal goals" (p. 480).

Observing the parallels between these abilities and the skills required of adults for success in our society, especially in competitive situations found in modern organizations, Lever (1978) then concludes with a speculation:

> One implication of this research is that boys' greater exposure to complex games may give them an advantage in occupational milieus that share structural features with those games. At the very least, the striking similarity between the formula for success in team sports and in modern organizations should encourage researchers to give serious attention to play patterns and their consequences. (p. 482)

In other words, the complexity of boy's play and games is seen to better prepare children to function as adults in our society and, hence, is developmentally advantageous as children move through adolescence and assume their productive and reproductive roles as adults. The complexity of girls' play and games goes unnoticed, and their difference is perceived as leaving them developmentally disadvantaged.

New Directions

As I noted at the start, this is an exploratory effort to pull together ideas from diverse bodies of literature. Hence, it is necessary to keep the following caveats in mind:

• The longitudinal research that will both systematically document the proposed links between the two moral voices and same-sex relationships and delineate their developmental consequences remains to be done.

- "Gender related" means we are more likely to see a characteristic in one gender than the other, not that any characteristic is gender specific (i.e., universally present in one gender and absent in the other).
- The topic of gender-related differences is a highly controversial one in our society as well as in developmental psychology.

With these caveats in mind, we can explore possible new directions for theory, research, and education that may help us to meet and master the old challenge of a male/justice bias and replace it with a more informed understanding of the potential developmental contributions and limitations of each orientation and each gender's perceptions and behaviors.

One first step is to identify the behaviors and concerns we see primarily in girls as a difference rather than as a deficit. This means we must come to grips with the values and ideals underlying our responses to the gender differences that we regularly observe and must address such critical questions as: How does the male/justice bias inform our interpretations of what we see? Is behavior we think of as typical or desirable more common in boys? Do we think of girls as doing nothing (or at least nothing important) when we see them standing on the playground talking while the boys are engrossed in a game of soccer? How does our own gender influence what we see and how we interpret it? Do we better understand and sympathize with children of our own gender? Do their experiences sometimes resonate too much? Given that historically males' perceptions have been recognized and valued in ways that those of girls and women have not, is it more difficult for males to recognize and value areas of difference? Does hierarchical ordering and reliance on rules seem more appealing and less wrenching? Do women's perceptions and experiences still largely remain within what Freud (1926/1961b) described as a "dark continent" (p. 212)?

In terms of curriculum, evidence that the ability to nurture entails experience, knowledge, and skills rather than being simply the product of "female intuition" points to possibilities for educating both genders about typical care orientation concerns. In general, we need to examine whether both moral voices are represented in the materials we present to children to foster their social and moral development. There have been recent successes in eliminating gender bias in obvious ways in school curricula by getting rid of books that show girls as helpless and weak and boys who would rather die than cry. But the observation that "boys do well [in school] by being bad," reported in an article entitled "Is school unfair to girls?" in a current issue of *Time* (1992) indicates we still overlook the more subtle ways the differential valuing of characteristics that boys and girls display is reflected in the curriculum. The educational setting is ideal in its opportunities to bring forward an awareness of the existence of both orientations and engage them in dialogue.

We must also consider the risks of overvaluing the male/justice perspective in boys. Are there weaknesses inherent in the type of interactions more typical of boys, and how might these limit boys' development of interpersonal skills? That speculation seems substantiated when we consider the social milieu of formal games, where rules and roles prescribe behavior and create a situation in which one does not really need to pay much attention to the particular characteristics or psychological needs of others or to display fully one's own. Yet interpersonal skills are the essential building blocks of a kind of flexible self-understanding that is required to adapt and function in contexts in which rules and roles are less clearly defined or absent. And such contexts constitute the bulk of our public and private adult lives.

Research on adults provides evidence that these limitations in the typical interactions of boys are more than mere speculation and may have long-range implications for their development in adulthood. That adult men have what Zick Rubin (1980) calls a "special difficulty" (p. 109) in forming intimate relationships is widely documented, and Rubin himself notes the potential tie between this and boys' experiences in same-sex groups in childhood. Research on friendships in adulthood also shows that in contrast to the shared interest and activity-based friendships of men, women's friendships with each other rest on shared intimacies, self-revelation, nurturance, and emotional support (Bell, 1981; Lowenthal & Haven, 1968; L. Rubin, 1985). Thus, we may also speculate that the interactions more typical of girls as early as the age of three also have long-range developmental consequences and that for both males and females, patterns of gender identity and moral orientation established in same-sex relationships of early and middle childhood create a core framework that is highly resistant to change.

As the unveiling of the male/justice bias makes clear, the danger of a gender-related tyranny that unnecessarily limits the opportunities for either males or females to develop capacities superficially ascribed by society to one gender or the other is real and ever present. But if we take the universality and potential developmental necessity of a preference for same-sex peers seriously, if the speculation about the early establishment and resistance of different gender-related frameworks of social understanding has validity, and if we assume that each orientation embodies valuable insights into the central moral question of human existence—How should we live and get along with others in the social world we share?—then we must also be wary of the equally real danger of ignoring gender differences and confusing equality with sameness. The popular view that insists that the male/justice bias be addressed by granting females the opportunity to do what males have always done in the ways they've always done them illustrates this confusion and why it is problematic: It leaves no room for difference. Neither does the recent "turning the tables" perspective that implies that there is something wrong with males because they are not like females. The challenge, then, may be best posed as a search for ways to value gender-related difference and simultaneously promote freedom from the tyranny of gender.

In contemporary society, this challenge requires us to resolve the discrepancy between what Robert May (1980) describes as our "political ideal" of the "dream of androgyny" and the reality of the differences we all observe in our own and others' behavior. The persistence, durability, and interrelatedness of patterns of gender differences such as those identified in this analysis are leading to a growing awareness that wishing that there were no important psychological differences between females and males won't make it so (Josselson, 1987; Miller, 1976; Paley, 1984). The psychological danger in this wish is the unrealizable expectation that we can make each gender into something it cannot become. But if we can enhance our capacity to say "different" without assuming "better" and "worse" and if we can appreciate that each perspective brings valuable and essential insights into human experience and that neither is complete without the other, the wish will no longer be necessary. And our energies can be directed toward freedom from the tyranny of gender by replacing false stereotypes of males and females as opposites with more accurate portraits of gender differences (e.g., females and males typically perceive relationships and are active and passive in different ways).

Conclusion

My goal in this chapter was to demonstrate that recognizing the connection between children's activities in same-sex peer relationships in early and middle childhood and the development of two moral orientations provides a starting place for identifying and understanding the developmental significance of girls' interactions. This recognition also yields a means to begin to eliminate the male/justice bias that has limited our understanding of the psychological meaning of the well-documented differences between males and females throughout the life cycle. The fact that these differences reflect the essence of what makes us distinctly human—concepts of self, gender, relationships, and morality—speaks to the significance of advancing our knowledge about them.

References

Bar-Yam, M., Kohlberg, L., & Naame, A. (1980). Moral reasoning of students in different cultural, social and educational settings. *American Journal of Education, 88,* 345–362.

Bell, R. (1981). Friendships of women and of men. *Psychology of Women Quarterly, 5,* 402–417.

Best, R. (1983). *We've all got scars.* Bloomington, IN: Indiana University Press.

Booth, A., & Hess, E. (1974). Cross-sex friendship. *Journal of Marriage and the Family, 36*, 38–47.

Bussey, K., & Maughan, B. (1982). Gender differences in moral reasoning. *Journal of Personality and Social Psychology, 42*, 701–706.

Damon, W. (1977). *The social world of the child.* San Francisco: Jossey-Bass.

Eder, D., & Hallinan, M. T. (1978). Sex differences in children's friendships. *American Sociological Review, 43*, 237–250.

Eisenberg-Berg, N. (1979). Development of children's prosocial moral judgment. *Developmental Psychology, 15*, 128–137.

Fishkin, J., Keniston, K., & MacKinnon, C. (1973). Moral reasoning and political ideology. *Journal of Personality and Social Psychology, 27*, 109–119.

Freud, S. (1961a). Some psychical consequences of the anatomical distinction between the sexes. In J. Strachey (Ed. and Trans.), *The standard edition of the complete psychological works of Sigmund Freud* (Vol. 19, pp. 248–258). London: Hogarth Press. (Original work published 1925.)

Freud, S. (1961b). The question of lay analysis. In J. Strachey (Ed. and Trans.), *The standard edition of the complete psychological works of Sigmund Freud* (Vol. 20, pp. 183–250). London: Hogarth Press. (Original work published 1926.)

Gibbs, J., & Wideman, K. (1982). *Social intelligence.* Englewood Cliffs, NJ: Prentice-Hall.

Gilligan, C. (1977). In a different voice: Women's conceptions of self and of morality. *Harvard Educational Review, 47*, 481–517.

Gilligan, C. (1982). *In a different voice: Psychological theory and women's development.* Cambridge, MA: Harvard University Press.

Gilligan, C., & Attanucci, J. (1988). Two moral orientations: Gender differences and similarities. *Merrill-Palmer Quarterly, 34*, 223–237.

Gilligan, C., Kohlberg, L., Lerner, J., & Belenky, M. (1971). *Moral reasoning about sexual dilemmas: The development of an interview and scoring system.* Technical report of the Commission on Obscenity and Pornography (Vol. 1). Washington, DC: Government Printing Office.

Goodwin, M. H. (1980). Directive-response speech sequences in girls' and boy's task activities. In S. McConnell-Ginet, R. Borker, & N. Furman (Eds.), *Women and language in literature and society* (pp. 157–173). New York: Praeger.

Grunebaum, H. (1976). Thoughts on sex, love and commitment. *Journal of Sex and Marital Therapy, 2*, 277–283.

Haan, N. (1977). *A manual for interpersonal morality.* Berkeley: University of California, Institute for Human Development.

Haan, N., Langer, J., & Kohlberg, L. (1976). Family patterns of moral reasoning. *Child Development 47*, 1204–1206.

Haan, N., Smith, M. B., & Block, J. (1968). Moral reasoning of young adults: Political-social behavior, family background, and personality correlates. *Journal of Personality and Social Psychology, 10*, 183–201.

Hallinan, M. (1979). Structural effects on children's friendships and cliques. *Social Psychology Quarterly, 42*, 43–54.

Hersh, R., Paolitto, D., & Reimer, J. (1979). *Promoting moral growth: From Piaget to*

Kohlberg. New York: Longman.

Holstein, C. (1976). Irreversible, stepwise sequence in the development of moral judgment: A longitudinal study of males and females. *Child Development, 47,* 51–61.

Hudgins, W., & Prentice, N. (1973). Moral judgment in delinquent and non-delinquent adolescents and their mothers. *Journal of Abnormal Psychology, 82,* 145–152.

Is school unfair to girls? (1992, February 24). *Time,* p. 62.

Jacklin, C., & Maccoby, E. (1978). Social behavior at thirty-three months in same-sex and mixed-sex dyads. *Child Development, 49,* 557–569.

Josselson, R. (1987). *Finding herself: Pathways to identity development in women.* San Francisco: Jossey Bass.

Kohlberg, L. (1966). A cognitive-developmental analysis of children's sex-role concepts and attitudes. In E. Maccoby (Ed.), *The development of sex differences* (pp. 82–172). Stanford, CA: Stanford University Press.

Kohlberg, L. (1969). Stage and sequence: The cognitive-developmental approach to socialization. In D. Goslin (Ed.), *Handbook of socialization theory and research* (pp. 347–480). Chicago: Rand McNally.

Kohlberg, L. (1971). From is to ought: How to commit the naturalistic fallacy and get away with it in the study of moral development. In T. Mischel (Ed.), *Cognitive development and epistemology* (pp. 151–235). New York: Academic Press.

Kohlberg, L. (1976). Moral stages and moralization: The cognitive-developmental approach. In T. Lickona (Ed.), *Moral development and behavior* (pp. 31–53). New York: Holt, Rinehart and Winston.

Kohlberg, L., & Kramer, R. (1969). Continuities and discontinuities in childhood and adult moral development. *Human Development, 12,* 93–120.

Kramer, R. (1968). *Moral development in young adulthood.* Unpublished doctoral dissertation, University of Chicago, Chicago.

Kuhn, D., Langer, J., Kohlberg, L., & Haan, N. (1977). The development of formal operations in logical and moral judgment. *Genetic Psychology Monographs, 95,* 97–188.

Langdale, S. (1983). Moral orientations and moral development: The analysis of care and justice reasoning across different dilemmas in females and males from childhood through adulthood. Doctoral dissertation, Harvard University. *Dissertation Abstracts International, 44,* 06B. (University Microfilms No. 83-20, 175).

Langdale, S. (1986). A Re-vision of structural-developmental theory. In G. Sapp (Ed.), *Handbook of moral development* (pp. 15–54). Birmingham, AL: Religious Education Press.

Lever, J. (1978). Sex differences in the complexity of children's play and games. *American Sociological Review, 43,* 471–483.

Lowenthal, J., & Haven, C. (1968). Interaction and adaptation: Intimacy as a critical variable. *American Sociological Review, 33,* 20–30.

Lyons, N. (1983). Two perspectives: On self, relationships and morality. *Harvard Educational Review, 53,* 125–145.

Maltz, D. N., & Borker, R. A. (1983). A cultural approach to male-female miscommunication. In J. J. Gumperz (Ed.), *Language and social identity* (pp. 195–216). New York: Cambridge University Press.

May, R. (1980). *Sex and fantasy: Patterns of male and female development.* New York: W.W. Norton.

Middleton, T. H. (1980, May). Boys and girls together. *Saturday Review of Literature*, p. 26.

Miller, J. B. (1976). *Toward a new psychology of women*. Boston: Beacon Press.

Munroe, R. H., Shimin, H. S., & Munroe, R. L. (1984). Gender understanding and sex role preference in four cultures. *Developmental Psychology, 20*, 673–682.

Omark, D., Omark, M., & Edelman, M. (1975). Formation of dominance hierarchies in young children: Action and perception. In T. R. Williams (Ed.), *Psychological anthropology*. The Hague: Mouton.

Paley, V. (1984). *Boys and girls: Superheroes in the doll corner*. Chicago: University of Chicago Press.

Parikh, B. (1980). Development of moral judgment and its relation to family environmental factors in Indian and American families. *Child Development, 1*, 1030–1039.

Piaget, J. (1965). *The moral judgment of the child*. New York: Free Press. (Original work published 1932.)

Pitcher, E., & Schultz, L. (1983). *Boys and girls at play: The development of sex roles*. New York: Praeger.

Rest, J. (1979). *Development in judging moral issues*. Minneapolis: University of Minnesota Press.

Rubin, L. (1985). *Just friends: The role of friendship in our lives*. New York: Harper & Row.

Rubin, Z. (1980). *Children's friendships*. Cambridge, MA: Harvard University Press.

Saltzstein, H. D., Diamond, R. M., & Belenky, M. (1972). Moral judgment level and conformity behavior. *Developmental Psychology, 7*, 327–336.

Serbin, L., Tonick, I. L., & Sternglanz, S. (1977). Shaping cooperative cross-sex play. *Child Development, 48*, 924–929.

Slaby, R. G., & Frey, K. S. (1975). Development of gender constancy and selective attention to same-sex models. *Child Development, 46*, 849–856.

Spivack, G., Marcus, J., & Swift, M. (1986). Early classroom behavior and later misconduct. *Developmental Psychology, 22*, 124–131.

Thorne, B. (1986). Girls and boys together . . . but mostly apart: Gender arrangements in elementary schools. In W. Hartup & Z. Rubin (Eds.), *Relationships and development* (pp. 167–184). Hillsdale, NJ: Lawrence Erlbaum.

Ullian, D. (1981). The child's construction of gender: Anatomy as destiny. In E. K. Shapiro & E. Weber (Eds.), *Cognitive and affective growth* (pp. 171–186). Hillsdale, NJ: Lawrence Erlbaum.

Waldrop, M. F., & Halverson, C. F. (1975). Intensive and extensive peer behavior: Longitudinal and cross-sectional analysis. *Child Development, 46*, 19–26.

Youniss, J. (1980). *Parents and peers in social development: A Sullivan-Piaget perspective*. Chicago: University of Chicago Press.

CHAPTER 3

Voices of Care and Justice in Children's Responses to Fable Dilemmas

Andrew Garrod and
Carole R. Beal

Dartmouth College and
University of Massachusetts at Amherst

Moral orientation is a recent and growing focus of research within moral psychology (Gilligan & Attanucci, 1988; Johnston, 1988; Pratt, Golding, Hunter, & Sampson, 1988; Walker, DeVries, & Trevethan, 1987). Until Gilligan's (1982) and Nodding's (1984) theorizing on the morality of care, the notion of moral orientation in moral development literature had been represented only in Kohlberg's stage theory of moral development (Colby et al., 1987). Kohlberg's hypothetical dilemmas can be coded for both moral development and moral orientation, according to established criteria in *The Measurement of Moral Judgment* (Colby et al., 1987). The four orientations that Kohlberg considers are normative, fairness, utilitarianism, and perfectionism.

Gilligan (1982, 1986) has elaborated the construct of moral orientations very differently from Kohlberg. Claiming that in its emphasis on justice as the core component of morality and in its use of hypothetical dilemmas Kohlberg's (1981) approach is biased and limited, Gilligan argues there is more to morality than justice. Specifically, justice is only one of two moral perspectives or orientations—the other being care. Her key claims are:

> (i) that justice and care are distinct moral orientations—i.e. two frameworks that organize thinking about what constitutes a moral problem and how to solve it, (ii) that most people in describing a moral problem and its resolution focus on one orientation and minimally represent the other, and (iii) that the direction of focus is associated with gender. (1986, p. 10)

Walker (1989) has emphasized the critical nature of the task in assessing moral orientation, arguing that the particular task may influence the orientation elicited. One alternative to Kohlberg's use of hypothetical dilemmas to evaluate moral orientation has been close analysis of the subject's self-generated moral dilemma. Several studies have shown that both orientations—justice and care—can appear in the real-life dilemmas reported by subjects and that the particular moral orientation represented in a dilemma appears to be linked with gender. Using data from a study of rights and responsibilities conducted by Gilligan (1982) and her colleagues, Lyons (1983) analyzed real-life moral problems reported by 36 upper-middle-class subjects ranging in age from 8 to 60 years. Lyons found that although men and women used both moral orientations, considerations of care seemed more likely to appear in the dilemmas reported by women, while concerns about issues of justice and rights tended to appear more often in the dilemmas described by men.

Similar patterns were reported by Gilligan and Attanucci (1988) in a study of real-life dilemmas described by adolescents and young adults. Gilligan and Attanucci tried to show that both moral orientations (justice and care) are present in the subjects' real-life dilemmas, that moral orientation is gender linked, and that although a given subject can generate considerations in both moral orientations, one orientation generally predominates. In the study, predominance was defined such that a real-life moral dilemma that consisted only of care considerations or of justice considerations was labeled "care only" or "justice only," respectively; a dilemma that consisted of 75% or more care or justice was labeled "care focus" or "justice focus," respectively. The results showed gender-linked patterns similar to those obtained by Lyons (1983). Thirty-five percent of the women versus only 2% of the men showed a care focus, but 65% of the men versus 30% of the women showed a justice focus.

There is also evidence for gender differences in moral orientation in adolescents as well as adults. Johnston, Brown, and Christopherson (1990) found gender-related differences in the moral conflicts described by adolescent boys and girls in a private school environment. Their results showed that although both boys and girls often described real-life moral conflicts in the context of a relationship, boys were more likely than girls to focus on the self as the context of the moral dilemma with no other relational context present. Significantly more girls than boys focused on concerns about the relationship rather than on concerns about the self.

Although these studies suggest that moral orientation is gender linked, at least when subjects are allowed to report their real-life moral conflicts, other studies have not obtained this pattern. Walker, DeVries, and Trevethan (1987) asked members of 80 family triads (mother, father, and child) to discuss Kohlbergian hypothetical dilemmas and to generate a real-life moral dilemma. The responses to the dilemmas were coded for the presence and dominance of the care/response or rights/justice moral orientation. Their results showed that few of the subjects showed consistent use of a single moral orientation across the two types of tasks. In addition, the evidence regarding the relation between gender and moral orientation was inconsistent.

In a longitudinal follow-up to this study, Walker (1989) also reported that there were no gender differences in moral orientation in the hypothetical dilemmas for either children or their parents. Gender differences in the real-life dilemmas were apparent only among the adults in the real-life dilemmas, and those differences disappeared when the content of the dilemma was controlled. Other researchers have also found that the specific content of the real-life moral dilemma has a strong influence on moral orientation.

Rothbart, Hanley, and Albert (1986) found that although both moral orientations were widely used by both men and women, women were more likely to employ predominantly care considerations. However, Rothbart, Hanley, and Albert also showed that the specific content of an individual's real-life moral dilemma had a strong influence on the use of moral orientation.

Similarly, Pratt, Golding, Hunter, and Sampson (1988) interviewed adults aged 18 to 75 about hypothetical and real-life moral dilemmas. Although they found that women were more likely to show a care orientation in their real-life dilemmas, the differences were not consistent as they were also influenced by the subjects' age, level of reasoning on the Kohlbergian interview, and type of real-life dilemma content recalled by the subjects for discussion.

Although current research provides some support for the existence of two moral orientations—an orientation to issues of justice and rights or to care and response—in subjects' real-life dilemmas, it is not yet clear whether the use of the orientations is actually gender linked, given that the use of a particular orientation seems highly influenced by the content of the dilemma. Concerns about the role of content are also problematic because there is not yet a consistent method for coding moral orientation in real-life dilemmas (Gilligan & Attanucci, 1988; Lyons, 1983; Walker, 1989).

It is also not yet clear when an orientation toward either justice or care might first appear in the life span and whether the use of a particular moral orientation might be gender linked in young children's reasoning. Donenberg and Hoffman (1988) conducted a study of moral orientation in hypothetical and real-life moral dilemmas among middle-class children and adolescents. Their results showed that girls emphasized the morality of care significantly more often than justice but that boys emphasized the morality of justice and care equally. Overall, the younger children emphasized the morality of care, while older children appeared more justice oriented. On the other hand, Walker, DeVries, and Trevethan (1987) found that concerns about rights and justice rather than care dominated children's real-life dilemmas. They also found that with maturity, there was increased use of a mixed orientation; this suggests that as children became more advanced in cognitive development, they might be better able to consider different points of view in a moral conflict.

Whereas both approaches to the study of moral orientation have been productive, each has limitations, particularly for investigating the development of moral orientation in young children. Kohlberg's hypothetical dilemmas are framed as problems of competing rights, making it difficult to detect concerns about care when such concerns are expressed. In addition, the hypothetical dilemmas often involve content that is remote from children's interests. On the other hand, although real-life moral dilemmas permit either moral orientation to be expressed, moral orientation may be confounded with dilemma content. It can also be difficult to elicit real-life problems from some young children. (One little boy seemed baffled by the question and told us, "I ain't had no problems yet.")

Johnston (1988) developed the fables task to address the limitations of existing approaches. The fables task uses standardized content, allows either moral orientation to be expressed, and involves content that is interesting and intelligible to young children as well as adolescents. In the task, children are presented with fables in which animal characters are faced with a conflict. For example, the "Porcupine and the Moles" fable (see Figure 6.1) describes a family of moles who generously invite a porcupine to share their warm cave for the winter, only to find that he is so large that his sharp quills make them uncomfortable. When they politely ask their guest to leave, he declines, saying that the cave "suits him very well." The problem can be framed in terms of competing rights: It is the moles' cave, and they have the right to determine who will live in their house, but they also made a promise to the porcupine and have an obligation to uphold it. The problem can also be framed in terms of concerns for the needs of each protagonist: The moles are miserable in their home, but the porcupine has nowhere to live and it is winter. The child is asked how the animals should solve their problem, if there is another solution, and what the best solution would be. In addition to probing for the child's use of a particular moral orientation in generating a solution, the interviewer can also present a different solution to see if the child can recognize and understand the alternative orientation even if he or she was not able to generate it spontaneously.

In her initial study, Johnston (1988) investigated how male and female adolescents aged 11 and 15 solved the moral problems embedded in the fables. She found that boys were more likely to adopt a rights orientation in discussing the fables—for example, by arguing that the moles should simply evict the porcupine because they were there first. In contrast, adolescent girls were more likely to exhibit a response solution to the fable problems—for example, by suggesting that the animals work together to enlarge the cave so that each would be comfortable and have a place to live. Johnston also obtained evidence that children's cognitive flexibility was implicated in their ability to think about both orientations. The older subjects were more likely to switch orientations when probed and to explain the logic of both orientations, which is consistent with the finding that older children seemed more aware of both orientations in their real-life moral dilemmas (Walker, DeVries, & Trevethan, 1987).

Johnston's findings suggest that an orientation toward justice/rights or response/care is apparent by early adolescence. However, little is known about when an orientation toward rights or response might develop in younger children and about whether such orientations are related to children's sex and cognitive flexibility. To investigate these issues, we conducted two studies of moral orientation in children and young adolescents, using Johnston's (1988) fable interviews.

Children's Responses to the Fable Dilemmas

In our first experiment (Garrod, Beal, & Shin, 1990), we included 54 children aged 6 to 11 years who attended schools in an upper-middle-class rural area in New England. The fables interview was administered to each child, and the children's responses were coded for the moral orientation used in their initial solution to the dilemma, their ability to think of a different way to solve the problem, their ability to explain both orientations when prompted, and their preferred moral orientation—that is, which solution they thought would be best. In addition, we investigated children's level of cognitive development as measured by several Piagetian tasks designed to assess concrete and early formal operational reasoning, and we included a measure of social perspective-taking skill (Selman, 1980).

The second experiment involved 132 children aged 5 to 13 years. We were interested in the possible effect of social class on the development of moral orientation; to investigate this factor, half of the children were drawn from a school in the same upper-middle-class rural neighborhood as those who participated in the first experiment. The remaining children attended a school in a larger working-class New England community. As in the first experiment, children received the fables interview and the battery of Piagetian tasks, but the social perspective-taking task was not included.

The fables task involves two different fables, the "Porcupine and the Moles" fable described earlier and the "Dog in the Manger" fable, in which an ox who is hungry from his long day's work returns to his stall, only to find a dog comfortably settled on the hay and refusing to move aside so the ox can have his dinner. Scoring was done by summing up the number of initial and preferred care-orientation responses provided by each child. Examples of responses showing the care and justice orientations are shown in Table 3.1. In both experiments, our analyses showed that there was no effect of grade; children in all grades tended to provide more care responses to the fable dilemmas.

Table 3.1. Examples of Care- and Justice-Oriented Responses in the Fables Task

Justice-Oriented Responses	Care-Oriented Responses
If somebody lets someone live with you . . . you should let them live with you forever. You just can't break your heart [promise]. (Boy, age 5)	They could cut the hay in half so that, well, the dog could have a little bit of the hay to sleep on, and the ox could eat the rest of it, then nobody would have gotten hurt, and they both would be satisfied. (Girl, age 8)
If there's a whole messload of dogs and a whole messload of oxes, they should have a big war to see who gets the hay. (Boy, age 8)	The porcupine could make a wall across the cave. 'Cause then they'd both have a home. (Boy, age 5)
Taking turns would keep the both of them from fighting and arguing about it. . . . If they were taking turns, it would be fair. (Boy, age 12)	They should cooperate. Maybe like if there was more rock they could try and blast out some more, and they would all help. And a few of 'em, maybe, ought to take care of the babies if they have some. (Girl, age 6)
They should put out a sign and it has a circle and a cross on it and a porcupine in the middle. And maybe they write in red on it that says "No porcupines allowed." (Boy, age 6)	Dig the place bigger so both of 'em can be in there. Then when they moved around they wouldn't get poked, 'cause there'd be more room to move around in. (Boy, age 6)
The porcupine should move because they [the moles] were there first, and if they left it wouldn't be fair, because they were there first. And the porcupine should move because they could hurt him, you know, really bad like that and stuff, and it's their home. (Girl, age 10)	They should all go on an expedition for marshmallows and stick the marshmallows on the porcupine's quills and then the moles will really, really, really not get pricked. Then the porcupine would be happy because he could live in the moles' house that suited him just fine and the moles could have tasty tidbits as well as a warm home because of the porcupine's body heat . . . and all would be happy. (Boy, age 8)
If you want to be treated nicely, you got to treat the other person nice, too. (Boy, age 12)	If they kicked the porcupine out, he'll be sad and he'll . . . it might die. And if the porcupine kicks them out, that would be the same thing. If they built another cave for the porcupine, then both of them would be happy and not have to worry about one of them getting hurt. (Boy, age 12)
The dog should move because the ox needs its own stall—and nobody wants someone in their home unless it's a visitor or a person you know, or it's someone babysitting you. (Girl, age 8)	The moles could dig another home for the porcupine. It would be generous of them, and they could make another friend if they did that. The more friends you have usually is the better. (Girl, age 12)

In addition, there was no effect of sex on children's tendency to provide care responses in either experiment. Finally, children were more likely to show a care orientation in their preferred solution than in their initial solution.

Although we found no evidence of sex or age differences in children's tendency to show a care orientation, there was evidence that children's ability to think about both moral orientations depended on their age and cognitive flexibility. After children had produced one solution to a fable problem, they were asked if there was "another way to solve the problem," to determine if they could switch between the care orientation and the justice/rights orientation spontaneously. In both experiments, we found that children who had reached the stage of early formal operations were more likely to switch moral orientations and to explain the logic of both orientations for at least one of the fables. In contrast, we found little evidence that social perspective-taking ability, as assessed by the Selman task in the first experiment, was related to children's moral orientation; although children's scores on the social perspective-taking task increased with grade, the frequency of care responses did not.

In the second experiment, we included children from working-class and upper-middle-class communities to investigate the possible role of social class on moral orientation. There was a marginally significant main effect for social class in the number of care responses offered by the children; upper-middle-class children were slightly more likely to show a care orientation than working-class children.

To summarize, the major findings of the two studies were that (1) there were no overall differences in moral orientation between boys and girls; (2) when asked for the best solution to the fable dilemmas, children preferred the care response; (3) children's ability to see both moral orientations depended on the use of abstract reasoning skills on beginning formal operational tasks; and (4) in the second study, there was a marginal but suggestive indication that upper-middle-class children were somewhat more likely to offer care solutions than working-class children were.

Before discussing these findings in relation to earlier research on moral orientation, it is helpful to examine how children of different ages respond to the fable questions. In the following example, Peter, a first-grader, generated two care solutions to the problem presented in the "Dog in the Manger" fable. Even with prompting, he was unable to generate a justice response. Here, he was asked to evaluate his answers:

I: Of all of the solutions we discussed, which one is the best one, do you think?
P: Sorting it out.
I: What do you mean by sorting it out?
P: The dog would get half and the ox half.
I: I see. Can you tell me why you think that would be the best way?

P: Because then there would be some [hay] for the dog and some for the ox, and it would be fairer.

I: What do you mean, that would be fairer?

P: Because then they would have the same amount, and then the dog could have somewhere to lay down, and the ox could have something to eat.

Despite his introduction of the comparative "fairer," which may sound suggestive of a rights orientation, clearly the major consideration for Peter is finding a solution that would make all the animals happy: "then the dog could have somewhere to lay down, and the ox could have something to eat." This desire for an inclusive solution is evidence, again, of the care orientation.

Another first-grader, Sally, is unable to generate an inclusive response to the "Porcupine and the Moles" fable that takes into account all the competing interests:

I: How would you solve this problem?

S: Just let the porcupine go.

I: Just let the porcupine go where?

S: Well, just tell the porcupine he had to go because it was [the moles'] house.

I: Why would that be a good way to solve it?

S: I don't know.

I: Can you think of any reason why you might want to do that? I mean, make the porcupine go? You said it was because it was the moles' house?

S: Yeah.

I: What does that mean?

S: The porcupine should go.

I: Do you think there's another way to solve the problem?

S: No.

I: No? How about, is there a way to solve the problem so that all the animals will be happy, both the porcupine and the moles?

S: No.

Sally can produce a solution to the problem without hesitation: "Just let the porcupine go." He is to be let go because it was the moles' house; in her emphasis on the moles' concrete and prior ownership rights, she demonstrates a justice response. Despite the prompting of the interviewer, who asks if there is a way to make all the animals happy, Sally cannot come up with another way to see or to solve the problem.

In contrast to the two first-graders, Penny, a fifth-grader in the stage of early formal operational reasoning, moves easily between the two orientations. She responds to the ox and the dog fable:

I: How do you think the animals should solve this problem?

P: Probably—well, I think the dog should get up and leave or something, because it's already slept there for a while, and the ox just wants to eat after it's been working all day.

I: So, you think the dog should just go.

P: Yeah. . . . The ox is trying to eat, but the dog has already taken a nap, so the dog, I think, should get up and go to another spot, because I'm sure there's plenty of hay around. . . . The dog should get up, because the ox wants to be there, and it's the ox's [place] and it's not really the dog's.

I: Is there any other way you can think of to solve this problem?

P: The ox could just, like, lay down for a while until the dog moved, and then he could go eat while the dog is gone.

I: What would be good about that way of solving the problem?

P: That way, then, there wouldn't be any fights or anything going on. . . . Probably the dog could just go and lay down someplace else because it's been laying there for a while and the ox has just come in because there should be lots of hay around so that he can lay on his own. . . . And that way, they could both get what they want.

Initially, Penny responds with what sounds like a turn-taking solution. The dog should get up and leave "because it's already slept there for a while, and the ox just wants to eat after it's been working all day." The rights orientation is confirmed by the consideration that it is "the ox's [place] and it's not really the dog's." With minimal probing, Penny suggests an alternative way of solving the problem; the merit in her second solution, she asserts, is that "that way, they could both get what they want." In sum, with her greater cognitive flexibility, Penny is able to generate two approaches to the problem and explain the logic underlying each solution.

Although the use of moral orientation was not found to be related to gender in our subjects, there was evidence among the older children of a greater commitment to a chosen orientation. For example, the following subjects, Leslie and Jesse, both 13 years old, illustrate flexibility in moving from one orientation to the other, but it is evident that each strongly prefers the initial solution offered. Leslie, a seventh-grader, sees the problem in terms of care:

L: Well, I guess the main problem is that the porcupine has no real home, and it's winter time. I suppose it's cold and snowy and stuff. It's not like he really has any other place to go. On the other hand, his prickly quills are scratching the moles, and that's the cause of the problem.

I: What do you think a solution to the problem might be?

L: I guess that they could try to make the cave bigger. That way, the porcupine's quills wouldn't bother the moles, and nobody would have to leave.

I: Why is it important that nobody has to leave?

L: Well, this way everybody can be happy, and I think that's really important. Besides, the porcupine doesn't have a family or a home, and the moles should take pity on him. Where's he going to go if they kick him out ?

After pursuing Leslie's reasoning on why she thinks it is important for all the animals to be happy and why she feels that the moles should be understanding toward the homeless porcupine, the interviewer asked Leslie if she could come up with another solution to the problem besides making the cave bigger for all the animals.

L: I guess the moles could try to find the porcupine another cave, although I suppose he'd still be lonely. Or they could kick him out, but I think that would be sort of mean.
I: Let's start with that first response, finding the porcupine another cave. Why is that a good answer?
L: Well, again, it's a solution that could make all of the animals happy, but like I said, the porcupine would probably still be lonely. Maybe the moles could help the porcupine locate another porcupine family and then everyone would be satisfied.
I: Could you elaborate on your response about kicking the porcupine out?
L: Well, you asked for all the solutions, and I guess this is a possibility, although I don't think that it is the best answer.
I: Why is that a good or bad solution?
L: I guess the fact that it is the moles' home is important, and if they simply cannot agree to cooperate, the moles might want to kick him out. I find it hard to believe, though, that they couldn't talk the whole thing through and come to some sort of agreement.

Leslie constantly seeks a solution that accommodates the interests of all the animals involved. She stresses the importance of talking things out, reaching agreement, and avoiding anyone being left out or feeling lonely—all factors that are clear indications of the care orientation. As illustrated near the end of this extract, when she talks about the importance of the cave being the moles' home, she can see the problem also from a rights perspective. However, regarding the problem from the care orientation is clearly preferable to her.

Jesse, another seventh-grader, focuses his initial response on the notion of rights and fairness:

J: The central problem, as I see it, is that the moles want the porcupine to leave and he's refusing. I think that they should kick him out. They were nice to let him in in the first place. And it's not their fault that he has quills. They have a right to be comfortable in their own home . . . they can do what they want in their cave. It's like if a homeless man moved into my home while my family was vacationing in Florida. We'd definitely call the police. Call it harsh, but it's reality.

I: Is there another way to solve the problem?

J: Another solution? Well, if they wanted to be kind, they could help him find another cave, but again, they don't have to. People should put themselves first.

I: Can you elaborate on that last comment?

J: Yeah, I mean people have to look after themselves. They can't always worry about what others think or want. Life's too short.

Individual rights, responsibility for self, and fairness—these seem to be central to the way Jesse sees and resolves the problem. When probed by the interviewer to see whether he can also view the problem from a care orientation, he offers a care solution (which needed further probing). It seems clear, however, that although Jesse has at his command the two moral voices, he clearly prefers the orientation of justice in resolving the fable problem.

Conclusion

Previous research has suggested that there may be gender-linked differences in moral orientation in adolescents and adults, although these findings have been questioned by other researchers (Gilligan & Attanucci, 1988; Lyons, 1983; Pratt, Golding, Hunter, & Sampson, 1988; Rothbart, Hanley, & Albert, 1986; Walker, 1989). Johnston (1988) investigated moral orientation in adolescents through the use of fables. In her sample of 11- and 15-year-olds, she found gender differences in the moral orientation used spontaneously and in the orientation chosen for best solution. In contrast, the present studies, with a wider age range (5-year-olds through 13-year-olds), did not find gender differences, suggesting that such differences may begin to emerge in adolescence. One may speculate that the greater commitment to one moral orientation that was shown by the older subjects in the second experiment might subsequently become linked with gender, as Johnston found in her early adolescent subjects.

Whereas Walker (1989) found a developmental pattern—with a focus on rights predominant in childhood and with increased use of a mixed orientation with maturity—this research found children of all ages to be generally care oriented. It should be noted, however, that Walker's findings were obtained with real-life dilemmas while the research reported here utilized a more standardized task, the fables. As Walker has argued, it may well be the nature of the task that determines which moral orientation will be employed by children as well as by adults (Walker, DeVries, & Trevethan, 1987; Walker, 1989).

An intriguing possibility raised by the second experiment is that moral orientation may be related to social class; upper-middle-class children were more likely to offer care solutions than working-class children. Although tentative, this finding is in line with Baumrind's (1969) research on parental instruction and parenting style. Baumrind distinguishes between "authoritative" parents and "authoritarian" parents: The former parents offer support, make standards clear, and emphasize the need for the child to develop self-control, while the latter parents value obedience, give orders, and are less likely to reason with the child. A sizable literature argues that variations in parenting style are related to social class (Kohn, 1977) and that a middle-class child is more likely to be punished on the basis of intent and a working-class child on the basis of consequences (Hill, 1980). It seems likely that the variables of parenting style, social class, and also minority status may be related to children's moral orientation. Gilligan and Attanucci (1988), looking at a racially diverse subsample in their study of moral orientation, found a relation between moral orientation and race for both men and women: The solutions presented by white students were more likely to fall in the care or justice category, while the solutions of minority students were more likely to fall in the justice focus category. This hypothesis about the relationship of moral orientation and class is supported by findings of Garrod and Webster (in preparation) who found that in a sample of urban, working-class adolescent and adult Native Canadians, there was no difference in moral orientation between adolescent and adult men and women. Thus, although a commitment to a particular moral orientation might develop with age, it appears that variables such as ethnicity, social class, and marginalization may well be as influential as gender in determining the predominant moral orientation.

Acknowledgments

The authors would like to thank the principals and teachers of the Bernice Ray Elementary School and the Richmond Middle School in Hanover, New Hampshire; the principal and teachers of the Hartland Elementary School in Hartland, Vermont; the principal and teachers of the Beech Elementary School in Manchester, New Hampshire; and the principal and teachers of the Thetford Elementary School in Thetford, Vermont, for their participation and cooperation in the second study. We are also grateful to Michael Campanale, Natalie Duval, Beth Hofman, and Paul Sawyer for assistance in data collection and to Matthew Houde for his coding of the data. Support for the research was provided by the Rockefeller Center at Dartmouth College.

References

Baumrind, D. (1969). Authoritarian versus authoritative parental control. *Adolescence, 3*, 255–272.
Colby, A., Kohlberg, L., Abrahimi, A., Gibbs, J., Higgins, A., Kauffman, K., Lieberman, M., Nisan, M., Reimer, J., Schrader, D., Snarey, J., & Tappan, M. (1987). *The measurement of moral judgment* (Vols. 1 & 2). Cambridge: Cambridge University Press.

Donenburg, G., & Hoffman, L. (1988). Gender differences in moral development. *Sex Roles, 18,* 701–717.

Damon, W. (1977). *The social world of the child.* San Francisco: Jossey-Bass.

Garrod, A., Beal, C., & Shin, P. (1990). The development of moral orientation in elementary school children. *Sex Roles, 22,* 13–27.

Garrod, A., & Webster, J. (in preparation). *Moral stage and moral orientation in Native Canadian adolescents and adults.*

Gilligan, C. (1982). *In a different voice: Psychological theory and women's development.* Cambridge, MA: Harvard University Press.

Gilligan, C. (1986, Spring). Letter to D. Baumrind. *Newsletter of the APA Division on Developmental Psychology,* pp. 10–13.

Gilligan, C., & Attanucci, J. (1988). Two moral orientations: Gender differences and similarities. *Merrill-Palmer Quarterly, 34,* 223–237.

Hill, J. P. (1980). The family. In M. Johnson (Ed.), *Toward adolescence: The middle school years.* (pp. 32–35). Chicago: National Society for the Study of Education (distributed by the University of Chicago Press).

Johnston, K. (1985). *Two moral orientations—Two problem-solving strategies: Adolescents' solutions to dilemmas in fables.* Unpublished doctoral dissertation, Harvard University.

Johnston, K. (1988). Adolescents' solutions to dilemmas in fables: Two moral orientations—Two problem-solving strategies. In C. Gilligan, J. Ward, J. Taylor, & B. Bardige (Eds.), *Mapping the moral domain.* Cambridge, MA: Harvard University Press.

Johnston, K., Brown, L., & Christopherson, S. (1990). Adolescents' moral dilemmas: The context. *Journal of Adolescence, 19,* 615–622.

Kohlberg, L. (1981). *Essays on moral development: Vol. 1: The philosophy of moral development.* San Francisco: Harper & Row.

Kohn, M. L. (1977). *Class and conformity* (2nd ed.). Chicago: University of Chicago Press.

Lyons, N. (1983). Two perspectives: On self, relationships, and morality. *Harvard Educational Review, 53,* 125–145.

Noddings, N. (1984). *Caring: A feminine approach to ethics and moral education.* Los Angeles: University of California Press.

Pratt, M. W., Golding, G., Hunter, W., & Sampson, R. (1988). Sex differences in adult moral orientations. *Journal of Personality, 56,* 373–391.

Rothbart, M., Hanley, D., & Albert, M. (1986). Gender differences in moral reasoning. *Sex Roles, 15,* 645–653.

Tietjen, A., & Walker, L. (1985). Moral reasoning and leadership among men in a Papau, New Guinean Society. *Developmental Psychology, 21,* 982–992.

Selman, R. (1980). *The growth of interpersonal understanding: Developmental and clinical analyses.* New York: Academic Press.

Walker, L. (1989). A longitudinal study of moral reasoning. *Child Development, 60,* 157–166.

Walker, L., DeVries, B., & Trevethan, S. (1987). Moral stages and moral orientation. *Child Development, 58,* 842–858.

Walker, L., & Richards, B. (1979). Stimulating transitions in moral reasoning as a function of stage of cognitive development. *Developmental Psychology, 15,* 95–103.

CHAPTER 4

Minding the Curriculum: Of Student Epistemology and Faculty Conspiracy

Robert Kegan

*Harvard University
and
Massachusetts School of Professional Psychology*

Most school faculties have factions. The junior/senior high school I taught at did, and nearly every faculty I've been privileged to teach or consult with in the 20 years since has had its subgroups that do battle with each other, usually in subtle but ongoing ways. The tensions that divide a group of teachers supposedly engaged in a common enterprise are not wholly a matter of differing personalities, generations, or gender. Much of the division is downright philosophical or ideological. The faculty members have different beliefs about what, fundamentally, they should be up to in teaching the young. Sometimes, these differing beliefs are discussed outright; more often, they are expressed indirectly through a faculty member's actions and reactions. Too often, they are experienced as unwelcome, unpleasant, and personal conflicts. Potentially, they amount to a fascinating *lived conversation* among equally respectable parties who care deeply about the outcome of a philosophical conflict because it has real implications for their own lives and for the lives of their students.

To oversimplify for a moment, these differing ideological positions could be placed on a continuum. At one end of this continuum is the curricular philosophy I'll call *back to basics,* and at the other end is the *whole child.* The curricular vision of back to basics stresses the acquisition and mastery of a generic set of cognitive skills that will equip learners for later life tasks, and of an ever

---

I dedicate this work to the memory of my friend, teacher, and colleague Lawrence Kohlberg, whose classic essay, "Development as the aim of education" (Kohlberg & Mayer, 1972), inspired it.

increasing fund of knowledge about the culture, past and present, in which they live. In the caricature of those who are critical of this vision, back to basics is an attention to rote learning, memorization, and the uncritical inculcation of the culture's historical values. It is possible, however, to hold the vision in a more sophisticated form that orients to the realization of an increasingly complex set of cognitive skills, including capacities for reflective and critical thought. From this point of view, back to basics is less a naive fundamentalism and more a stand against neglecting the need for a solid foundation in youth out of misguided deference either to faddish pursuits of relevance, or to a particular set of values not necessarily shared by the full range of students' families in a pluralistic society.

The vision of the *whole child,* in contrast, declares that cognitive development is valuable, but only as part of a curricular agenda that must include equal respect for the students' emotional and social development. It, too, has a common caricature in the hands of its antagonists: intrusive, quasipsychiatric forays into the feelings and valuing of students (to which their families might appropriately say, "None of your business") and social engineering according to the blueprint of one faction of society that feels it has the right to define mental health and good social order for all the rest of society. But it is also possible to see in the curricular vision of the whole child an old-fashioned and long-esteemed conviction that good schooling should nurture "the wit and character" of the young (Graham, 1983)—that if we are not to become captives of our own increasingly mechanized society, the young must not only be smart but also capable of conviction and self-defined purpose.

The way these competing visions get discussed in educational circles is often historical or sequential: Back to basics became a dominant vision in the late 1950s and early 1960s in reaction to presumed Soviet scientific accomplishments symbolized by the launching of Sputnik. The whole-child ideology arose in the later 1960s and early 1970s as a pedagogical expression of the more general cultural rediscovery of humanism and romanticism, in reaction to the manifest contradictions within the public and private institutions of a democratic society. Then, in the later 1970s and the 1980s, the pendulum swung to back-to-basics for reasons depending largely on one's view of recent history. Some would argue that the reascendance of this vision is made necessary by the inevitable costs of the conception of schooling as a solution to social problems and is made possible by the relative amelioration of those problems (reduced racial, ethnic, and gender discrimination and the end of the war in Vietnam). Others would argue that the reascendance of the back-to-basics vision is a defensive reaction to the deeply disturbing and still largely unanswered questions raised by the cultural critique of the 1960s. Whatever one's explanation for such a sequence, the problem with thinking about these ideologies primarily in such linear historical terms is that the reality of life within contemporary school faculties is obscured. In real faculties at any point in time, these competing ideologies are coexistent; teachers today experience the tension between these ideologies—within their faculty and even perhaps within themselves as well.

Although these tensions are no one's fault, they are costly. They tie up energies—within a faculty, in which teachers of one persuasion may actually believe that teachers of the other are ill serving the young, and within teachers' relationships to themselves, in which they may feel at times constrained or even paralyzed by their own recognition of the competing wisdoms expressed in each view. These tensions tie up energies that could be put to better use by being released into the shared purposes of the school—if only some integrating vision of that purpose might be found.

In this chapter, I argue that such a vision—a vision that does not award victory to either side but that clarifies a common enterprise hospitable to both—is possible and transforming. I propose a view of the curricular mission that recognizes and indeed celebrates the inevitable diversity of teacher temperament, personal preference, and educational ideology, but one that also goes beyond an eclectic spirit of uncritical tolerance—a vision that provides a way for very different kinds of teachers to look across the faculty room at each other and think, "That guy has an entirely different way of going about it than I do, *but we are both pulling in the same direction.*"

Proposing a Solution: A Curriculum for the Growth of the Mind

At the heart of my argument is the claim that teachers' common enterprise is epistemological—that however diverse the teaching goals that emanate from the competing ideologies, each of these goals when properly understood amounts not only to a concern for the students' minds but also to the same kind of concern. Without keener recognition of the epistemological basis of their own goals, educators of any ideological stripe lose the opportunity for a more extensive and less fractious colleagueship and increase the likelihood that their own favorite programs will more closely resemble their antagonists' caricatures of what they are up to. The vision I suggest may more powerfully advance the agenda dear to the hearts of both groups, and it is simply stated: the growth of the student's mind, no more and no less. In practice, the realization of the vision requires a greater familiarity with what a philosophy-laden developmental psychology has to teach us about the regular forms and transformations of the human mind over the course of the life span.

To discuss this subject at some depth within this short chapter, I will focus on a particular period in the life span: early adolescence and the junior high years. Although the argument applies to any schooling period, I have chosen this one because of my high regard for the junior high teacher, an unrecognized national treasure. (I've long been struck by the fact that although people in different regions of the United States may agree on little else, they do concur that it is impossible to teach the eighth grade!)

In Table 4.1, the reader will find a shorthand description of the regular transformations of mind in childhood and adolescence in three different domains: the logical-cognitive, the social-cognitive, and the intrapersonal-affective. In each of these domains, three different eras are described: one common to early childhood and the preschool years, a second common to the latency age or elementary school years, and a third beginning sometime in adolescence (Kegan, 1982, 1986). The reader will note that people of junior high age may be in the second era, the third era, or, most commonly, in transition between the two. Such a variety of possibilities is an immediate indicator of the complexities of teaching this age group.

The reader will also note that each era can do what the preceding era cannot: Each era contains abilities of the preceding ones, organized at a greater level of complexity. For example, consider the logical-cognitive domain. Imagine this syllogistic question put to children in all three eras: "All purple snakes have fifteen legs, I am holding a purple snake in my hands; how many legs does it have?" (Kagan, 1972). Adolescents in the third era are able to accept for the sake of argument the concrete "facts" of purple snakes and 15-legged snakes, and can subordinate these facts to the abstract relation between them, understood in the first premise of the syllogism—namely, if X, then Y. They are aware that X and Y may not be true, but they are also aware that the question is not so much about the truth status of X and Y as about what can be concluded given the relation between the two stated in the first premise. Adolescents in the third era can think propositionally, hypothetically, and, in other words, abstractly, and will answer that the snake you say you have, which is purple, must also have 15 legs if it is true that all purple snakes have 15 legs.

Children and adolescents who organize their logical-cognitive thinking according to the second era, however, are not capable of relativizing the concrete to some higher-order context, such as necessary and sufficient relations between concrete facts. The realm of what is actual, factual, and observable as opposed to what is merely imagined, fantastic, and illogical is itself the basic context for making the crucial conclusions, and the conclusions that children and adolescents in this era are likely to make in answer to the same question are thus likely to be along the lines of the improbability or unreality of purple snakes or 15-legged snakes.

Finally, young children in the first era do not yet even construct the category of the durable fact, let alone subordinate facts to abstraction. So, not only is the actual reality of X and Y not an issue, but young children do not understand the logical link of "if . . . then" between the two; thus, their answer

Table 4.1 Three Eras of Meaning Organization

	Era 1 Normal age: roughly 2–6 years	Era 2 Normal age: roughly 6 years to teens	Era 3 Normal age: teenage years and beyond
Logical-Cognitive Domain			
	Can: recognize that objects exist independently of one's own sensing of them ("object permanence") *Cannot:* distinguish one's perception of an object from the actual properties of the object; construct a logical relation between cause and effect (Piaget's stage of "pre-operational thought")	*Can:* grant to objects their own properties irrespective of one's perceptions; reason consequentially, that is, cause and effect; construct a narrative sequence of events; relate one point in time to another; construct fixed categories and classes into which things can be mentally placed *Cannot:* reason abstractly; subordinate concrete actuality to possibility; make generalizations; discern overall patterns; form hypotheses; construct ideals (Piaget's stage of "concrete operational thought")	*Can:* reason abstractly, that is, reason about reasoning; think hypothetically and deductively; form negative classes (for example, the class of all not-crows); see relations as simultaneously reciprocal *Cannot:* systematically produce all possible combinations of relations; systematically isolate variables to test hypotheses (earliest form of Piaget's stage of "formal operations")
Social-Cognitive Domain			
	Can: recognize that persons exist separate from oneself	*Can:* construct own point of view and grant to others their distinct point of view; take the role of another person; manipulate others on behalf of one's own goals; make deals, plans, and strategies	*Can:* be aware of shared feelings, agreements, and expectations that take primacy over individual interests

Cannot: recognize that persons have their own purposes independent of oneself; take another person's point of view as distinct from one's own

(Kohlberg's stage of "heteronomous morality")

Intrapersonal Affective Domain

Can: distinguish between inner sensation and outside stimulation

Cannot: distinguish its impulses from itself, that is, is embedded in or driven by its impulses

(Kegan's "impulsive self")

Cannot: take own point of view and another's simultaneously; construct obligations and expectations to maintain mutual interpersonal relationships

(Kohlberg's stage of "instrumentalism")

Can: drive, regulate, or organize impulses to produce enduring dispositions, needs, goals; delay immediate gratification; identify enduring qualities of self according to outer social or behavioral manifestations (abilities—"fast runner", preferences—"hates liver", habits—"always oversleep")

Cannot: internally coordinate more than one point of view or need organization; distinguish its needs from itself; identify enduring qualities of the self according to inner psychological manifestations

(Kegan's "imperial self")

Cannot: construct a generalized system regulative of interpersonal relationships, and relationships between relationships

(Kohlberg's stage of "interpersonal concordance")

Can: internalize another's point of view in what becomes the co-construction of personal experience, thus creating new capacity for empathy and sharing at an internal rather than merely transactive level; coordinate more than one point of view internally, thus creating emotions experienced as internal subjective states rather than social transactions

Cannot: organize own states or internal parts of self into systematic whole; distinguish self from one's relationship

(Kegan's "interpersonal self")

Source: R. Kegan. The child behind the mask. In W. H. Reid, D. Door, J. I. Walker, & J. Bonner (Eds.), *Unmasking the Psychopath*, 1986, pp. 45–77. New York: W.W. Norton. Copyright 1986 by W.W. Norton. Adapted by permission.

might well be something that sounds to us less like an answer than a spontaneous association, as in "My brother has a snake!"

Thus, the relation between the three eras is not merely additive or cumulative—an accretion of skills. Rather, the relation is qualitative or incorporative. The very way of making sense (e.g., the concrete fact in era 2) becomes an element of a more complex way of making sense in era 3.

A geometric analogy for the relation between these three eras in the logical-cognitive domain might be that of the point, the line, and the plane, with each subsequent geometric form containing the last. A line is a metapoint in a sense; it contains an infinite number of points, but as elements subordinated to the more complex organizational principle of the line, where earlier the point was itself an organizational principle. Similarly, a plane is a metaline, an organizational principle containing line as an element.

One can see the analogy almost literally at work when considering how persons in the three eras might explain a movie such as *Star Wars,* which had a broad age appeal because it was no doubt interesting to a variety of organizational principles. The young children in era 1 demonstrate no sense of a story or logical connection from one part of the movie to another. Instead, they talk about a single *point* in time in the movie or a single character, with no indication of their understanding of his importance to the story ("I loved Chewbaka; he was so big and hairy"). The children in era 2 can subordinate point to line but not line to plane; they can string the events together to create a linear narrative of the story at a concrete level, but they do not organize an abstract theme of which the particular story is an expression. "What the movie is about" is the linear sequence of events that happened in the movie (as any exasperated parent knows who has asked this question, without being prepared for a marathon recounting of the entire story of the movie). It is only in era 3 that the movie might "be about the battle between good and evil," for example, or some such other thematic abstraction, in which the line of the story's plot is subordinated to a bigger field or plane of consideration.

What we have said about different eras of the logical-cognitive domain is that each is organized by a more complex or inclusive principle of organization in which the very principle of a prior era becomes an element that can itself be organized by the new era's principle of organization. What this means is that the relation between the principles is essentially developmental (each one is included in the next) and that the organizational principles themselves are essentially epistemological: Their structure can be described in terms of what is taken as subject (the principle of organization) and what is taken as object (the element that can be organized). The eras, thus, are not so much about what the mind knows but about how it knows, with each era describing a different system of knowing, and the sequence of eras describes an evolutionary development of mind in the logical-cognitive domain.

The reader can see that the same can be said of the social-cognitive and intrapersonal-affective domains—that is, they too trace a development in which the prior era's principle of knowing becomes an element in the next principle. For example, in the social-cognitive domain of era 2, children are able to distinguish their own point of view from another's, and they can see that others' actions issue from their own purposes and intentions, which may not be the same as their own purposes and intentions.

Consider one favorite story about which Piaget (1948) asked children: There are two children. One is told by his mother not to touch a collection of cups, and he deliberately picks one up and drops it, and it breaks. The other child is told nothing but sees that his mother needs a tray of cups taken into the kitchen; while carrying them, he slips and *all* the cups break. Which child is naughtier? Children and adolescents in era 2 see that the first child is naughtier because they orient to the child's point of view or intention, but children in the earlier era orient to the result ("he broke all the cups"), do not distinguish between points of view, and think that the second child is naughtier.

What those in era 2 cannot do is subordinate the category of point of view to an even broader context that will relate points of view together. Selman (1980), for example, asked children who correctly recited the golden rule what it told them to do if someone hit them. "Hit 'em back!" is a common answer among the era 2 children: "Do unto others as they do unto you." Only in era 3, in which one can hold multiple points of view simultaneously, can one come to a different understanding of the golden rule.

If we can thus describe a sequence of qualitative developments in the way one knows in the organizing of the physical, social, and personal spheres, this question naturally arises: Are we describing an evolution of three different minds that any person has, or are these the expression, in three different domains, of a single mind's development? This turns out to be a complicated question, with important theoretical, empirical, and practical implications. Some researcher theorists in this tradition seem almost to argue for the multiple minds side of this controversy, especially in light of the inevitable unevenness in some people's development. Although this is not the place for a full-scale account of the debate, I think it is much more plausible to consider that what we are looking at in these developments is the evolution of a single mental activity and that the unrecognized common link between the domains is the subject-object relation and its natural evolution.

In other words, just to take an example, the principle of organization in era 2 can be seen to be the same principle of organization whether we are looking at organizing physical, social, or internal experience. What is this principle? Consider these apparently disparate discoveries: (1) The quantity of liquid is not changed by its being poured into a smaller glass; (2) a person who could have no way of knowing you would be made unhappy by his actions cannot be said to be mean; and (3) when I tell you, "I don't like spinach," or think to myself, "I'm a Catholic girl," I mean that these are things that are ongoing about me, not just how I feel or think now—these are how I am or tend to be. Now, as different as these discoveries are (they are about one's understanding of the physical, social, and personal world), it is the same single epistemological principle or way of knowing that makes these discoveries possible. In each case, the discovery arises out of the same single ability to see that the phenomenon being considered (thing, others, or self) has its own properties, which are elements of a class to which these properties belong, and that the phenomenon (thing, others, or self) is, itself, known as this class (which, like all classes, has durable, ongoing rules that create the idea of class membership and regulate that membership). "Liquid" is a class that has as a member the property of quantity, and that property is not regulated by my perception; "other person" is a class that has as a member the property of intention, and that property is not determined by my wishes; "self" is a class that has as members the properties of preference, habit, and ability, and—the self being a class, something that has properties—these are things about me in some ongoing way, as opposed to just what I want to eat now, for example. Hence new *ways of knowing* in such disparate domains as the inanimate, the social, and the introspective may all be occasioned by a single transformation of mind.

An interesting, if unwitting, confirmation of this line of argument comes from a new player in the school reform movement: the Coalition of Essential Schools Project, led by Theodore Sizer and his colleagues (1984). Sizer's group makes the compelling and provocative point that as schools have become impossibly overburdened by being made the repository of nearly all society's hopes for the young (school as parent, school as church, school as physician), accepting such expectations is a guarantee of disaster. Instead, the coalition suggests, schools would be better off identifying fewer—not more—goals and pursuing a very few well rather than very many poorly. Well and good, we might say, but what should the favored few goals be? Sizer and his colleagues considered this question deeply and consulted widely. The short list they came up with as goals for an adolescent curriculum is a fascinating one. Stated most concisely, the goals are that adolescents should be able to (1) think well, (2) be decent, and (3) plan for the future. When the fuller meaning of the goals is unpacked, they might be put this way:

1. Adolescents should be able to think reflectively, abstractly, and critically.
2. They should be able to take out membership in and maintain loyalty to a human community greater than one—greater than their own self-interest—and they should be capable of being trustworthy and supportive participants in private relations and civic life.

3. They should be able to defer short-term gratifications in favor of longer-term goals and satisfactions.

I say this is an interesting list for the present conversation because whatever else one wants to say about the goals, they are appropriate aspirations for the culmination of the teen years precisely because each amounts to an identical epistemological expectation—a way of knowing—that it would be appropriate to hope for in people as they graduate from high school. They are goals in the cognitive, social, and personal domains, respectively, and the underlying and possibly unrecognized epistemological principle that each embodies is reflected in the third era as described in Table 4.1.

That Sizer's group should come up with a collection of goals that match perfectly a single era in the table is confirmation of the work of researcher theorists by school practitioners. But if my claim—that the epistemological demands implicit in all three goals are essentially a same single demand—has merit, then the theory also has important implications for the carrying out of Sizer's vision. Even if a school does accept the three goals (and such a consortium of Essential Schools now exists) and even if faculty agree that the goals are appropriate to the high school student, it makes a very big difference to the operation of such a school whether one views these as essentially three compatible but independent goals—as goals to be pursued independently—or as three expressions of a single goal collectively pursued. This brings us naturally to a discussion of the general implications of the vision of a curriculum for the growth of the mind.

Considering the Implications

What happens if we take seriously the possibility that schools could have a single mission equally hospitable to competing factions? In fact, a very great deal could happen in terms of both faculty collegiality (considered by some to be the most crucial feature in the effectiveness of a school [Barth, 1980; Waller, 1932]) and quality of instruction in each individual classroom.

If five lamps are lit in a large living room, how many sources of light are there? We might say there are five sources of light. If each lamp has its own tint of glass, its own design, and its own bulb wattage, each will throw off a different kind of light. Perhaps the maker of each lamp, genuinely committed to bringing you into the light, will be partial to his or her own and will bid you to come to his or her source of light. Or at best, some generous spirit of eclectic relativism may obtain, and the lamp makers may concede there is a benefit to your being exposed to each of the lamps, each separate source having little to do with the other except that, like the food groups of a well-balanced diet, each has a partial contribution to make to a well-rounded, beneficial whole.

But there is quite a different answer possible to the question of how many sources of light there are in the room: namely, that there is only one source. All five lamps work because they are plugged into sockets that draw power from a single source: the home's electrical system. In this view, each lamp is neither a contender for the best source of light nor a mere part of a whole. Each lamp is powered by the whole and expressive of the whole. And if the lamp maker's mission is not first of all to bring you to the light of his or her particular lamp but to bring you to the light of this single source, he or she can delight equally in the way his or her particular lamp makes use of this source and in the way other lamps that he or she would never think to create do also. The lamp maker's relationship to the other lamp makers is neither rivalrous nor laissez-faire but conspiratorial; the lamp makers breathe together.

The ultimate goal of any school leader is to get the faculty to breathe together, but this cannot be done by firing the troublemakers, burying the conflicts, and hiring a crew who all make their lamps in the same way. It can only be done by identifying a mission that pays the greatest respect to the diverse lamp designs, while at the same time keeping in the foreground the common source of power that illuminates the lamps and to which the different designers share loyalty.

The development of the student's mind is such a mission. The vital force of mental development (an energy no educator brings to the school, classroom, or student, but, rather, finds there) is the common source. But such a vision does not transform a school if it only lives rhetorically or is espoused in the abstract, even an abstract disguised as parable.

It lives in the nitty-gritty operations of the classroom and in the school as a whole. It lives through faculty members' considerations—be they back to basics or whole child advocates—as to whether the way we teach "plugs into" the developmental source. Let us consider, for example, two junior high English teachers each teaching a unit on the short story. Teacher A and Teacher B couldn't be more different in their temperaments, life-styles, or educational philosophies. Teacher A fought in the Korean War, still wears a crew cut, and remembers with fondness the days when "students would never think of talking back to their teachers." Teacher B refused to serve in his generation's war, only recently cut off his ponytail, and remembers with fondness the days when "kids cared more about causes than designer clothes." Teacher A sees English class as, first of all, a place to teach kids how to read and write intelligently. He uses the short story as a vehicle to teach the kids both, challenging them to get as much meaning out of the story as the author put into it and taking the story apart to show the kids how it is made. Teacher B sees English class as, first of all, a place to engage the valuing side of his students. He respects good reading and writing and wants to see it in his students, but he believes the overall school curriculum is already weighted much more heavily on the cognitive side and that English class is an opportunity to teach about values and social relations. He uses the short story as a vehicle to engage the kids' philosophies and to enhance their abilities to respect each other in spite of the fact they may disagree.

Now, we might ask of Teacher A and Teacher B: Are they good teachers? Is one better than the other? Are they collaborating or competing? Do they respect each other? Do they experience each other as true colleagues, breathing together, or do they at best put up with each other? The answer to all these questions, from a developmental view, is that we do not yet have enough information to know. We know that one teacher is partial to back to basics and the other to the whole child, but this doesn't tell us who is the better teacher. We know that the two have dramatically different educational philosophies, but this doesn't necessarily tell us that they are pulling in different directions.

So, let's get more information. The short story that each is teaching is O. Henry's "Gift of the Magi." Teacher A on this particular morning wants to get across the concept of irony to his seventh-graders. He asks for a definition, and the first student responds, "Like when the husband sold his watch to get his wife the combs for her hair, but then she had sold her hair to get him a chain for his watch—that's irony." Now, how does Teacher A respond to this? One sort of Teacher A might respond, "Well, that's not really a definition of anything, that's an example. Depending on what you think that example means, it might even be a correct example of irony, but it's certainly not a definition. Now, can someone give me a definition of irony, not an example?" The probable sequence of events is now something like this: (1) A few more examples of irony, which the teacher does not accept as definitions of irony, follow; (2) there is eventual silence on the part of the class; (3) and finally there is an occasion for the teacher, having stumped the class, to define the term irony, possibly writing the definition on the blackboard for students to copy into their notebooks, memorize, and file away for the exam. And perhaps from the perspective of this sort of Teacher A, he created a heightened readiness and interest in learning a concept before he provided the answer.

Another sort of Teacher A (A') might respond differently: "Well, that's a terrific example of irony, all right. Let's put that one up on the blackboard and circle it. Okay, can someone give me another example of irony? It doesn't have to be from the story, it can be anything." The probable sequence of events goes like this: First, the students offer many more examples of irony: "It was ironic that Samantha Smith, that girl who went to Russia for world peace, then dies in a plane accident"; "It was ironic that Dennis Eckersley, who used to pitch for the Red Sox, was the one who ended up beating the Red Sox for the pennant"; and so on. Teacher A' salutes each example, puts it up on the board, and draws a circle around it. Next, the teacher says, "Let's stop and take a look at all these great examples of irony." She then draws one big circle enclosing all the separate circles. "Now can anyone tell me what *irony* is in a way that would be true for all these examples?" At this point, the students collectively struggle toward a generalization that can be checked against all the particulars.

Both sorts of Teacher A are back to basics oriented; both want to teach about a cognitive concept. And both know how to teach; each is able to foster a process that creates the "teachable moment." The difference is that Teacher A creates a teachable moment in order to teach rote learning, memorization, and an increasing fund of knowledge. What is Teacher A' doing with the teachable moment? She is engaging the developing mind of her students, their evolving epistemological capacities. How so? Rather than demonstrating to the students their inability to generalize for the purpose of making the concept into a kind of concretion they can handle by memorizing, Teacher A' directly engages their growing edge, which is expressed in their inability to move smoothly from the concrete to the abstract (which subtends the concrete). If you reconsider the second era of Table 4.1, you will see that the teachers' requests (to define) exceed the limits of this way of making sense. The difference between the definition and an example is precisely the difference between abstract generalization and a concrete fact. By welcoming the concrete as a route to the abstract, Teacher A' creates a teachable moment that involves an epistemological stretch just a little beyond most of her students. She invites her students to take the concrete examples as objects and to create some new knowledge structure that will contain all these objects. This new knowledge structure, which the students struggle collectively to create, will here express itself as the capacity to define rather than merely to exemplify, but, of course, it is the much bigger capacity depicted in era 3 in Table 4.1.

Now let's turn to Teacher B. He's teaching O. Henry, too, but he's not teaching the concept of irony. On this particular morning, as the students are engaged in heated controversy, the learning goal on his mind has to do with the very way the students listen to each other—or, more precisely, the way they do not. He's struck by the way they interrupt each other and by the way that, even when they take turns, they seem to ignore completely or distort what the previous speaker said in order to return to the point they favor. Teacher B does not think about this as just a class management issue that must be resolved in order to get the kids back on track for learning; he regards this as part of the track, an opportunity for learning, an opportunity for teaching them important lessons about respect, good listening, and learning from others. Now, how does Teacher B teach this? One sort of Teacher B may elect any of the following approaches: (1) He establishes rules for proper conduct in conversations, along with consequences for violating the rules (e.g., if you interrupt, you can't speak again for 15 minutes), or he gives each student three tokens, and one token is spent each time a student speaks, so that no student can speak more than three times; (2) he stops the discussion and gives a sincere, eloquent, hortatory speech on the importance of the students' treating one another better; or (3) he stops the discussion and runs a brief "therapy group" in which students are encouraged to talk about how they feel when they are interrupted or ignored.

Another sort of Teacher B (B') might teach the lesson this way. He lets the conversation/debate proceed, but he institutes one new requirement. Before any speaker may make a point, she must restate the preceding speaker's point with sufficient accuracy that the preceding speaker agrees his point has been adequately restated. At first, the students try to fulfill the agreement by restating the points in the straw-man fashion they are prepared to attack, but they do not get to the attack because, amid laughter and hooting, the preceding speaker objects, requiring the speaker to restate the opposing view in a nondistorting, noneditorializing fashion, however maddening it may be to do so.

Again, both Teacher B and Teacher B' share a whole child philosophy: They want their class to affect the students' social development as well as their intellectual development. And, again, both know how to teach. But what they know how to teach differs. The Teacher B who establishes rules for respectful behavior may actually possess, whether he knows it or not, a theory of education vis-à-vis social development that bears remarkable similarity to that of Teacher A, who teaches the rote learning of concepts. Although Teacher A directs the teaching to controlling the internal operations of the mind and this Teacher B directs the teaching to the external operations of the body, both essentially make good teaching about the effective shaping of inner or outer behavior. The Teacher B who preaches a sermon directs his teaching to winning souls, converting the junior high heathen, and the Teacher B who runs the therapy-type discussion group directs his teaching to the healing of the psyche. All three kinds of Teacher B are coming out of a whole child agenda, but in contrast to teaching social development from the stance of behavioral engineer, secular minister, or amateur psychiatrist, only Teacher B' pursues the same agenda in a way that makes good teaching about the growth of the students' minds. All the teachers have a vision or metaphor that animates the teaching, but in contrast to the actions of control, conversion, or healing, only Teacher B' supports a motion or telos that does not get its start from him. What is the teaching action for Teacher B'?

Teacher B' is supporting motion that comes from his students' own vitality rather than from himself; he is supporting their natural epistemological development as it expresses itself in the realm of social understanding. And what makes him a good teacher of the mind is that he devises a way to engage both the strengths and limits of the students' current epistemological predicament— he engages them "where they are" but invites them to step beyond that limit. How so? Looking once again at the much consulted Table 4.1, we can see that the little rule that Teacher B' adds to the "game" of class conversation ingeniously transcends mere classroom management and joins the students' natural curriculum. Students' era 2 capacity to take another's perspective allows them to stand in a classmate's shoes and restate the classmate's position, but the *incapacity* to hold multiple points of view simultaneously and to integrate them means that when the students do stand in their classmate's shoes, they experience the temporary surrender of their own preferred view. He will not necessarily enjoy doing this, as the initial attempts to distort tendentiously the others' views demonstrates, but out of the desire to express the view they favor, they will accept the unwelcome route. The trick is that this unwelcome route, first seen as a mere means to an end, has the promise of itself becoming an end: The continuous consideration of another's view in an uncooptive fashion, which requires the continuous stepping out of one's own view, is a definite move toward making one's own view object rather than subject and considering its relation to other views.

Teachers A, A', B, and B' thus demonstrate two important points with respect to the ideological factions that divide faculties. First, in the context of a curricular vision of the growth of the mind, the distinction between better and poorer teaching has nothing whatever to do with the distinction between fundamentalist visions and humanist visions. On the contrary, as Table 4.2 indicates, the examples help us to suggest what stronger and weaker teaching might look like in each of the approaches. Second, as the developmental column of Table 4.2 indicates, as different as teachers in the two factions might be, were each to practice his or her vision in the context of supporting the growth of the mind, the bigger truth would be the complementary and collaborative nature of their teaching venture, not its antagonism.

The "prime" teachers in the examples just given, A' and B', may be of different generations, political persuasions, and life-styles. But the deep structures of their practice and their attention to enhancing the structures and processes of their students' meaning making are remarkably similar, however disparate their practices may appear on the surface.

Hoping to develop faculties that breathe together, school leaders may understandably throw up their hands as they confront among faculty differences in qualities that greatly influence the nature of a teacher's engagement of his or her students—differences of temperament, social and interpersonal style, preference, or comfort as to which aspects of a child's mind a teacher seeks to engage. But these differences do not need to defeat the hope of a conspiratorial faculty. The more that teachers can be prime teachers, whatever their vision, the greater likelihood they will come to see that their fellow prime teachers, whatever their vision, are joined with them in a common pursuit. Teacher B' may never want to use an O. Henry story to teach the concept of irony, as A' does. But they are on the same team: They know that each in his or her own way is trying to accomplish the very same thing.

Table 4.2. Nondevelopmental and Developmental Approaches to Fundamentalist and Humanist Curricular Visions

Curricular Vision	Developmental Approaches	Nondevelopmental Approaches
Fundamentalist (back to basics)	Support for cognitive construction	Shaping of cognitive behavior
	Exercise of cognitive structures	Rote learning, information transfer
	Opportunities for the relativizing (objectifying) of cognitive structures	Increase in fund of knowledge
	Support for the integration of relativized structures into new structures	Teaching of cognitive skills as distinct and separate operations, and building up of the number of such skills
Humanist (the whole child)	Support for social, affective, and intrapersonal constructions	Shaping of social and emotional behavior
	Exercises of social, affective, and intrapersonal structures	Preachment, suasion, social pressures, and secular conversion
	Opportunities for the relativizing (objectifying) of social, affective, and intrapersonal structures	Quasitherapeutic supports and interventions
	Support for the integration of relativized structures into new structures	Teaching of each social or emotional skill as a distinct and separate operation, and building up of the number of such skills

References

Barth, R. (1980). *Run school run.* Cambridge, MA: Harvard University Press.

Graham, P. (1983, October). *Wit and character.* Speech delivered to the National Forum of the College Board, Dallas, TX.

Kagan, J. (1972). A conception of early adolescence. In J. Kagan & R. Coles (Eds.), *Twelve to sixteen: Early adolescence* (pp. 90–105). New York: Norton.

Kegan, R. (1982). *The evolving self.* Cambridge, MA: Harvard University Press.

Kegan, R. (1986). The child behind the mask. In W. H. Reid, D. Door, J. I. Walker, & J. Bonner (Eds.), *Unmasking the psychopath* (pp. 45–77). New York: Norton.

Kohlberg, L., & Mayer, R. (1972). Development as the aim of education. *Harvard Educational Review, 42,* 449–496.

Piaget, J. (1948). *The moral judgement of the child.* Glencoe: Free Press.

Selman, R. (1980). *The growth of interpersonal understanding.* New York: Academic Press.

Sizer, T. (1984). *Horace's compromise.* Boston: Houghton-Mifflin.

Waller, W. (1932). *The sociology of teaching.* New York: John Wiley.

PART II

Adolescence

CHAPTER 5

The Case of the Missing Family: Kohlberg and the Study of Adolescent Moral Development

Joseph Reimer

Brandeis University

In the moral development literature, there are two substantial longitudinal studies of the development of moral judgment from adolescence into adulthood. The first is a study that Kohlberg began in Chicago for his doctoral dissertation and that was continued for 20 years as the definitive case study on stage and sequence (Colby & Kohlberg, 1987). The second was begun by Kohlberg in 1969 on an Israeli kibbutz and was continued during the following decade by Snarey and myself (Snarey, Reimer, & Kohlberg, 1985a). It is the kibbutz study that will be the focus of my attempt to explore the case of the missing family—the question of why in the study of the moral development of adolescents Kohlberg and his colleagues (myself included) consistently excluded the family as a relevant factor in understanding the course of that development.

The background for Kohlberg's entry into the study of adolescent moral development on a kibbutz begins with the 1969 publication of Bruno Bettelheim's influential *The Children of the Dream*. As a graduate student, Kohlberg studied with Bettleheim at the University of Chicago and was clearly both influenced and disturbed by Bettelheim's psychoanalytically based analysis of child and adolescent development on the kibbutz. Although Bettelheim began his study with an enthusiastic embrace of the kibbutz approach to child rearing, he concludes that kibbutz education works well at the earlier stages of childhood but falls short in adolescence. Bettelheim writes bitingly of the conformity and emotional restrictions of the kibbutz adolescents and concludes that these adolescent children of the kibbutz founders simply cannot stand up to their domineering parents and thus pay a high personal price for their submissiveness.

Kohlberg could not agree with Bettleheim's descriptions; they simply made no sense to him. Kibbutz education, at least in theory, looked much like what Kohlberg envisioned as an almost ideal setting for adolescent moral education. Kibbutz education places great stress on the values of justice and equality. It is nonhierarchical in encouraging adolescents to democratically govern themselves through a peer group structure, and it allows for grappling with real-life moral dilemmas through group discussion. Given his theoretical assumptions, Kohlberg (1971) hypothesized that kibbutz education could stimulate higher stages of moral judgment, and he set out to empirically prove his point.

A decade of study confirmed his hypothesis. The longitudinal data show that kibbutz adolescents develop in their moral judgment at a reasonably accelerated pace and that the kibbutz also succeeds in stimulating the moral judgment of lower- and working-class urban youth who come to live and study on the kibbutz during high school and remain in later years as young adult members of the kibbutz (Snarey, Reimer, & Kohlberg, 1985a).

In a subsequent article, we (Snarey, Reimer, & Kohlberg, 1985b) spelled out our view of what about kibbutz secondary education accounts for stimulating the adolescents' rate of moral development. We cited aspects of the adolescents' experiences in school, in their peer groups, and in their general contact with kibbutz society.

What we left out is any consideration of the adolescents' experiences with their families—be they the biological families of the kibbutz-born youth or the "adopted" families of the city-born youth studying on the kibbutz. (Upon entering the kibbutz, a city-born youth was assigned an adopted family with whom to visit each day after school during the regular at-home hours.) Although this omission may make sense if one assumes the common stereotype of kibbutz society as a nonfamilial environment, both Snarey and I were participant observers on the kibbutz (Reimer, 1977; Snarey, 1982) and knew that beyond that stereotype lay the social reality of the emergence of the family as a powerful force in kibbutz life. Why, then, did we make no reference to the influence of the family? It was, I am retrospectively suggesting, the frame of cognitive-developmental theory that led to the omission; it was working with the assumptions of Kohlberg's theorizing about adolescent moral development that led to our not knowing how to meaningfully incorporate observations of family life into an explanation of the phenomena we were studying.

To make this point more clearly, I need to make reference first to kibbutz social history and next to a review of Kohlberg's and Piaget's writings on the family and moral development.

Kibbutz Social History

As kibbutz culture emerged during the 1920s through the 1940s, there was a decidedly strong ideological stance against replicating the nuclear family of the

European Jewish community. For both these ideological and other practical reasons, kibbutzim instituted the system of collective education, which substantially reduced the authority of parents over their children and the cohesion and prominence of the familial bond (Bettelheim, 1969; Spiro, 1963).

However, it is also true that observers of kibbutz culture began to notice by the 1950s, when the first large cohort of kibbutz children was born, that the balance was beginning to shift and that kibbutz members were asking to play a more active role in raising their children (Talmon, 1972). By the 1970s, when we were conducting our study, the balance had shifted much further, and numbers of kibbutzim (although not the one we studied) were deciding to enlarge members' living quarters so that children up to elementary school age could live at home with their parents. That trend has continued into the 1980s and represents a major shift in kibbutz educational practice. We noted its occurrence in our ethnographic notes but did not realize its significance for the study of moral development.

Piaget and Kohlberg on the Family

To retrospectively understand this missing link, I returned to Kohlberg's earlier writings and those of his predecessor, Piaget, to see how they viewed the role of the family in children's moral development. What I found convinced me that our leaving out the kibbutz adolescents' connections to their families was but a symptom of a larger phenomenon of the missing family in cognitive developmental theory. Writing from within that perspective led us to *not* see a connection between family life and adolescent moral development.

To begin with Piaget's (1965) classic, *The Moral Judgment of the Child,* there is a distinctly negative portrayal of the role that parents play in their children's moral development. A few quotes will make the point clearly.

> Egocentricism results from the unequal relation between child and adult. . . . The very nature of the relationship between child and adult places the child apart . . . shut up in his own point of view. . . . (pp. 35–36)
>
> It looks as though, in many ways, the adult did everything in his power to encourage the child to persevere in its specific tendencies . . . whereas given sufficient liberty of action the child will spontaneously emerge from his egocentricism, the adult most of the time acts in such a way to strengthen egocentricism in its double aspect, intellectual and moral. . . . (p. 190)
>
> The average parent is like an unintelligent government that is content to accumulate laws in spite of the contradictions and ever-increasing mental confusion . . . [and takes] pleasure in inflicting punishments [and] using authority. . . . (p. 192)
>
> The sense of justice, though capable of being reinforced by the precepts

and examples of the adult, is largely independent of these influences and requires nothing more for its development than the mutual respect and solidarity which holds among children themselves. (p. 198)

For Piaget, the child's social world divides into two domains: the unequal relationship between child and adult and the equal relationship among peers. The first is not much better than a necessary evil and certainly is not designed to promote the child's moral development. The latter, the society of peers, represents the way out from the trap of the first. By achieving mutuality and solidarity among peers, children can emerge from the egocentricism their parents promote and develop a sense of justice, which is the hallmark of moral maturity.

Kohlberg is less extreme in his position than Piaget. Not negative about the family's influence on children's moral development, he is decidedly neutral, as this quote from his article Stage and Sequence (1969) shows.

> For the developing child there is presumably a rough sequence of groups or institutions in which he participates. The first, the family, has received the most attention. . . . From our point of view, however, (1) Family participation is not unique or critically necessary for moral development and (2) the dimensions on which it stimulates moral development are primarily general dimensions by which other primary groups stimulate moral development, i.e., the dimensions of creation of role-taking opportunities. (p. 399)

Reacting strongly against the psychoanalytically based trend to see moral development as a product of the early parent-child relationship, Kohlberg was making the valid points that moral development includes more of the child's experience than being at home with one's parents, continues beyond early childhood into adolescence and early adulthood, and involves the young person's cognitive processing of a broad range of social and interpersonal experiences. These include participation in school and peer life and interaction with the political and social institutions of larger society.

However, in making these points, Kohlberg not only calls into question the unique role of the family but also its role as "critically necessary for moral development." To show that family life may not be necessary for moral development, Kohlberg (1969) turns to the example of the kibbutz.

> There is no evidence that the family is a uniquely necessary setting for normal moral development. . . . On the same Piaget measures on which institutionalized children are more backward than children in families, kibbutz children are equal to city children living in families. In general, kibbutz children are "normal" in moral development in spite of marked reduction in amount of interaction with their parents. (p. 399)

Kohlberg (1969) claims there is no evidence that "the family is a uniquely necessary setting" and cites children who grow up on kibbutz being normal in moral development "in spite of marked reduction in amount of interaction with their parents." However, Kohlberg slips here in assuming that being provided with less interaction time with one's parents is the same as having no family life. The kibbutz is not and never was a nonfamilial environment comparable to an orphanage. To have your parents, siblings, and possibly extended family living in your village and visiting with you daily is to have a family life, although differently organized than in a nuclear family. Kibbutz children's growing up normal does not illustrate that family is not necessary to moral development. It may illustrate that the amount of daily parent-child interaction alone cannot predict the course of moral development.

In reacting against the psychoanalytic position, Kohlberg not only misread the kibbutz reality as being nonfamilial but also ended up equating family life with a certain pattern of parent-child interaction. In rejecting the view of moral development as based primarily in early parent-child interaction, Kohlberg, as Piaget before him, missed the opportunity of seeing that there is far more to ongoing family life than the early experience of the child with his or her parents. He thus ended up dismissing any distinctive role for the family in children's moral development rather than investigating whether other dimensions of family life may play an influential role in children's moral maturation over time.

Subsequent Research

Neither Piaget's negativism nor Kohlberg's neutrality has stood well the test of time. Piaget's position has received its most convincing restatement by Youniss (1980), who believes it remains valuable to distinguish between child-parent interaction, which has as its primary aim the child's learning to conform to social convention, and peer interaction, which is more cooperative in nature and promotes mutuality and adjustment of views. Yet even he admits "neither relation is pure; child-adult relations must have moments when direct reciprocal exchange is enacted and children recognize that adults are making adjustments to children's needs and interests" (p. 263). Furthermore, Youniss notes that by adolescence, children still do relate to their parents in terms of conformity and nonconformity but also try actively to integrate into that relationship elements of friendship and mutual adjustment. Youniss' recognition that the parent-child relationship is not necessarily frozen in one stance but may develop over time is an important advance over Piaget's negativism.

As to Kohlberg's assumptions about family, it was only a matter of time before his colleagues and students would bring them to the court of empirical investigation. A number of studies (Holstein, 1969; Parikh, 1975; Speicher, 1982; Stanley, 1980) have assessed the relationship between parents' and adolescent children's levels of moral judgment and the relationship between certain variables of family life and children's levels of moral judgment.

Although none of these studies produced definitive results that could con-
vincingly suggest a positive relationship between any given family variable and
adolescent children's moral development, ground-breaking work has been done
by Sally Powers (1982; Powers, Hauser, Schwartz, Noam, & Jacobson, 1983)
and her colleagues (Hauser et al., 1984). Theirs is the first empirical work that
suggests the need to revise fundamentally the assumptions that led Kohlberg to
neutralize the family's role in studies of adolescent moral development.

The Powers Study

Powers begins with assumptions borrowed from Kohlberg's neutral stance. If
an adolescent's family were to be an ongoing factor in his or her moral development, the family—or, more specifically, the parent-child interaction—
would have to share with other social environments the general characteristics
shown in the literature to be stimulating to the development of moral reasoning: namely, cognitive conflict and role-taking opportunities. The family environment would have to be like a good classroom or peer interaction: characterized by lively, challenging discussion of moral issues in which members
participate by presenting their views, listening to others, weighing accurately
the differences, critiquing others, but also trying to resolve differences by
stretching their own assumptions (Berkowitz, Gibbs, & Broughton, 1980; Blatt
& Kohlberg, 1975).

   However, Powers and her colleagues went one step beyond these assumptions by hypothesizing that it is not sufficient to consider only behaviors associated with raising cognitive conflict and providing role-taking opportunities.
One must also consider the family's affective climate—the degree to which discussions in the family of differences of viewpoints are supportive or conflictful.
Family members may focus on issues, present their positions, and challenge
the positions of others in ways that either encourage or discourage the free
exchange of views. The researchers hypothesize that affective support versus
affective conflict may be a significant factor in the relationship between family
environment and adolescent development.

   To test these hypotheses, Powers and her colleagues observed 59 upper-
and middle-class adolescents (average age, 14-1/2 years) and their parents discussing as families differences of perspective that had arisen when each had
responded to the three moral dilemmas of Kohlberg's moral judgment interview. (Two features of the sample were that these were all two-parent families
and that while half of the adolescents were students at a high school, the other
half were hospitalized in a psychiatric hospital.) The discussion of differences
was audiotaped, transcribed, and analyzed by individual speech using the
developmental environment coding system (DECS). Powers devised the DECS

for this study to reliably categorize eight kinds of verbal behaviors: six associated with the cognitive climate and two with the affective climate. Four behavioral categories (focusing, competitive challenging, noncompetitive sharing of perspectives, and affective support) were hypothesized to stimulate adolescent moral development, and four others (avoidance, distortion, rejection of task, and affective conflict) were hypothesized to inhibit development.

When these categories of family behavior were related to the levels of justice reasoning of the participants, the results were dramatic. None of the behavioral categories thought to be associated with cognitive conflict and role-taking opportunities were significantly related to levels of adolescent development. But mothers' and fathers' levels of affective support were significantly and positively related to levels of adolescent development. Additionally, mothers' and families' levels of affective conflict were significantly and negatively related to levels of adolescent development. A cluster analysis revealed that adolescent development was most advanced when families presented a high amount of noncompetitive sharing of perspectives or of challenging behavior within a context of high affective support or low affective conflict.

These results show that family interaction is not a neutral factor in adolescent moral development, at least for the populations studied. It may either stimulate or inhibit development, as Powers hypothesized. What stands out most clearly is that Kohlberg's assumption quoted earlier—that "the dimensions on which it [family life] stimulates moral development are primarily general dimensions . . . , i.e., . . . role-taking opportunities"—does not receive empirical support. Even when operationalized into observable behaviors, these "general dimensions" become factors only in the context of the family's affective climate, a dimension Kohlberg did not consider relevant.

Families are not simply outgrown, shed like skin when a child reaches adolescence. There are families in which adolescent children are entitled to views of their own and are supported for discussing and exploring those differences. There are also families in which the raising of differences is a flag for emotional conflict and yet others in which the message is: If differences arise, let's avoid them and discuss something else. Powers and her colleagues are suggesting, based on their correlational data, that living in one family or another bears a relation to adolescent moral development.

Strangely, though, Powers and her colleagues seem not to articulate the full potential theoretical implications of their work, which extend to the domain of ego development as defined by Loevinger (1976) as well as moral development. What they have found, if replicated, would suggest not only that Piaget was wrong to have dismissed the family as a necessarily negative factor in the child's moral development but that Kohlberg's (1969) insistence that "for the developing child there is presumably a rough sequence of groups or institutions in which he participates" (p. 399) is also misguided. If sequence is meant to suggest that the maturing child leaves behind one group—the family—to participate in the next set of groups—school and peer life—there is much prior evidence to suggest that this is not necessarily the case (Bronfenbrenner, 1970). Now, this important study shows that there are families that continue to meet the adolescent need for "support with room to grow." As it was too simplistic for Kohlberg to have assumed that "good" families operate like "good" classrooms in stimulating adolescent moral reasoning primarily through raising cognitive conflict and providing role-taking opportunities, so, too, the notion of sequence is too simplistic to capture the ongoing interaction of effects of school and home on the adolescent's moral development.

Family Dynamics and Moral Development

Powers and her colleagues, based on their data, cannot inform us about interactive effects between family and school on the development of these adolescents. But were they to further interpret their data, they could tell us more about the nature of the family dynamics they observed when watching these families interact. There are interesting but underdeveloped implications in this study concerning family influence.

One example concerns the role of mothers and fathers in influencing adolescent moral development. In Kohlberg's view, the gender of the parent (as of the teacher) is not a relevant variable; what matters is how either parent encourages certain gender-free interactions with the child. In Powers' data, however, the gender of the parent makes a difference.

Powers shows the significant relationships between affective support and conflict and the level of adolescent development. On closer inspection, it is the mothers' but not the fathers' use of the conflictual mode that significantly and negatively relates to adolescent development. Likewise, mothers' but not fathers' level of justice reasoning positively relates to supportive interactions. Also, although mothers are equally supportive of sons and daughters, fathers of daughters are significantly more supportive of their daughters than are fathers of sons supportive of their sons.

Although we ought to be careful about generalizing from Powers' small sample of parents, it is interesting to note that in a parallel study reported in the same volume by Bell and Bell (1983), there also emerged significant unexpected differences between the impact of mothers' and fathers' supportive behavior on adolescent (girls') development. Bell and Bell, who are more attentive to theories of family dynamics than are Powers and her colleagues, seize on these unexpected differences to explore how in family life it may make a difference who is giving support to whom and for what reasons. So, too, might we speculate that an adolescent being put down or attacked by mother might have a different meaning than if he or she had received similar treatment from father.

Finally, the most interesting question to emerge from Powers' study is how we might understand the differences between families that are most supportive and stimulating to their adolescent's development and those that are not. One thing is clear: The difference is not simply a matter of the parents' individual level of development. There is no significant correlation between parent levels and child levels of moral development when socioeconomic status, level of education, and religion are controlled for. And as noted, although mothers' level of justice reasoning is significantly related to affective support (positively) and conflict (negatively), the same is not true for fathers.

If parents' individual levels of development cannot account for the differences between families, it makes sense to look to family dynamics, as do Bell and Bell (1983). Perhaps there are family characteristics that best account for why some families are supportive of adolescent initiative in the face of differences while others find that initiative hard to tolerate. Perhaps moral development theory is ready not only to explicitly recognize the ongoing role played by families in adolescent moral development but also to seek a linkage to family life-cycle theory (Carter & McGoldrick, 1988) to help explain how adolescent development is sponsored or inhibited within the family context.

Sociologists of the family (Duvall, 1962) and family therapists (Bowen, 1978; Haley, 1973; Minuchin, 1974) have spoken of the need to understand the family as a dynamic system that transforms itself over time. They have introduced the notion of stages of family development to refer to the phases of family organization that undergo transformation at nodal moments in the lives of family members. Carter and McGoldrick (1988) have systematized these notions of family development into a more comprehensive scheme of "the family life cycle."

What would it mean for moral development theory to seek linkage with the family life cycle, as presented by Carter and McGoldrick?

1. It would place the drama of adolescent moral development within the context of a family trying to respond to the challenges of living with an adolescent child. As Jim and Jill are struggling to reformulate their primary moral concepts, they are often throwing their parents, grandparents, and siblings off balance by the newness of their responses and by the turmoil of their uncertainty. What does it take for a family to rise to this challenge and to welcome the new ideas as exciting and accept the turmoil as a necessary moment of transition? What are the consequences of a family's tightening up and rejecting new thinking as alien or rebellious?

2. By placing the drama of adolescent development within a family context, this linkage might balance the tendency in Kohlberg's writing, picked up

by Powers, to identify the family with parent-child interaction. In a powerful article on the family as educator, Leichter (1977) stresses how in families the influences on learning and development come from many directions. When parents are not available or functional, siblings, grandparents, aunts, and uncles can step in to play crucial educative roles. In almost all cases, families present a multiplicity of human resources to interact with the developing child and provide diverse avenues for growth and exploration.

3. Families come in many configurations with variations due to culture, socioeconomic and historic factors, natural causes, and marital changes. Powers and colleagues, as Bell and Bell, have studied two-parent, white, middle-class families. Other types of families may show different patterns of handling the transition to adolescence. Instead of falling into the old trap of asking which type of family configuration is best for promoting moral development (for example, by engaging in family meetings or moral discussions), this linkage could provide ways of looking at different types of families and of asking: How can we help them to build on their existing family patterns to support and encourage the moral development of their adolescent children?

Conclusion

To return to the kibbutz study from which we began, a family perspective would have allowed Snarey, Reimer, and Kohlberg (1985b) to see the family presence on the kibbutz. Simply because kibbutz parents and children do not live together under one roof and interact like American middle-class nuclear families, we cannot dismiss their coherence as a family or ignore their need for reorganization to help negotiate together the tasks of adolescence. Some, as in Powers' study, seem to succeed at the task with greater facility than others. But it will take an expanded theoretical framework for future researchers to understand how on the kibbutz or elsewhere adolescent moral development proceeds within a family context or in the interaction between the family and other salient institutions.

References

Bell, D., & Bell, L. (1983). Parent validation and support in the development of adolescent daughters. In H. R. Grotevant & C. R. Cooper (Eds.), *Adolescent development in the family* (pp. 27–42). San Francisco: Jossey-Bass.

Berkowitz, M. W., Gibbs, J. C., & Broughton, J. M. (1980). Structure and process: An experimental inquiry into the "what" and "how" of moral judgment development. In *Proceedings of the eighth annual international conference on Piagetian theory and its implications for the helping professions, I.* Los Angeles: University of Southern California Press.

Bettelheim, B. (1969). *The children of the dream*. New York: Macmillan.

Blatt, M., & Kohlberg, L. (1975). The effects of classroom discussion upon children's level of moral judgment. *Journal of Moral Education, 4,* 129–161.

Bowen, M. (1978). *Family therapy in clinical practice.* New York: Jason Aronson.

Bronfenbrenner, U. (1970). *Two worlds of childhood.* New York: Russell Sage Foundation.

Carter, B., & McGoldrick, M. (Eds.). (1988). *The changing family life cycle: A framework for family therapy* (2nd ed.). New York: Gardner Press.

Colby, A., & Kohlberg, L. (1987). *The measurement of moral judgement*. New York: Cambridge University Press.

Duvall, E. M. (1962). *Family development*. Philadelphia: Lippincott.

Haley, J. (1973). *Uncommon therapy: The psychiatric techniques of Milton H. Erickson, M.D.* New York: Norton.

Hauser, S. T., Powers, S. I., Noam, G. G., Jacobson, A. M., Weiss, B., & Follansbee, D. J. (1984). Familial context of adolescent ego development. *Child Development, 55,* 195–213.

Holstein, C. B. (1969). *Parental consensus and interaction in relation to the child's moral judgment*. Unpublished doctoral dissertation, University of California, Berkeley, CA.

Kohlberg, L. (1969). Stage and sequence: The cognitive developmental approach to socialization. In D. A. Goslin (Ed.), *Handbook of socialization theory and research* (pp. 347–480). Chicago: Rand McNally.

Kohlberg, L. (1971). Cognitive-developmental theory and the practice of collective moral education. In M. Wolins & M. Gottesman (Eds.), *Group care: An Israeli approach* (pp. 342–371). New York: Gordon and Breach.

Leichter, H. J. (Ed.). (1977). *The family as educator*. New York: Teachers College Press.

Loevinger, L. (1976). *Ego development: Conceptions and theories*. San Francisco: Jossey-Bass.

Minuchin, S. (1974). *Families and family therapy*. Cambridge, MA: Harvard University Press.

Parikh, B. (1975). *Moral judgment and its relation to family environmental factors in Indian and American upper middle class families*. Unpublished doctoral dissertation, Boston University, Boston, MA.

Piaget, J. (1965). *The moral judgment of the child*. New York: Free Press.

Powers, S. I. (1982). *Family interaction and parental moral development as a context for adolescent moral development*. Unpublished doctoral dissertation, Harvard University, Cambridge, MA.

Powers, S. I., Hauser, S. T., Schwartz, M. M., Noam, G. G., & Jacobson, A. M. (1983). Adolescent ego development and family interaction: A structural-developmental perspective. In H. R. Grotevant & C. R. Cooper (Eds.), *Adolescent development in the family* (pp. 5–26). San Francisco: Jossey-Bass.

Reimer, J. (1977). *A study in the moral development of kibbutz adolescents*. Unpublished doctoral dissertation, Harvard University, Cambridge, MA.

Snarey, J. (1982). *The social and moral development of kibbutz founders and sabras: A cross-sectional and longitudinal cross-cultural study*. Unpublished doctoral dissertation, Harvard University, Cambridge, MA.

Snarey, J., Reimer, J., & Kohlberg, L. (1985a). Development of social-moral reasoning among kibbutz adolescents: A longitudinal cross-cultural study. *Developmental Psychology, 21*, 3–17.

Snarey, J., Reimer, J., & Kohlberg, L. (1985b). The kibbutz as a model for moral education: A longitudinal cross-cultural study. *Journal of Applied Developmental Psychology, 6*, 151–172.

Speicher, B. (1982). *Relationships between parent moral judgment, child moral judgment and family interaction: A correlational study.* Unpublished doctoral dissertation, Harvard University, Cambridge, MA.

Spiro, M. E. (1963). *Kibbutz: Venture in utopia.* New York: Schocken Books.

Stanley, S. F. (1980). The family and moral education. In R. L. Mosher (Ed.), *Moral education: A first generation of research and development* (pp. 341–355). New York: Praeger.

Talmon, Y. (1972). *Family and community in the kibbutz.* Cambridge, MA: Harvard University Press, Cambridge, MA.

Youniss, J. (1980). *Parents and peers in social development: A Sullivan-Piaget perspective.* Chicago: University of Chicago Press.

CHAPTER 6

Adolescent Development Reconsidered

Carol Gilligan

Harvard University

In talking about adolescent development, how will one respond to the adolescent's questions or the questions behind the adolescent's questions: What is true? What is of value? Who am I now? Where is my home?

In an essay, "On the Modern Element in Modern Literature," Trilling (1967) writes of his discomfort in teaching the course in modern literature at Columbia College. No literature, he observes, "has ever been so shockingly personal as ours—it asks every question that is forbidden in polite society. It asks us if we are content with our marriages, with our family lives, with our professional lives, with our friends. . . . It asks us if we are content with ourselves, if we are saved or damned" (pp. 164–165). How is one to teach such literature? After addressing the technicalities of verse patterns, irony, and prose conventions, the teacher must confront the necessity of bearing personal testimony, "must use whatever authority he may possess to say whether or not a work is true, and if not, why not, and if so, why so." Yet one can do this only at considerable cost to one's privacy. What disturbs Trilling is that in the absence of such confrontation, the classroom lesson exemplifies the very problem displayed in the novels—the costs of detachment and dispassion in the face of what is most intensely passionate and personal.

To talk about health of adolescents raises a similar problem. Once we have covered the technicalities of physical disease and psychic mechanisms, how will we respond to the adolescent's questions, or the questions behind the adolescent's questions: What is true? What is of value? Who am I now? Where is

The research discussed in this chapter was supported by grants from Marilyn Brachman Hoffman, the Geraldine Rockefeller Dodge Foundation, the Rockefeller Foundation, the Joseph S. Klingenstein Foundation, and the Lilly Foundation.

my home? I have studied identity and moral development by listening to the ways in which people speak about themselves and about conflicts and choices they face. In this context, I have thought about the nature of psychological growth as it pertains to questions of truth and of value. Adolescence is a naturally occurring time of transition—a time when changes happen that affect the experience of self and relationships with others. Thus adolescence is a situation for epistemological crisis, an age when issues of interpretation come to the fore. The turbulence and indeterminacy of adolescence, long noted and often attributed to conflicts over sexuality and aggression, can also be traced to these interpretive problems. In this chapter, I will join concerns about the development of contemporary adolescents with concerns about questions of interpretation within psychology. I will begin by specifying four reasons for reconsidering the psychology of adolescence at this time and then offer a new framework for thinking about adolescent development and secondary education.

Four Reasons for Reconsidering Adolescent Development

First, the view of childhood has changed. Since adolescence denotes the transition from childhood to adulthood, what constitutes development in adolescence hinges on how one views the childhood that precedes it and the adulthood that follows. Recent research on infancy and early childhood reveals the young child to be far more social than psychologists previously imagined, calling into question most descriptions of the beginnings or early stages of cognitive, social, and moral development. Stern's recent book, *The Interpersonal World of the Infant* (1985) and Kagan's *The Nature of the Child* (1984) document the interpersonal capabilities and the social nature of young children: their responsiveness to others and their appreciation of standards. Previously described as "locked up in egocentrism," as "fused" with others, as capable only of "parallel play," the young child now is observed to initiate and sustain connection with others, to engage in patterns of social interaction with others and thus to create relationships with them. Emde, Johnson, and Easterbrooks' (1987) research shows that nine-month-old babies prefer mothers to respond to their actions rather than to mimic, or mirror, their behavior. In addition, infants by this age have established distinctive patterns of social interaction with others, so that their relationships can be differentiated in these terms by the researcher, and presumably by the baby, since the patterns repeat. Thus relationships, or connections with others, are known to the young child as patterns of interaction that occur in time and that extend through time: themes and variations.

It may well be that the tension between this felt knowledge of human connection, this earliest grasp of what relationship means, and the ability to represent this knowledge in language underlies many psychological problems people experience and also many problems within the field of psychology itself. Despite the fact that psychologists constantly talk about interaction or relationship—between self and others, between person and environment—the language of psychology is filled with static, visual images of separation. Thus psychologists delineate borders and boundaries in an effort to classify and categorize and ultimately to predict and control human behavior, whereas behavior, especially when observed in its natural settings, often resists such classification. At present, Hoffman's (1976) observations of empathy and altruism in young children and Gottman's (1983) monograph "How Children Become Friends"—studies that derive from watching children in the natural settings of their daily lives—challenge existing stage theories of social and moral development by revealing the disparity between the stage theory description of the young child as asocial or amoral and the intensely social and also moral nature of the young child's relationships with others. Like Bowlby (1973, 1980), who observed the young child to grieve the loss that separation entails, Hoffman saw young children perceive and respond to the needs of others, and Gottman saw children remember their friends—even after surprisingly long intervals of physical distance and time.

These radical changes in the view of childhood necessitate a revision in the description of adolescent development, since they alter the foundation on which psychologists have premised development in the teenage years. If social responsiveness and moral concern are normally present in early childhood, their absence in adolescence becomes surprising. Rather than asking why such capacities have failed to emerge by adolescence, implying that the child is stuck at some earlier or lower stage, one would ask instead what has happened to the responsiveness of infancy, how have the child's capacities for relationship been diminished or lost? This change in perspective also offers a new way of thinking about resistance—especially the signs of resistance often noted among teenage girls (Gilligan, 1986a). Rather than signaling conflicts over separation, such resistance may reflect girls' perception that connections with others are endangered for girls in the teenage years on a variety of levels.

The second reason for reconsidering what is meant by development in adolescence follows directly from this observation. Repeatedly, the inattention to girls has been noted as a lacuna in the literature on adolescence (Bettelheim, 1962; Adelson & Doehrman, 1980)—which raises the question: What has been missed by not studying girls? The answer generally is felt to be something about relationships, and those who have studied girls and women confirm this speculation. Konopka (1966), who entered the locked world of delinquent girls to learn about their own stories, found that these stories were centrally about "loneliness accompanied by despair" (p. 40)—a desperation of loneliness "based on a feeling of being unprotected, being incapable of making and finding friends, being surrounded by an anonymous and powerful adult world" (p. 40). Konopka observed that although the need for connection with others, which means involvement with others who are "real friends" or with an adult who appears as "a person," is unusually intense among delinquent girls, the "need for dependence . . . seems to exist in all adolescent girls" (p. 41). Miller (1976), writing about women who come for psychotherapy, noted that women's sense of self is built around being able to make and then maintain connections with others and that the loss of relationships is experienced by many women as tantamount to a loss of self. Listening to girls and women speaking about themselves and about their experiences of conflict and choice, I heard conceptions of self and morality that implied a different way of thinking about relationships—one that often had set women apart from the mainstream of Western thought because of its central premise that self and others were connected and interdependent.

Thus to say what is true—that girls and women have not been much studied—is only to begin to appreciate what such study might entail. To reconsider adolescent development in light of the inattention to girls and women is to hold in abeyance the meaning of such key terms of psychological analysis as self and development and perhaps above all relationship.

For the present, to take seriously psychologists' past omission of girls and women and to see this absence as potentially significant means to suspend for the moment all discussion of sex differences until the standards of assessment and the terms of comparison can be drawn from studies of girls and women as well as boys and men. The deep sense of outrage and despair over disconnection, tapped by Konopka, Miller, myself, and others—the strong feelings and judgments often made by girls and women about excluding, leaving out, and abandoning, as well as the desperate actions girls and women often take in the face of detachment or indifference or lack of concern—may reflect an awareness on some level of the disjunction between women's lives and Western culture. Yet the equally strong feelings often expressed by girls and women that such feelings are illegitimate and the judgments often made that such exclusion is justified or deserved serve to undercut this awareness. What Adelson and Doehrman (1980) call "the inattention to girls, and the processes of feminine development in adolescence" (p.114) tacitly supports the suspicion of girls and women that nothing of importance or value can be learned by studying them. In the moral conflicts adolescent girls and women describe, a central and searing dilemma is about this problem of disconnection: Is it better, women ask, to turn away from others or to abandon themselves? This question—whether to be selfish or selfless in choosing between self and others—rests on the premise that genuine connection must fail. One reason for reconsidering the psychology of adolescence is to examine this premise.

The third reason for reconsideration pertains specifically to cognitive development and involves the definition of cognition—what knowing and also thinking mean. Following Sputnik in the late 1950s, Americans became concerned about the state of math and science education as part of an effort to "catch up with the Russians." The revival of Piaget's work in the early 1960s provided a psychological rationale for this endeavor, since in Piaget's view cognitive development was identical to the growth of mathematical and scientific thinking (see, for example, Inhelder & Piaget, 1958). This conception of cognitive development conveys a view of the individual as living in a timeless world of abstract rules. Within this framework, there is no rationale for teaching history or languages or writing or for paying attention to art and music. In fact, the flourishing of Piagetian theory within psychology over the past two decades has coincided with the decline of all these subjects in the school curriculum.

Educators looking to psychology to justify curriculum decisions still can find little basis for teaching history or for encouraging students to learn more than one language or for emphasizing complex problems of interpretation and the strategies needed for reading ambiguous texts. In the timeless world of critical thinking, the fact that one cannot say exactly the same thing in French and in English becomes in essence irrelevant to the development of intelligence. Ravitch (1985) recently has chronicled the decline of historical knowledge among high school students and lamented the transposition of history into social science. Yet the humanities, in order to gain funding or to defend their place within the curriculum, have often had to justify their educational value in terms psychologists have derived from analyzing the structure of mathematical and scientific reasoning.

The ahistorical approach to human events underlies the fourth reason for reconsideration: namely, the overriding value psychologists have placed on separation, individuation, and autonomy. To see self-sufficiency as the hallmark of maturity conveys a view of adult life that is at odds with the human condition—a view that cannot sustain the kinds of long-term commitments and involvements with others that are necessary for raising and educating a child or for citizenship in a democratic society (see Arendt, 1958). The equation of development with separation and of maturity with independence presumes a radical discontinuity of generations and encourages a vision of human experience that is essentially divorced from history or time. The tendency for psychologists to characterize adolescence as the time of second individuation (Blos, 1967) and to celebrate an identity that is self-wrought (Erikson, 1958) encourages a way of speaking in which the interdependence of human life and the reliance of people on one another become largely unrepresented or tacit. The way in which this value framework colors the interpretation of research findings is exemplified by an article recently published by Pipp and others (1985), who set out to discover how adolescents view their relationships with their parents over time—what changes they see in such connections from early childhood to late adolescence. Thus college sophomores were asked through drawings and questionnaire ratings to indicate the nature of their relationship with their parents at five points in time ranging from early childhood to the present. The authors note two distinct trends. One was expected and is familiar to anyone conversant with developmental theory: a linear progression whereby incrementally over time child and parent move from a relationship of inequality toward an ideal of equality. Thus the child is portrayed as gaining steadily in responsibility, dominance, and independence in relation to the parents, who correspondingly decline on all these dimensions. With this shift in the balance of power, child and parent become increasingly alike or similar over time. The other trend was unanticipated and showed a striking discontinuity. With respect to variables pertaining to love and closeness, college sophomores saw their relationships with their parents as closer at present than in the years preceding, more similar in this respect to their relationships with their parents in early childhood. In addition, differences emerged along these two dimensions between the ways students represented their relationships with their mothers and fathers in that they felt more responsibility toward their mothers, whom they perceived as especially friendly, and they felt more similar to their fathers, whom they perceived as more dominant.

The unexpected finding of two asymmetrical lines of development tied to different dimensions of relationship is of great interest to me because it corroborates the developmental model I have derived from analyzing the ways people describe themselves and make moral judgments—a model built on the distinction between equality and attachment as two dimensions of relationship that shape the experience of self and define the terms of moral conflict. For the moment, however, I wish to focus on the way Pipp and others interpret their findings, specifically to note that in discussing their results, they collapse the two trends they have discovered and in doing so reveal an overriding concern with equality and independence. The fact that nineteen-year-olds describe themselves as their parents' children thus is taken by Pipp and others (1985) as a sign of limitation, an indication that the process of individuation is not yet complete.

> Although [our subjects] felt themselves to be more independent of the relationship than their parents were, there were indications that they still felt themselves to be their parents' children. . . . The results suggest that the individuation process is still ongoing at the age of 19. It would be interesting to see whether it continues throughout adulthood. (p. 1001)

With this interpretation, the authors align themselves with the field of psychology in general. Viewing childhood attachments as a means to separation, they portray continuing connections between adolescents and parents as a sign of dependence, negatively valued, and considered as a source of limitation.

To summarize this first section, the need to reconsider adolescent development at present stems from changes in the understanding of infancy and childhood, from the recognition that girls have not been much studied and that studies of girls are overlooked or not cited, from the observation that Piagetian theories of cognitive development provide no rationale for roughly half of what has traditionally been regarded as the essence of a liberal arts or humanistic education, and from the fact that a psychology of adolescence, anchored in the values of separation and independence, fails to represent the interdependence of adult life and thus conveys a distorted image of the human condition, an image that fosters what is currently called the culture of narcissism.

I take from these observations several cautions: that there is a need for new concepts and new categories of interpretation; that the accumulation of data according to old conceptual frameworks simply extends these problems; that the assessment of sex differences cannot be undertaken until female development is better understood; that such understanding may change the description of both male and female development; and that the approach to the psychology of adolescence and to subjects pertaining to adolescent development and education must be informed by the insights of such disciplines as anthropology, history, and literature. Specifically, psychologists need to incorporate anthropologists' recognition of the dangers in imposing one set of ethnocentric categories on a different population and to take on the concerns of anthropologists, historians, and literary critics with the complexity of interpretation and the construction of alternative world views.

Formulating an Approach

In the 1971 issue of *Daedalus* devoted to the subject of early adolescence, several articles addressed the question of values. If the high school does not have a coherent set of values or a moral philosophy, Kagan argued (as did Kohlberg and myself), it cannot engage the commitment of its students. The school and the culture at large must offer some justification for learning to adolescents who are distracted by other concerns, who are capable of spotting contradiction, who have a keen eye for adult hypocrisy, and who are unwilling to put their self-esteem on the line when failure seems inescapable. Bettelheim (1965) linked the problems of youth to the problem of generations: "Whenever the older generation has lost its bearings, the younger generation is lost with it. The positive alternatives of emulation or revolt are replaced with the lost quality of neither" (p. 106). Erikson (1975), writing at a time when the dissent of contemporary youth was rising, noted that for adults "to share true authority with the young would mean to acknowledge something which adults have learned to mistrust in themselves: a truly ethical potential" (p. 223). To Erikson, ethical concerns were a natural meeting ground between adults and adolescents, both rendered uncertain by the predicament of modern civilization.

Yet if ethical questions are inescapable in relations between adults and adolescents, if the problems of adolescents are in some sense a barometer of the health of civilization, a measure of the culture's productive and reproductive potential, the issues raised by Trilling become central: How are adults to address the ethical problems of modern society? What claims to moral authority do the teachers of adolescents possess? The great modern novels that Trilling was teaching had as a central and controlling theme "the disenchantment of our culture with culture itself . . . a bitter line of hostility to civilization" (1967, p. 60). Thus the urgency of the questions: Are we content with our marriages, our work, and ourselves? How do we envision salvation? What wisdom can we pass on to the next generation? Twentieth-century history has only heightened ambivalence toward the life of civilization by demonstrating in one of the most highly educated and cultured of nations a capacity for moral atrocity so extreme as to strain the meaning of words. In light of this history, any equation of morality with culture or intelligence or education is immediately suspect, and this suspicion has opened the way for the current revival of religious fundamentalism and of terrorism, as well as for the present skepticism about nineteenth-century ideas about development or progress. The idea of "surrendering oneself to experience without regard to self-interest or conventional morality, of escaping wholly from the societal bonds, is," Trilling (1967, p. 82) notes, "an 'element' somewhere in the mind of every modern person." This element is manifest in one form or another in many of the problems of today's adolescents.

The awesome power of the irrational in human behavior is the subject of both classical tragedy and modern psychology, each attempting in different ways to untangle and explain its logic, to understand why people pursue paths that are clearly marked as self-destructive—why, for example, teenagers stop eating, take drugs, commit suicide, and in a variety of other ways wreak havoc with their future. Two approaches currently characterize the response of professionals to these signs of disease. One relies on the imposition of control, the effort to override a tortuous reason with behavior modification and biofeedback, to focus attention simply on physical survival by teaching skills for managing stress and regulating food and alcohol consumption. The other approach reaches into reason and joins the humanistic faith in the power of education with the insights of modern psychology. Positing human development as the aim of education, it turns attention to the question: What constitutes and fosters development?

My interest in adolescence is anchored in the second approach. It was spurred by Erikson's attention to the relationship between life history and history and by two insights in the work of Kohlberg: First, that following the Nazi holocaust, psychologists must address the question of moral relativism, and second, that adolescents are passionately interested in moral questions. Thus adolescence may be a crucial time for moral education. Erikson's study of Luther highlighted the central tie between questions of identity and questions of morality in the adolescent years. But it also called attention to a set of beliefs that extend from the theology of Luther's Reformation into the ideology of contemporary psychology: a world view in which the individual is embarked on a solitary journey toward personal salvation, a world view that is centered on the values of autonomy and independence. Luther's statements of repudiation and affirmation, "I am not" and "Here I stand," have become emblematic of the identity crisis in modern times—a crisis that begins with the separation of self from childhood identifications and attachments and ends with some version of Luther's statement: "I have faith, therefore I am justified." In a secular age, the faith and the justification have become psychological. The limitations of this vision have been elaborated by a variety of social critics and are closely connected to the reasons I have given for reconsidering the psychology of adolescence: the view of childhood attachments as dispensable or replaceable, the absence of women from the cosmology, the equation of thinking with formal logic, and the value placed on self-sufficiency and independence. Such criticisms are augmented by the facts of recent social history: the rise in teenage suicides, eating disorders, and educational problems. The need at present for new directions in theory and practice seems clear.

Two Moral Voices: Two Frameworks for Problem Solving

My approach to development is attentive to a moral voice that reveals the lineaments of an alternative world view and is grounded in seemingly anomalous data from studies involving girls and women (Gilligan, 1977, 1982, 1986b)— moral judgments that did not fit the definition of moral and self-descriptions at odds with the concept of self. The data that initially appeared discrepant became the basis for a reformulation, grounds for thinking again about what self, morality, and relationship mean. Two moral voices that signal different ways of thinking about what constitutes a moral problem and how such problems can be addressed or resolved draw attention to the fact that a story can be told from different angles and a situation seen in different lights. Like ambiguous figure perception where the same picture can be seen as a vase or two faces, the basic elements of moral judgment—self, others, and relationship—can be organized in different ways, depending on how relationship is imagined or construed. From the perspective of someone seeking or loving justice, relationships are organized in terms of equality, symbolized by the balancing of scales. Moral concerns focus on problems of inequality or oppression, and the moral ideal is one of reciprocity, or equal respect. From the perspective of someone seeking or valuing care, relationship connotes responsiveness, or attachment, a resiliency of connection that is symbolized by a network, or web. Moral concerns focus on problems of detachment or disconnection or abandonment, and the moral ideal is one of attention and response. Since equality and attachment are dimensions that characterize all forms of human connection, all relationships can be seen in both ways and spoken of in both sets of terms. Yet by adopting one or another moral voice or standpoint, people can highlight problems that are associated with different kinds of vulnerability and focus attention on different types of concern.

Evidence that justice and care concerns can be distinguished in people's narratives about moral conflict and choice and that these concerns organize people's thinking about decisions they make comes from a series of studies in which people were asked to discuss conflicts and choices that they faced. In essence, by asking people to speak about times when they confronted dilemmas, it was possible to examine how people think about the age-old questions of how to live and what to do. Most of the people who participated in these studies, primarily North American adolescents and adults, raised considerations of both justice and care when describing an experience of moral conflict. Yet they also tended to focus their attention on one set of concerns and minimally represent the other. The surprising finding of these studies was the extent of this "focus" phenomenon. For example, in a study (Gilligan & Attanucci, 1985) where focus was defined as 75% or more considerations pertaining either to issues of justice or to issues of care, fifty-three out of eighty educationally advantaged adolescents and adults, or two thirds of the sample, demonstrated focus. The remaining third raised roughly equal numbers of justice and care considerations.

The tendency for people to organize experiences of conflict and choice largely in terms of justice or in terms of care has been a constant finding of the research on moral orientation, ranging from Lyons' (1983) and Langdale's (1983) reports of orientation predominance, to the more stringent analysis of orientation focus by Gilligan and Attanucci (1985), to the most recent analysis of narrative strategies (Brown et al., 1987). This takes into account not simply the number or proportion of justice and care considerations raised but also the way in which concerns about justice and care are presented in relation to one another and in relation to the speaker or narrator of the dilemma—whether justice and care are presented as separate concerns or integrated, whether one or both sets of concerns are aligned with the narrator or claimed as the speaker's own terms. The fact that two moral voices can repeatedly be distinguished in narratives of moral conflict and choice and the fact that people tend to focus their attention either on problems of unfairness or problems of disconnection

give credence to the interpretation of justice and care as frameworks that organize moral thinking and feelings. The focus phenomenon, however, suggests
that people tend to lose sight of one perspective or to silence one set of concerns
in arriving at decisions or in justifying choices they have made.

The tendency to focus was equally characteristic of the men and the
women studied, suggesting that loss of perspective is a liability that both sexes
share. There were striking sex differences, however, in the direction of focus.
Of the thirty-one men who demonstrated focus, thirty focused on justice; of
the twenty-two women who demonstrated focus, ten focused on justice and
twelve on care. Care focus, although not characteristic of all women, was
almost exclusively a female phenomenon in Brown and others' study of educationally advantaged North Americans. If girls and women were eliminated
from the study, care focus in moral reasoning would virtually disappear.

With this clarification of the different voice phenomenon—the thematic
shift in outlook or perspective, the change in the terms of moral discourse and
self description, and the empirical association with women—it becomes possible to turn to new questions about development in adolescence and psychological interpretation, as well as to concerns about moral relativism and moral
education. It is noteworthy that both sexes raise considerations of care in
describing moral conflicts they face and thus identify problems of care and
connection as subjects of moral concern. Yet it is women's elaboration of care
considerations that reveals the coherence of a care ethic as a framework for
decision—its premises as a world view or way of constructing social reality, its
logic as a problem-solving strategy, and its significance as a focal point for evaluating actions and thinking about choice. The description of care concerns as
the focus of a coherent moral perspective rather than as a sign of deficiency in
women's moral reasoning or a subordinate set of concerns within a justice
framework (such as special obligations or personal dilemmas) recasts the
moral domain as one comprising at least two moral orientations. Moral maturity presumably would entail an ability to see in both ways and to speak both
languages, and the relationship between these two moral perspectives or voices
becomes a key question for investigation.

The significance of the concept of moral orientation for thinking about
development in adolescence is illuminated by a brilliant study designed and
conducted by Johnston (1985). Johnston set out to examine Polanyi's (1958)
suggestion that there are two conflicting aspects of formalized intelligence: one
that depends on the acquisition of formalized instruments (such as proposi-
tional logic) and one that depends on the "pervasive participation of the knowing person in the act of knowing" (p. 70). Polanyi (1958) considers this latter
kind of intelligence to rest on "an art which is essentially inarticulate" (p. 70).
Johnston's question was whether this way of knowing could be articulated. Her
approach to this question was informed by Vygotsky's (1978) theory that all of

the higher cognitive functions (voluntary attention, logical memory, formation of concepts) originate as actual relations between individuals, so that in the course of development "an interpersonal process is transformed into an intrapersonal one" (p. 57). This is a theory that allows for individual differences and that can explain how different experiences of relationships might lead to different ways of thinking about a problem—such as the sex differences in early childhood relationships that Chodorow (1978) has described. Furthermore, groups like women whose experience in general has been neglected in considering the sources of cognitive and moral proficiency may exemplify ways of knowing or thinking that appear, in the present context, to be inarticulate. Johnston's question was whether tacit knowledge, or intuitive forms of knowing—what Belenky and others (1986) have subsequently called connected knowing—might appear as different forms of moral problem solving.

Thus Johnston asked sixty eleven- and fifteen-year-olds from two schools in a typical middle-class suburb to state and to solve the problem posed in two of Aesop's fables. Of the sixty children, fifty-four (or fifty-six, depending on the fable) initially cast the problem either as a problem of rights or as a problem of response, framing it either as a conflict of claims that could be resolved by appealing to a fair procedure or a rule for adjudicating disputes or as a problem of need, which raised the question of whether or how it was possible to respond to all of the needs. Each way of defining the problem was associated with a different problem-solving strategy, thus tying moral orientation to the development of different kinds of reasoning. For example, in the fable, "The Porcupine and the Moles" (see Figure 6.1 and Table 3.1), a justice strategy focused on identifying and prioritizing conflicting rights or claims. ("The porcupine has to go definitely. It's the moles' house.") In contrast, a care strategy focused on identifying needs and creating a solution responsive to all of the

Figure 6.1 The Porcupine and the Moles

It was growing cold, and a porcupine was looking for a home. He found a most desirable cave, but saw it was occupied by a family of moles.

"Would you mind if I shared your home for the winter?" the porcupine asked the moles.

The generous moles consented, and the porcupine moved in. But the cave was small, and every time the moles moved around, they were scratched by the porcupine's sharp quills. The moles endured this discomfort as long as they could. Then at last they gathered courage to approach their visitor. "Pray leave," they said, "and let us have our cave to ourselves once again."

"Oh no!" said the porcupine. "This place suits me very well."

---

needs. ("Cover the porcupine with a blanket [so that the moles will not be stuck and the porcupine will have shelter]" or "Dig a bigger hole.") It is important to stress that these two approaches are not opposites or mirror images of one another (with justice uncaring and care unjust). Instead, they constitute different ways of organizing the problem that lead to different reasoning strategies—different ways of thinking about what is happening and what to do.

The brilliance of Johnston's design lay in the fact that after the children had stated and solved the fable problem, she asked, "Is there another way to think about this problem?" About half of the children, somewhat more fifteen- than eleven-year-olds, spontaneously switched orientation and solved the problem in the other mode. Others did so following a cue as to the form such a switch might take. ("Some people say you could have a rule; some people say you could solve the dilemma so that all of the animals will be satisfied.") Then Johnston asked, "Which of these solutions is the better solution?" With few exceptions, the children answered this question, saying which solution was better and explaining why it was preferable.

This study is a watershed about developmental theory and research practices. The fact that people solve a problem in one way clearly does not mean that they do not have access to other approaches. Furthermore, a person's initial or spontaneous approach to a problem is not necessarily the one he or she deems preferable. Eleven- and fifteen-year-olds are able to explain why they adopt problem-solving strategies that they see as problematic, to give reasons for why they put aside ways of thinking that in their own eyes seem preferable. Whether there are reasons other than the ones they cite is, in this context, beside the point. The fact that some boys choose justice strategies but say they prefer care solutions, while also considering care solutions to be naive and unworkable, is in itself significant. For example, in one high school, students of both sexes tended to characterize care-focused solutions or inclusive problem-solving strategies as utopian or outdated; one student linked them with impractical Sunday school teachings, one with the outworn philosophy of hippies. Presumably, students in the school who voiced care strategies would encounter these characterizations.

The tendency for children to define the fable problem in terms either of rights or of response, combined with their ability to switch orientations, heightens the analogy to ambiguous figure perception but also raises the question: Why do some people focus on justice and some on care when considering the same problem? Furthermore, why do some people see rights solutions as better and others see response solutions as preferable in the same situation? Johnston found sex differences in both spontaneous moral orientation and preferred orientation, with boys more often choosing and preferring justice formulations and girls more often choosing and preferring care strategies. In addition, she found fable differences, indicating that moral orientation is associated both with the sex of the reasoner and with the problem being considered. (See Langdale, 1983, for similar findings.)

Since people can adopt at least two moral standpoints and can solve problems in at least two different ways, the choice of moral standpoint, whether implicit or explicit, becomes an important feature of moral decision making and of research on moral development. The choice of moral standpoint adds a new dimension to the role commonly accorded the self in moral decision making. Traditionally, the self is described as choosing whether or not to enact moral standards or principles, as having or not having a good will. Yet the self, whether conceived as a narrator of moral conflict or as a protagonist in a moral drama, also chooses, consciously or unconsciously, where to stand—what signs to look for and what voices to listen to in thinking about what is happening (what is the problem) and what to do. People may have a preferred way of seeing and may be attuned to different voices, so that one voice or another is more readily heard or understood. Johnston demonstrated that at least by age 11, children know and can explain the logic of two problem-solving strategies and will indicate why they see one or the other as preferable. In adolescence, when thinking becomes more reflective and more self-conscious, moral orientation may become closely entwined with self-definition, so that the sense of self or feelings of personal integrity become aligned with a particular way of seeing or speaking.

But adolescence, the time when thinking becomes self-consciously interpretive, is also the time when the interpretive schemes of the culture, including the system of social norms, values, and roles, impinge more directly on perception and judgment, defining within the framework of a given society what is the "right way" to see and to feel and to think—the way "we" think. Thus adolescence is the age when thinking becomes conventional. Moral standpoint, a feature of an individual's moral reasoning, is also a characteristic of interpretive schemes, including the conventions of interpretation or the intellectual conventions that are taught in secondary education. The justice focus, which is explicit in most theories of moral development (see Freud, 1923/1961; Piaget, 1932/1965; Kohlberg, 1969), also characterizes and makes plain the correlation found between tests of moral development and tests of cognitive and social and emotional development; although measuring different things, all these tests may be measuring from the same angle. Thus a care focus that otherwise can be viewed as one aspect of moral reasoning becomes a crucial perspective on an interpretive level, challenging the prevailing world view. Here the questions raised by Trilling become especially pertinent, articulating a central theme in modern culture that is at odds with the dominant viewpoint in contemporary psychology—the theme of disenchantment. Psychology's response to the moral crisis of modern civilization has become a kind of heady optimism, reflected in the language of current stage theories and intervention promises, conveying the impression that the nature of moral maturity is dear and the road to development apparent. To bring in a standpoint missing from such theories enlarges the definition of cognition and morality and renders the portrayal of human development and moral dilemmas more complex. The following example, taken from a study of high school students, speaks directly to these questions and suggests how a prevailing justice orientation may impinge on the judgments adolescents make, influencing both the concerns that they voice and also what they hold back or keep silent. The example contains both a theoretical point and a methodological caution: Two judgments, one directly stated and one indirectly presented, highlight a developmental tension between detachment and connection and underscore the limitations of data gathered without attention to the issue of standpoint or the possibility of alternative frameworks or world views. At the heart of this illustration of alternative world views and the problems posed by alternative world views is a critical but subtle shift in perspective, caught colloquially by the difference between being centered in oneself and being self-centered.

An Example of Alternative World Views

A high school student, Anne, was attending a traditional preparatory school for academically talented and ambitious students, a boy's school that in recent years became coeducational. When asked to describe a moral conflict she faced, Anne spoke about her decision not to buy cigarettes for someone who asked her to do so. Her reasoning focused on considerations of justice: "If I am against smoking, but yet I buy cigarettes for a person, I think I am contradicting myself." Noncontradiction here means reciprocity in the sense of applying the same standard to herself and to others, treating others as she would treat herself or want to be treated by them, and thereby showing equal respect for persons. Asked if she thought she had done the right thing, she answers, "Yes. . . . I think it was, because I did not contradict myself, because I held with what I believed." Thus she assesses the rightness of her decision by examining the consistency between her actions and her beliefs, justified on grounds of respect for life and valuing health. Then she is asked, "Is there another way to see the problem?" and she says:

> Well, no. I mean yes. It is not as simple as buying cigarettes or not. It has a lot to do with everything that I believe In . . . In another sense, it represents how I deal with what I believe. I try not to break down just because somebody pressures me, but I don't feel like I get into situations like they always write about in books. . . . I don't think people are represented the way they are sometimes.

It is important to emphasize that this intimation of another way of seeing, and the suggestion that the way people and situations are commonly represented may not be an accurate representation, occurs only after the interpretive question "Is there another way to see the problem?" is raised. And the interpretive question leads to confusion, to a dense statement that appears to alternate between two perspectives, one elaborated and one implied. The implied perspective, which "has a lot to do with everything that I believe in," is only clarified when Anne speaks about a friend whom she characterizes as "self-centered." In this context, the meaning of being self-centered shifts from "holding with what I believe" to "not thinking about how one's words or actions affect other people." With this shift, the alternative world view and the problem posed by alternative world views become clear.

Anne says that her friend does not recognize how what she says affects other people: "She does not think about how it affects them, but just about the fact that she told them." In other words, she acts as if speaking could be divorced from listening, or words from interpretation. Because her friend is inattentive to differences in interpretation, she "does not always recognize that what she likes to hear is not what other people like to hear, but may hurt their feelings." She is self-centered in that she does not realize that "other people are not all like her."

Thus attention to differences in interpretation is central to making connection with others. The interpretive question raised by the researcher that leads Anne to attend to the issue of perspective also leads her into a way of thinking where the failure to see differences becomes morally problematic, signifying carelessness or detachment (being self-centered) and creating the conditions for the unwitting infliction of hurt. This is a very different set of concerns from the concerns about noncontradiction and acting consistently with her beliefs, which characterized Anne's justice reasoning. With the shift in perspective, the word autonomy takes on different connotations: To be self-regulating or self-governing can mean being centered in oneself but it also can mean not attending or responding to others. The tension between these two ways of seeing and listening creates a conflict that, as Anne says, is "not as simple as buying cigarettes or not," a conflict that in addition is not well represented by the common depiction of adolescent moral conflicts as peer-pressure problems.

Asked if she had learned anything from the experience, Anne speaks in two voices. She asserts her satisfaction with her ability "to stay with what I believe, and as far as learning something from it, I was able to say no and so I could say it again." But she also asserts her unease about shutting herself off from others, about becoming impervious to the changing circumstances of her life and unresponsive to the people around her.

But I don't know that I will always say no to everything. You can't all the time, and as you make better friends and as you are under different circumstances and different situations, I think my answers will change—as I become more like the people in this school. Because no matter where you are, you tend to become at least a little like the people around you.

Anne does not doubt the wisdom or the rightness of her decision to say no in this instance, but the incident raises a further question: How can she stay with herself and also be with other people? Viewing life as lived in the changing medium of time and seeing herself as open to the people around her, she believes that in time both she and her answers will change. The dilemma or tension she faces is not that of peer pressure—how to say no to her friends or classmates. Instead, it stems from a different way of thinking about herself in relation to others, a way that leads into the question of what relationship, or in this instance friendship, means.

The ability to sustain two perspectives that offer divergent views of a scene or to tell a story from two different angles can be taken as a marker of cognitive and moral growth in the adolescent years—a sign perhaps in the context of ordinary living of what Keats called "negative capability," the ability of the artist to enter into and to take on ways of seeing and speaking that differ from one's own. For example, with respect to the question of separation or individuation as it pertains to adolescents' perceptions of their relationships with their parents, one teenager says, "I am not only my mother's daughter, I am also Susan." Another, describing her anger at her holding-on mother, recalls herself as saying to her mother, "You will always be my mother. . . . I will always be your daughter, but you have to let go." These not only/but also constructions used by teenage girls in describing themselves in relation to their mothers convey a view of change as occurring in the context of continuing attachment and imply a vision of development that does not entail detachment or carry the implication that relationships can be replaced. From this standpoint, the moral problems engendered by the transformations of relationships in adolescence pertain not only to injustice and oppression but also to abandonment and disloyalty. Thus seen, development in adolescence takes on new dimensions. The much discussed problem of moral relativism is joined by the problem of moral reductionism, the temptation to simplify human dilemmas by claiming that there is only one moral standpoint.

A study conducted at a high school for girls clarified the ways in which moral conflicts in adolescence catch the transformation of relationships along the two dimensions of equality and attachment, highlighting problems of unfairness but also problems of disconnection. As the balance of power between child and adult shifts with the child's coming of age, so too the experience and the meaning of connection change. What constitutes attachment in early childhood does not constitute connection in adolescence, given the sexual changes of puberty and also the growth of subjective and reflective thought. Thus the question arises: What are the analogues in adolescence to the responsive engagement that psychologists now find so striking in infancy and early childhood? What constitutes genuine connection in the adolescent years?

I raise this question to explicate a point of view that at first glance may seem inconsequential or even antithetical to concerns about adolescent development and health. One can readily applaud Anne's decision not to buy cigarettes for another (argued in terms of justice) and see her ability to say no as one that will stand her in good stead. My intention is not to qualify this judgment or to diminish the importance of this ability but to stress the importance of another as well. Like concerns about submitting or yielding to pressure from others, concerns about not listening or becoming cut off from others are also vital concerns. The ability to create and sustain human connection may hinge in adolescence on the ability to differentiate true from false relationship—to read the signs that distinguish authentic from inauthentic forms of connection and thus to protect the wish for relationship or the openness to others from overwhelming disappointment or defeat. The capacity for detachment in adolescence, heightened by the growth of formal operational thinking and generally prized as the hallmark of cognitive and moral development, is thus double-edged, signaling an ability to think critically about thinking but also a potential for becoming, in Anne's terms, self-centered. Although detachment connotes the dispassion that signifies fairness in justice reasoning, the ability to stand back from oneself and from others and to weigh conflicting claims evenhandedly in the abstract, detachment also connotes the absence of connection and creates the conditions for carelessness or violation, for violence toward others or oneself.

The adolescent's question "Where am I going?" is rendered problematic because adolescents lack experience in the ways of adult work and love. High school students, including inner-city youth living in poverty, often speak about their plans to work and have a family. Yet even if such goals are clearly envisioned, teenagers have no experience of how to reach them. When you do not know where you are going or how the route goes, the range of interpretation opens up enormously. The adolescent's question "Where is my home?" is commonly raised for college students who wonder, is it here at school, or back in Ohio, or in Larchmont? Where will it be in the future? How do I interpret whatever new moves I make in my life?

These interpretive questions fall on the line of intellectual and ethical development that Perry (1970) traced—a line leading from the belief that truth is objective and known by authorities to the realization that all truth is contextually relative and responsibility for commitment inescapable. Yet Perry, although addressing the existential dilemma, leaves open the issue of detachment that bothered Trilling, posing the teaching quandary Trilling raised: What commitments can one defend as worth making and on what basis can one claim authority? Erikson (1958) wrote about the penchant of adolescents for absolute truths and totalistic solutions, the proclivity to end, once and for all, all uncertainty and confusion by seizing control and attempting to stop time or blot out, or eliminate, in one way or another the source of confusion—in others or in oneself. Many destructive actions on the part of adolescents can be understood in these terms. Because adolescents are capable not only of abstract logical thinking but also of participating in the act of knowing; because they are in some sense aware of subjectivity and perspective, or point of view; because they are therefore able to see through false claims to authority at the same time as they yearn for right answers or for someone who will tell them how they should live and what they should do; the temptation for adults dealing with adolescents is to opt for the alternatives of permissiveness or authoritarianism and to evade the problems that lie in taking what Baumrind (1978) has called an authoritative stance.

Resisting Detachment

One problem in taking an authoritative stance with adolescents is that many of the adults involved with adolescents have little authority in this society. Therefore, although they may in fact know much about teenagers' lives, they may have little confidence in their knowledge. Rather than claiming authority, they may detach their actions from their judgment and attribute their decisions to the judgments of those who are in positions of greater social power. But another problem lies in the perennial quandary about adolescents: what actions to take in attempting to guide teenagers away from paths clearly marked as destructive and how to read the signs that point in the direction of health. To reconsider the nature of development in adolescence itself raises a question of perspective: From what angle or in what terms shall this reconsideration take place?

Recent studies of adolescents in families and schools have been discovering the obvious, although the need for such diversity also seems obvious since the implications are repeatedly ignored. The studies find that adolescents fare better in situations where adults listen and that mothers and teachers are centrally important in teenagers' lives. Mothers are the parent with whom adolescents typically have the most contact, the one they talk with the most and perceive as knowing most about their lives (Youniss & Smollar, 1985). Most researchers consider it desirable for fathers to be more involved with adolescents, but they find, in general, that fathers do not spend as much time or talk as personally with their teenage children. In studies of schools, teachers are cited as central to the success of secondary education. The good high schools identified by Rutter and others (1979) and by Lightfoot (1983) are characterized by the presence of teachers who are able, within the framework of a coherent set of values or school ethos, to assume authority and to take responsibility for what they do. Yet mothers of adolescents are increasingly single parents living in poverty, and teachers at present are generally unsupported and devalued. Psychological development in adolescence may well hinge on the adolescent's belief that her or his psyche is worth developing, and this belief in turn may hinge on the presence in a teenager's life of an adult who knows and cares about the teenager's psyche. Economic and psychological support for the mothers and the teachers who at present are the primary adults engaged with teenagers may be essential to the success of efforts to promote adolescent development.

The question of what stance or aim or direction to take is focused by the research on moral orientation, which points to two lines of development and to their possible tension. If a focus on care currently provides a critical interpretive standpoint and highlights problems in schools and society that need to be addressed, how can this perspective be developed or even sustained? The evidence that among educationally advantaged North Americans care focus is demonstrated primarily by girls and women raises questions about the relationship between female development and secondary education. But it also suggests that girls may constitute a resistance to the prevailing ethos of detachment and disconnection, a resistance that has moral and political as well as psychological implications. Thus the question arises as to how this resistance can be educated and sustained.

In tracing the development of women's thinking about what constitutes care and what connection means, I noted that a critical junction for women had to do with their inclusion of themselves (Gilligan, 1982). This inclusion is genuinely problematic, not only psychologically for women but also for society in general and for the secondary school curriculum. As self-inclusion on the part of women challenges the conventional understanding of feminine goodness by severing the link between care and self-sacrifice, so too the inclusion of women challenges the interpretive categories of the Western tradition, calling into question the description of human nature and holding up for scrutiny the meanings commonly given to relationship, love, morality, and self.

Perhaps for this reason, high school girls describing care focus dilemmas will say that their conflicts are not moral problems but just have to do with their lives and everything they believe in—as Anne said when she intimated that in fact she had another way of seeing the dilemma that she had posed in justice terms. From a care standpoint, her otherwise praiseworthy ability to say no to others seemed potentially problematic: What had seemed a valuable ability to stay centered in herself, to hold with what she believed, now seemed in part self-centered, a way of cutting herself off from the people around her. Thus development for girls in adolescence poses a conundrum, and at the center of this puzzle are questions about connection: How does one stay in touch with the world and others and with oneself? What are the possibilities for and the nature of genuine connection with others? What are the signs that distinguish true from false relationship? What leads girls to persist in seeking responsive engagement with others? What risks are attendant on this quest? And finally, what are the moral, political, and psychological implications of resisting detachment? If one aim is to educate this resistance, secondary education may play a crucial role in this process.

Bardige (1983, 1985), analyzing the journals kept by seventh- and eighth-graders as part of the social studies curriculum, *Facing History and Ourselves: Holocaust and Human Behavior* by Strom and Parsons (1982), found evidence of moral sensibilities that seemed to be at risk in early adolescence. Specifically, she observed that the journal entries written by 8 of the 24 girls and 1 of the 19 boys in the two classes studied showed the children's willingness to take evidence of violence at face value, and to respond directly to the perception that someone was being hurt. Because this responsiveness to evidence of violence was associated with less sophisticated forms of reasoning and because detachment and dispassion were linked with the ability to see both sides of a story and to reflect on the multiple lenses through which one can view or present a set of events, the tension between responsiveness and detachment poses an educational dilemma: How can one develop moral sensibilities anchored in commonsense perception while at the same time developing the capacity for logical thinking and reflective judgment? The present skewing of the secondary school curriculum, both in the humanities and the sciences, toward reasoning from premises and deductive logic, with emphasis placed on critical thinking, defined as the ability to think about thinking in the abstract, leaves uneducated or undeveloped the moral sensibilities that rely on a finely tuned perception— the ability to take one's responses to what is taken in by seeing and listening as evidence on which to recognize false premises, as grounds for knowing what is happening and for thinking about what to do.

Given the heightened self-consciousness of teenagers and their intense fear of ridicule or exposure, secondary education poses a major challenge to teachers: how to sustain among teenagers an openness to experience and a willingness to risk discovery. The responsiveness of the relationship between teacher and student, the extent to which such connections involve a true engagement or meeting of minds, may be crucial in this regard. Yet when reliance on human resources is construed as a sign of limitation and associated with childhood dependence, the ways in which people can and do help one another tend not to be accurately represented. As a result, activities of care may be tacit or covertly undertaken or associated with idealized images of virtue and self-sacrifice. This poses a problem for teachers, parents, and adolescents, one which, for a variety of reasons, may fall particularly heavily on girls.

Psychologists recently have sought to understand the terms in which girls and women speak about their experience and have drawn attention to terms of relationship that suggest both a desire for responsive engagement with others and an understanding of what such connection entails (see Belenky et al., 1986; Josselson, 1987; Miller, 1984, 1986; Surrey, 1984). In addition, Steiner-Adair (1986), studying the vulnerability of high-school-age girls to eating disorders, found that girls who articulate a critical care perspective in response to interview questions about their own future expectations and societal values for women are invulnerable to eating disorders, as measured by the Eating Attitudes Test. The critical care perspective provided a standpoint from which to reject the assumptions embodied in the media image of the superwoman—assumptions that link separation and independence with success both in work and in love. Steiner-Adair found that in the educationally advantaged North American population where eating disorders currently are prevalent, girls who implicitly or explicitly take on or endorse the superwoman image, who do not identify a conflict between responsiveness in relationships and conventional images of femininity or of success, are those who appear vulnerable to eating disorders. Thus girls who show signs of vulnerability to eating disorders seem to be caught within a damaging framework of interpretation; when discussing their own future wishes and societal values, they do not differentiate signs of responsiveness and connection from images of perfection and control.

Along similar lines, Attanucci (1984) and Willard (1985), studying educationally advantaged North American mothers of young children, noted a disparity between mothers' own terms in speaking about their experiences as mothers and the terms used to characterize mothers and mothering in contemporary cultural scripts. Mothers' own terms included terms of relationships that convey mothers' experience of connection with their children, so that caring for children is neither selfish nor selfless in these terms. In contrast, the terms used by psychologists to describe good or good enough mothers convey the impression that women, insofar as they are good mothers, respond to their children's needs rather than to their own, whereas women, insofar as they are psychologically mature and healthy persons, meet their own needs and separate themselves from their children. Willard found that mothers who draw on their own experience of connection with their children in making decisions about work and family (whatever the specific nature of these decisions) do not suffer from symptoms of depression. In contrast, women who cast employment decisions in terms derived from cultural scripts, whether for good mothers or for superwomen, show signs of depression, suggesting that cultural scripts for mothers at present are detrimental to women. What differentiates these scripts for mothering from mothers' own terms is the division made between the woman herself and her child, so that mothers in essence are portrayed as caught between themselves and their child. The ability of adolescent girls and adult women to define connection and care in terms that reflect experiences of authentic relationship or responsive engagement with others and that encourage inclusive solutions to conflicts was associated in these three different studies by Steiner-Adair, Attanucci, and Willard with resistance to psychological illness—with invulnerability to eating disorders and the absence of depressive symptoms.

But the importance of reconsidering what is meant by care and connection as well as what responsiveness in relationship entails is underscored also by recent studies of inner-city youth (see Gilligan et al., 1985; Ward, 1986). The ability of teenagers living in the inner city to reason about care was often far more advanced than the level of their justice reasoning. In addition, they often spoke clearly about the necessity for care and the reliance of people on human resources. For example, a fifteen-year-old, when asked to describe a moral conflict he had faced, spoke of a time when he wanted to go out with his friends after a dance but his mother wanted him home. He decided to go home, he said, to avoid "getting into trouble with my mother." However, when asked if he thought he had done the right thing, he spoke about the fact that he knew, from watching what had happened when his older sister stayed out late, that his mother would not sleep until he came home. His reason for going home was not simply grounded in a desire to avoid punishment (Stage I reasoning in Kohlberg's terms) but also in a wish not to hurt his mother and not to "just think about myself."

> My mother would have been worried about me all night if I stayed out. . . . [When] my sister used to do it to her, she didn't get any sleep all night. . . . I would be pretty bad if I kept her up like that, you know, just thinking about myself and not thinking about her. . . . Why should I just go off and not worry about her and just think about myself?

Hearing this teenager's concerns about avoiding punishment and getting into trouble, the psychologist schooled in the conventions of developmental psychology might well suspend further questioning, assuming a match with a codable low-level classification, a match rendered plausible because of this teenager's low socioeconomic status. Yet when the researcher, perhaps rejecting a Stage I depiction of a fifteen-year-old as implausible, chooses another line of questioning and pursues the boy's recognition that his actions can hurt his mother, the boy's moral strengths appear. He expresses concern about hurting his mother, and his awareness of how he can do so reveals a care perspective. Furthermore, his knowledge of what actions will cause hurt is based on his observations. Thus he does not need to put himself in his mother's place (which would earn him a higher score on stages of social, moral, and ego development) because he knows from experience with his mother how she will feel.

The change in assessment that follows from listening for two voices in the moral conflicts related by inner-city teenagers is further illustrated by a twelve-year-old girl who, asked for an example of moral conflict and choice, described a decision she made to override her mother's rules (Gilligan et al., 1985). Having laid out the moral world in terms of a stark contrast between "good guys" and "bad guys," she also contrasted this familiar moral language with the language of necessity. "Good guys," she explained, sustaining both languages, "know what's wrong and what's right and when to do right, and they know when it's necessary to do wrong." Her example of moral conflict involved precisely this judgment. A neighbor who had cut herself badly called because she needed bandages; the twelve-year-old had been told by her mother that she was not to leave the house. Discussing her decision to leave, she speaks repeatedly of the fact that she had to, referring to the neighbor's need and to her own judgment that it was absolutely necessary to help: "She needed my help so much, I helped her in any way I could. I knew that I was the only one who could help her, so I had to help her."

This example also contains a contrast between a seemingly simplistic moral conception (here a notion of absolute rules that determine right and wrong, irrespective of intention or motivation—a heteronomous morality in Piaget's terms or a low-stage morality in Kohlberg's terms) and a more sophisticated moral understanding, captured by the language of necessity—the need of people for help and the ability of people to help one another. Although the seeming inability of this girl to anticipate her mother's approval of her decision would qualify her for a low level of interpersonal perspective taking in Selman's (1980) terms, her insistence that "I did the right thing" and her belief that her actions would have been right even if her mother had disagreed with her decision suggest a more autonomous moral sense. Her decision in the instance she describes was guided by her judgment that help must be provided when it is needed and where it is possible: "You can't just stand there and watch the woman die" (Gilligan et al., 1985). This disparity, between seemingly low stages of social and moral development, as measured by conventional psychological standards, and evidence of greater moral understanding and sensibilities than the developmental stage descriptions imply, was encountered repeatedly in the study of inner-city teenagers, raising the kinds of questions about the moral life of children that have been articulated so pointedly by Coles (1986).

The collective implication of these studies is that interpretive problems cannot be separated from the consideration of adolescent development and that these problems raise questions not only about adolescents but also about the society and culture in which these teenagers are coming of age. The observation often made by teachers that girls, in general, become less outspoken following puberty, less likely to disagree in public or even to participate in classroom discussions, together with the observation that school achievement tends to drop off in adolescence for the children of ethnic minorities suggest that secondary education, or the interpretive frameworks of the culture, may be more readily accessible and comprehensible to those students whose experience and background are most similar to that of those who shape the frameworks. If, at present, a care perspective offers a critical lens on a society that seems increasingly justice focused, it is also one that clarifies and makes sense of the activities of care that teenagers describe—not only helping others but also creating connections with others, activities they link with times when they feel good about themselves.

Gender differences along the same lines as those found among educationally advantaged teenagers were also observed among inner-city teenagers. Nine of 11 boys who described moral dilemmas involving friends focused their attention on the question of resisting peer pressure, while 6 of the 10 girls whose dilemmas involved friends focused on questions of loyalty in relationship, citing as moral problems instances of abandonment, disconnection, and exclusion. In addition, girls in the inner city were more likely than boys to describe dilemmas that continued over time, rather than dilemmas portrayed as one-time occurrences or repeated instances of the same problem. Perhaps as a result, girls were more likely to seek inclusive solutions to the problems they described, solutions that contributed to sustaining and strengthening connections in that they were responsive to the needs of everyone involved. While girls were apt to talk about staying with a problem in relationships and with the people involved, boys were more likely to talk about leaving. The one boy in the study who described a continuing dilemma to which he sought an inclusive solution spoke about his problems in maintaining a relationship with both of his divorced parents. Thus the tendency to voice concerns about connection and to seek and value care and responsiveness in relationships was associated in these studies both with social class and with gender (see also Stack, 1974, and Ladner, 1972), like the findings reported by Johnston (1985) and Langdale (1983) that moral orientation, or the standpoint taken in solving moral problems, is associated both with gender and with the problem being considered.

The language of necessity that distinguishes the moral discourse of inner-city youths offers a compelling rendition of a care perspective in an environment characterized by high levels of violence. Ward's (1986) study of the ways in which adolescents living in the inner city think about the violence they witness in the course of their daily lives reveals the strengths of a focus on issues of care and connection—the association with nonviolent responses to violence and with holding off from violent response (often cast in the logic of retributive justice). Ward's study also reveals the importance accorded by teenagers to mothers who label violence in the family as violence (rather than speaking about love or not talking about what is happening) and who take action to stop it. The clear sex differences with respect to violent action and the effects of these differences on male and female adolescents are curiously overlooked in current discussions about sex differences in moral development. Yet such differences pose major questions for theory and research.

Reconsidering adolescence from the two standpoints of justice and care and thinking about what constitutes development in both terms also spur a reappraisal of traditional research methods, specifically a rethinking of the detachment that has been embedded in research practice. When interviewing pregnant teenagers who were considering abortion, I was struck by the fact that most of them knew about birth control. Their pregnancies seemed in part to have resulted from actions that comprised sometimes desperate, misguided, innocent strategies to care for themselves or others, to get what they wanted, or to avoid being alone. Engaging with these teenagers in the context of inquiring about their moral conflicts and interpretive quandaries raised a question about the effects of research as an intervention with both clinical and educational implications. What lessons are taught about connection and detachment, about care and justice, through the practice of asking teenagers, in the context of a research interview, about their experiences of moral conflict?

It may be that asking teenagers to talk about their own experiences of moral conflict and choice in itself constitutes an effective intervention, as some preliminary evidence suggests. Such questioning may reveal to teenagers that they have a moral perspective, something of value at stake, and thus that they have grounds for action in situations where they may have felt stuck or confused or unable to choose between alternative paths. The efficacy of the intervention may depend on the responsiveness of the research relationship, on whether the researcher engages with the teenager's thinking rather than simply mirroring or assessing it. For the adolescent, the realization that he, and perhaps especially she, has a moral perspective that an adult finds interesting, or a moral voice that someone will respond to, shifts the framework for action away from a choice between submission and rebellion (action defined in others' terms) and provides a context for discovering what are one's own terms. In adolescence, this discovery galvanizes energy and stimulates initiative and leadership.

But the same is true for teachers as well. The interpretive and ethical questions raised by considering adolescent development form a basis for genuine collaboration between psychologists and secondary school teachers. Such collaboration joins a naturalistic approach to research with what is perhaps the oldest strategy of education: not to teach answers but to raise questions that initiate the search for knowledge and, in the spirit of discovery, to listen for what is surprising. If the "modern" element in modern literature is the theme of disenchantment with the idea of culture or civilization, the challenge to those of us who would speak about development in adolescence, psychological health, or education is to take seriously the questions about truth and values that are raised by adolescents coming of age in modern culture and then, in responding to these questions, to imagine that this generation may hear different voices and may see from a new angle.

Acknowledgments

The author is very grateful for the help of Mrs. Hoffman, Scott McVay, Valerie Peed, Phoebe Gottingham, Joseph Klingenstein, Susan Wisely, the principals and teachers who joined in this collaboration, and the leaders of the Boys' and Girls' Clubs of Boston. Special thanks is extended to Bernard Kaplan, Jane Lilienfeld, Jim Gilligan, and Diana Baumrind for their criticisms and responses to the research. Thanks is also due to Mary Hartman, dean of Douglass College, and Ferris Olin, as well as the members of the Laurie Chair seminars for a stimulating and responsive environment in which to work. For the invitations that stimulated both the writing and rewriting of this chapter, the author is grateful to Robert Blum.

References

Adelson, J., & Doehrman, M. (1980). The psychodynamic approach to adolescence. In J. Adelson (Ed.), *The handbook of adolescent psychology* (pp. 99–116). New York: Wiley.

Arendt, H. (1958). *The origins of totalitarianism.* New York: Harcourt Brace Jovanovich.

Attanucci, J. (1984). *Mothers in their own terms: A developmental perspective on self and role.* Unpublished doctoral dissertation, Harvard Graduate School of Education, Cambridge, MA.

Bardige, B. (1983). *Reflecting thinking and prosocial awareness: Adolescents face the holocaust and themselves.* Unpublished doctoral dissertation, Harvard Graduate School of Education, Cambridge, MA.

Bardige, B. (1985). *Things so finely human: Moral sensibilities at risk in adolescence.* Unpublished manuscript, Harvard Graduate School of Education, Center for the Study of Gender, Education, and Human Development, Cambridge, MA.

Baumrind, D. (1978). Parental disciplinary patterns and social competence in children. *Youth and Society, 9,* 239–276.

Belenky, M., Clinchy, B., Goldberger, N., & Tarule, J. (1986). *Women's ways of knowing.* New York: Basic Books.

Bettelheim, B. (1962). The problem of generations. *Daedalus, 91,* 68–96.

Blos, P. (1967). The second individuation process of adolescence. *The Psychoanalytic Study of the Child, 22,* 162–186.

Bowlby, J. (1973, 1980). *Attachment and loss* (Vols. 2 & 3). New York: Basic Books.

Brown, L., Argyris, D., Attanucci, J., Bardige, B., Gilligan, C., Johnston, K., Miller, B., Osborne, R., Ward, J., & Wilcox, D. (1987). *A guide to reading narratives of moral conflict and choice for self and moral voice.* Unpublished manuscript, Harvard Graduate School of Education, Center for the Study of Gender, Education, and Human Development, Cambridge, MA.

Chodorow, N. (1978). *The reproduction of mothering.* Berkeley, CA: University of California Press.

Coles, R. (1986). *The moral life of children.* Boston: Atlantic Monthly Press.

Emde, R. N., Johnson, W. E., & Easterbrooks, M. A. (1987). The do's and dont's of early moral development. In J. Kagan & S. Lamb (Eds.), *The emergence of morality in young children* (pp. 245–276). Chicago: University of Chicago Press.

Erikson, E. (1958). *Young man Luther.* New York: Norton.

Erikson, E. (1975). Reflections on the dissent of humanist youth. In E. Erikson (Ed.), *Life history and the historical moment* (pp. 193–224). New York: Norton.

Freud, S. (1961). Some psychical consequences of the anatomical differences between the sexes. In J. Strachey (Ed. and Trans.), *The standard edition of the complete psychological works of Sigmund Freud* (Vol. XIX). London: Hogarth Press. (Original work published 1923.)

Gilligan, C. (1977). In a different voice: Women's conceptions of self and of morality. *Harvard Educational Review, 47,*481–517.

Gilligan, C. (1982). *In a different voice: Psychological theory and women's development.* Cambridge, MA: Harvard University Press.

Gilligan, C. (1986a). Exit-voice dilemmas in adolescence. In A. Foxley, M. McPherson, & G. O'Donnell (Eds.), *Development, democracy, and the art of trespassing: Essays in honor of Albert O. Hirschman* (pp. 283–300). Notre Dame, IN: University of Notre Dame Press.

Gilligan, C. (1986b). Remapping the moral domain: New images of the self in relationship. In T. C. Heller, M. Sosna, & D. E. Wellbery (Eds.), *Reconstructing individualism.* Stanford, CA: Stanford University Press.

Gilligan, D., & Attanucci, J. (1985). *Two moral orientations: Implications for developmental theory and assessment.* Unpublished manuscript, Harvard Graduate School of Education, Center for the Study of Gender, Education, and Human Development, Cambridge, MA.

Gilligan, C., Bardige, B., Ward, J., Taylor, J., & Cohen, G. (1985). *Moral and identity development in urban youth.* Report to the Rockefeller Foundation.

Gottman, J. M. (1983). How children become friends. *Monographs of the Society for Research in Child Development, 48*(3), 1–86.

Hoffman, M. (1976). Empathy, role-taking, guilt, and the development of altruistic motives. In T. Lickona (Ed.), *Moral development and behavior* (pp. 124–143). New York: Holt, Rinehart & Winston.

Inhelder, B., & Piaget, J. (1958). *The growth of logical thinking from childhood to adolescence.* New York: Basic Books.

Johnston, D. K. (1985). *Two moral orientations; two problem-solving strategies: Adolescents' solutions to dilemmas in fables.* Unpublished doctoral dissertation, Harvard Graduate School of Education, Cambridge, MA.

Josselson, R. (1987). *Finding herself: Pathways to identity development in women.* San Francisco: Jossey-Bass.

Kagan, J. (1971). A conception of early adolescence. *Daedalus, 100,* 997–1012.

Kagan, J. (1984). *The nature of the child.* New York: Basic Books.

Kohlberg, L. (1969). Stage and sequence. In D. Goslin (Ed.), *Handbook of socialization theory and research* (pp. 347–480). Chicago: Rand McNally.

Kohlberg, L., & Gilligan, C. (1971). The adolescent as a philosopher. *Daedalus, 100,* 1051–1086.

Konopka, G. (1966). *The adolescent girl in conflict.* Englewood Cliffs, NJ: Prentice Hall.

Ladner, S. (1972). *Tomorrow's tomorrow.* New York: Anchor Books.

Langdale, S. (1983). *Moral orientation and moral development: The analysis of care and justice reasoning across different dilemmas in females and males from childhood through adulthood.* Unpublished doctoral dissertation, Harvard Graduate School of Education, Cambridge, MA.

Lightfoot, S. L. (1983). *The good high school.* New York: Basic Books.

Lyons, N. P. (1983). Two perspectives: On self, relationships, and morality. *Harvard Educational Review, 53,* 125–146.

Miller, J. B. (1976). *Toward a new psychology of women.* Boston: Beacon Press.

Miller, J. B. (1984). The development of women's sense of self. *Work in Progress, 12.*

Miller, J. B. (1986). What do we mean by relationships? *Work in Progress, 22.*

Perry, W. (1970). *Forms of intellectual and ethical development in the college years.* New York: Holt, Rinehart & Winston.

Piaget, J. (1965). *The moral judgement of the child.* New York: Free Press. (Original work published 1932.)

Pipp, S., Shaver, P., Jennings, S., Lamborn, S., & Fischer, K. (1985). Adolescents' theories about the development of relationships with parents. *Journal of Personality and Social Psychology, 48,* 991–1001.

Polanyi, M. (1958). *Personal knowledge.* Chicago: University of Chicago Press.

Ravitch, D. (1985, November 17). Decline and fall of teaching history. *New York Times Sunday Magazine,* p. 50.

Rutter, M., Maughan, B., Mortimore, P., Ouston, J., & Smith, A. (1979). *Fifteen thousand hours.* Cambridge, MA: Harvard University Press.

Selman, R. (1980). *The growth of interpersonal understanding.* New York: Academic Press.

Stack, C. (1974). *All our kin.* New York: Harper & Row.

Steiner-Adair, C. (1986). The body politic: Normal female adolescent development and the development of eating disorders. *Journal of the American Academy of Psychoanalysis, IV,* 95–114.

Stern, D. (1985). *The interpersonal world of the infant.* New York: Basic Books.

Strom, M., & Parsons, W. (1982). *Facing history and ourselves: Holocaust and human behavior.* Watertown, MA: International Education.

Surrey, J. (1984). The self-in-relation. *Work in Progress, 13.*

Trilling, L. (1967). On the modern element in modern literature. In I. Howe (Ed.), *The idea of the modern in literature and the arts* (pp. 59–82). New York: Horizon Press.

Vygotsky, L. (1978). *Mind in society.* Cambridge, MA: Harvard University Press.

Ward, J. (1986). *A study of urban adolescents' thinking about violence following a course on the holocaust.* Unpublished doctoral dissertation, Harvard Graduate School of Education, Cambridge, MA.

Willard, A. K. (1985). *Self, situation, and script: A psychological study of decisions about employment in mothers of one-year-olds.* Unpublished doctoral dissertation, Harvard

Graduate School of Education, Cambridge, MA.
Youniss, J., & Smollar, J. (1985). *Adolescents' relations with mothers, fathers, and friends.* Chicago: University of Chicago Press.

Bibliography

Adelson, J. (Ed.). (1980). *The handbook of adolescent psychology.* New York: Wiley.

Brown, L. (1986). *When is a moral problem not a moral problem?* Unpublished manuscript, Harvard Graduate School of Education, Cambridge, MA.

Gilligan, C. (1984). The conquistador and the dark continent: Reflections on the psychology of love. *Daedalus, 113,* 75–95.

Gilligan, C. (1986). Reply. *Signs, 11,* 324–333.

Gilligan, C., & Wiggins, G. (1987). The origins of morality in early childhood relationships. In J. Kagan & S. Lamb (Eds.), *The emergence of morality in young children* (pp. 277–305). Chicago: University of Chicago Press.

Kohlberg, L. (1968). *Education for justice: A modern statement of the platonic view.* Cambridge, MA: Harvard University Press.

Konopka, G. (1976). *Young girls: A portrait of adolescents.* Englewood Cliffs, NJ: Prentice-Hall.

Osborne, R. (1987). *Good-me, bad-me, true-me, false-me: A dynamic multidimensional study of adolescent self-concept.* Unpublished doctoral dissertation, Harvard Graduate School of Education, Cambridge, MA.

Wiggins, G. (1986). *Thoughtfulness as an educational aim.* Unpublished doctoral dissertation, Harvard Graduate School of Education, Cambridge, MA.

CHAPTER 7

Luck, Ethics, and Ways of Knowing: Observations on Adolescents' Deliberations in Making Moral Choices

Nona P. Lyons

Brown University

Having learned that she is to be sent to Lowood, a charity school for girls, in part because she is a "deceitful child," Charlotte Bronte's Jane Eyre confronts her Aunt Reed with a harsh truth (Bronte, 1846/1960). Faced with her aunt's failure to acknowledge Jane's suffering at the hands of Reed's son, John, or the punishment of being locked in the isolated Red Room, inflicted by her aunt, Jane decides: "Speak, I must . . . against what is 'unjust.'" Then, addressing her guardian and the charge that she is deceitful, 10-year-old Jane declares:

> I am not deceitful: if I were, I should say I loved *you*. But I declare I do not love
> you: I dislike you the worst of anybody in the world except John Reed. . . .
>   I am glad you are no relation of mine: I will never call you aunt again as
> long as I live . . . if anyone asks me how I liked you and how you treated
> me, I will say the very thought of you makes me sick, and that you treated me
> with miserable cruelty. (p. 36)

When Mrs. Reed demands, "How dare you affirm that, Jane Eyre?" Jane continues:

> How dare I, Mrs. Reed? How dare I? because it is the truth. You think I have
> no feelings, and that I can do without one bit of love or kindness; but I cannot
> live so: and you have no pity. . . . I will tell anybody who asks me questions,
> this exact tale. People think you are a good woman, but you are bad; hard-
> hearted. You are deceitful. (p. 37)

Mrs. Reed, visibly frightened by Jane's eruption, leaves to hasten her departure for Lowood. Alone, "winner of the field," Jane contemplates her "victory." At first elated with a sense of freedom and triumph, Jane suddenly finds her pleasure ebbing as she sees the dreariness of "her hated and hating position: A child cannot quarrel with its elders, as I had done, cannot give its furious feelings uncontrolled play, as I had given mine, without experiencing afterwards the pang of remorse and the chill of reaction" (p. 37). But elaborating a new insight, Jane goes on:

> Willingly would I now have gone and asked Mrs. Reed's pardon; but I knew, partly from experience and partly from instinct, that was the way to make her repulse me with double scorn, thereby exciting every turbulent impulse of my nature. I would fain exercise some better faculty than that of fierce speaking. (p. 38)

Thus Jane prepares to leave forever the house of her Aunt Reed.

Through a moment of choice, Jane Eyre defines an emerging reality. Seeing that she had to speak, to act ethically, to right a wrong, Jane acts, but comes to know something else: To acknowledge what is—to engage in "fierce speaking"—may come at a cost, to entrust oneself to a relationship of love may involve great risks, and to expect control in one's life may be false. Life is contingent on other people or events—what some call luck. Jane Eyre's experience illuminates not just the existential reality of an unexpected and inescapable life happening, but also its delicate interconnection in acknowledging oneself and what one cares about, acting morally, and being in relation to others. This way of knowing and understanding—one that Jane will experience on her journey to adulthood—points to a set of ideas that are central to today's adolescents as well: ideas about self and relationships, about ways of seeing and resolving ethical conflict, and about how one comes to know and consider life's chance events in making moral choices.

This chapter is a preliminary examination of the issue of chance in adolescents' ethical decision making. Following the work of philosopher Martha Nussbaum (1986, 1990), a chance event is defined here as one of the happenings that are part of an individual's life experiences and circumstances over which he or she may not have control. Hence, one can be subject to chance or change through occurrences that were unforeseen or unforeseeable. These events can, as Nussbaum suggests, be a powerful component of one's ethical development.

My interest in these ideas first emerged from observations made in a study of students at the Emma Willard School, a private school for girls in Troy, New York (Gilligan, Lyons, & Hanmer, 1990). In open-ended interviews, girls participating in the study were asked to describe themselves, their relationships with others, and ethical conflicts they had experienced. Initiated in 1981 by the Emma Willard School, the study was undertaken as a collaboration between the school and a group of Harvard researchers under the direction of Carol Gilligan and myself. This project, which followed girls over their four years of high school, had two purposes: to help Emma Willard teachers and administrators to better understand girls' ways of knowing, learning, and making choices, including ethical choices; and to begin mapping the largely neglected domain of adolescent girls' development (Gilligan, Lyons, & Hanmer, 1990; Gilligan, 1990). Under particular scrutiny was how girls might make use of two moral orientations in their ethical decision making: an orientation toward concerns of justice, rights, and fairness (the traditionally identified ethic of justice [Kohlberg, 1969]) or an orientation toward concerns of responsiveness to the needs of oneself and others (an ethic of care [Gilligan, 1977, 1982; Lyons, 1982, 1983]). The results of this work were presented in the book *Making Connections: The Relational World of Adolescent Girls at Emma Willard School* (Gilligan, Lyons, & Hanmer, 1990).

But in a subsequent reexamination of these data, a new dimension emerged: Girls' descriptions of their ethical deliberations revealed their awakening responses to life's realities—like Jane Eyre's—and showed how sometimes seemingly simple chance events entered into their thinking, their moral decision making, and their relationships to others. In this chapter, I return to interviews from the Emma Willard study—ones I previously examined for girls' ideas about morality, moral orientation, and self (Lyons, 1990)—but now I explore the role of chance in adolescents' thinking about ethical conflicts and consider how chance or luck may influence their development.

The potential connection of chance to ethical decision making or development has not been seriously examined in adolescent theory building. Indeed, the concept of chance, with its insistence on the particular and the concrete, the real rather than the ideal, counters traditional views of adolescence, which posit adolescence as a time of preoccupation with idealism and ideology (Erikson, 1968), with the achievement of abstract thinking (Piaget, 1968; Piaget & Inhelder, 1958), and with the emergence of transcendent ethical values (Kohlberg, 1969, 1984; Marcia, 1980). In its suggestion that one important but little explored strand of adolescent development may be coming to see, acknowledge, and deal with life's inescapable realities, this chapter does, however, resonate with earlier, sometimes puzzling research and with more recent findings.

For example, in 1971, Joseph Adelson reported a finding he describes as unexpected. In a study of the emergence of political thought in adolescence, he not only found little evidence of political idealism in the adolescents he studied, but he also noted an anti-utopian streak held with "fierce strength." Adelson observed that although idealism is present, "it is by no means modal, let alone universal, and is less common than skepticism, sobriety, and caution as a characteristic political affect" (p. 1027). Twenty years later, Michelle Fine (1991) offers a related finding in a study of New York City high school dropouts. Her research shows that compared with their classmates who stayed in school—teenagers more likely to be depressed, conformist, and self-critical—dropouts were more realistic, significantly less depressed, and more likely to see their problems as related to the poverty and racism of their lives as well as to their own characters. This observation, Fine argues, indicates that dropping out could be recast as a strategy for taking control of one's life. Recently, Carol Gilligan has been exploring the shift into adolescence of girls aged 11 to 13. At this time, Gilligan argues, some girls are likely to go "underground," reducing their responses to a characteristic "I don't know," when only shortly before they were confident, "fierce speakers" and accurate readers of the world around them (Gilligan, 1990; Brown, 1989). Gilligan believes that girls' realistic knowledge of the world comes in conflict with what their culture tells them is possible in their lives. Confronting this contradiction, they go underground, disavowing what they in fact know.

These researchers underscore the importance of describing systematically how adolescents see, uncover, and deal with the actualities and sometimes inescapable chance contingencies of their lives as they grow older and closer to adulthood, and how they go on to gain or regain a way to voice them and to live or not live in their acknowledgement.

Contexts

Two lines of research converge to provide a context for this discussion. One strand, the psychological research that examines women's moral decision making, first linked ideas of relationships with ideas of morality and self and called attention to the need for a study that focused on adolescent girls (Gilligan, 1977, 1982; Lyons, 1982, 1983; see also Adelson, 1980; Adelson & Doehrman, 1980; Belenky, Clinchy, Goldberger, & Tarule, 1986; Douvan & Adelson, 1966; Johnston, 1985; May, 1980; Miller, 1976; Piaget, 1965). The second strand concerns recent developments in moral philosophy, especially the writings of philosopher Martha Nussbaum. Nussbaum traces the interconnection of the ideas of luck (chance) and ethics in classical Greek thought and literature; she illuminates an element missing not just in contemporary moral philosophy but in moral psychology as well (Nussbaum, 1986, 1990; Williams, 1981).

This work in philosophy suggests, too, why this topic may not have been addressed in adolescent psychology: This line of thinking about chance, however compelling, has been almost eliminated from Greek thought and our own. Through certain powerful ethical traditions beginning with Plato and including Kant, Nussbaum (1986) argues, "the goodness of a good human life has been made safe from luck" (p. 4) by placing it under the power of reason. "Putting that life . . . under the control of the agent, an element of reliance upon the external and undependable was removed" (p. 4). Kantians, for example, believe that there is only one domain of value, the domain of moral value, and that it is immune from the assaults of luck. This is so, Kant would claim, because a genuine moral obligation, by its very nature, can never conflict with another genuine obligation. By construing conflicting claims into a hierarchical, ranked order, one can always determine which is the first and only duty or obligation or right choice.

However, Nussbaum finds, the Greeks offered no such comfort, and playwrights like Aeschylus, Sophocles, and Euripides, through such characters as Agamemnon or Antigone, tended to consider unalterable human predicaments as part of human experience and of a valued human life. While Nussbaum sees stark examples in these Greek plays—for example, Agamemnon confronting the sacrifice of his daughter—she also finds similar ones in the more mundane though nonetheless significant moments in our daily lives. She gives the example of a young professional woman who, already scheduled to present an important paper at a scholarly conference, discovers that her daughter has just been chosen for a leading part in a school play to be performed on the same day as the conference (Nussbaum, 1989). Nussbaum articulates the ethical dimensions of these events: that in the most vulnerable of human activities, in our relations with others, when we care deeply and simultaneously for more than one thing that cannot be ranked, we face the possibility of human conflict in which there may be no way to avoid harm. Thus, the inescapable and unalterable experiences may be significant and deeply at work in the conflicts we encounter and in our deliberative thinking about them and about how to live a good human life.

But the rational, ranking model of ethical decision making is reflected as well in moral psychology. Indeed, the dominant model in the field, Kohlberg's justice model, is itself hierarchically organized. It offers a way to consider, reason, and rank situations and values in determining how to make moral choices. Similarly, in using an ethic of care, one can assume that it is possible to decide whom one is to care for first.

Nussbaum's work in philosophy, however, alerts us to ask how people, like high school students, might come to know and to act on the unalterable situations they find in their relations to others, considering the givens of their lives—what they can and cannot control, what they care about deeply—and how they come to realize and act on these perceptions.

Drawing on data from interviews with students at the Emma Willard

School, this chapter takes up two contrasting case studies to examine the ethical conflicts that girls (16 to 18 years old) reported during their high school years. Each student presents a different predominant moral orientation in her thinking: One student's moral orientation focuses on care, with a characteristic assumption that relationships are interdependent. The other student's moral orientation focuses on justice, with a characteristic assumption that relationships are reciprocal. (Table 7.1 describes these conceptualizations and the interconnection of ideas of self and relationships to moral orientation.) In a clearly speculative but highly detailed way, these cases trace how life's ordinary chance events are entwined in girls' ethical decision making and may be embedded in their development.

The results of this presentation suggest at least three hypotheses: (1) Regardless of moral orientation, the experiencing of life's inescapable chance events, ones over which one has no control, can precipitate ethical conflict; (2) these situations generate ethical conflict precisely because they involve and reveal the individual's deepest values, values that cannot be ranked; and (3) the discovery of conflict in turn triggers ethical deliberation that expands the ability to see and to be responsive to one's self and to the others involved in their unique particularity. This deliberative activity might be said, as Nussbaum suggests, to engage one's moral imagination.

The implications of this research are also discussed to reveal ideas that have significance for practitioners and for ethical, intellectual, and developmental theorists. Although this study relies on the experiences of girls in one setting and this research needs to be extended systematically to a more inclusive range of adolescent girls and boys, the analysis does suggest that the issues that young Jane Eyre uncovered are part of the life experiences of today's adolescents and are likely to follow them throughout adulthood.

A Case Study: Intersecting Issues of Development— Ideas of Self, Relationships, and Life's Contingencies

Asked to describe herself, Anne, a high school sophomore, hesitated at first because "It's really hard to do this." Then, however, she began to respond. As she did so, she laid out a set of interconnected ideas:

> Describe myself? Um—I guess I'm a pretty outgoing person, likes people. I'm a pretty intelligent person when I put my mind to it. It's really hard to do [this]. . . . Describe myself, like to me? . . . I try to be generous to people. It is very important to me not to be selfish. Have very high standards for myself and for others, and that's not always good, but I have them.

In this response, three themes appear that may not at first seem important, yet they became central to Anne's growth and to her conflicts in subsequent years. The themes are selfishness ("It is very important to me not to be selfish"), generosity ("I try to be generous to people"), and having high standards. As Anne elaborated on the interconnectedness of her values, however, she begins to reveal why generosity and unselfishness would become issues in her relations with others and how the idea of accepting people as they are emerged in her thinking.

When asked by the interviewer why it is not good to have high standards for yourself and others, Anne explained:

> Sometimes people are the way they are and you have to accept them the way they are and you can't say that this person is not good enough for me. . . . Somebody who maybe is an alcoholic or maybe . . . they are on drugs or something like that, I sometimes look at and say that person isn't you know, blah, something like that. But I shouldn't do that *because that is the way they are* and I think that . . . that is one of the bad things about having such high standards. And, I like a lot of people around me.

Anne's concerns about standards arose from her desire to accept people "the way they are." Her tag line, "I like to have a lot of people around me," suggests an unelaborated coupling of these ideas. She went on to talk about how she tried to be generous:

> I like to do things for other people . . . to give somebody something that they don't have or help with work or even if they need money. . . . I like to know, I go down and buy a flower for my mother or something. I like to do things like that.

Thus, for Anne, connection to others was a central value, an orientation toward others that is part of the way she thinks about herself. Its importance lies not only in liking the people around her, but in "the feeling you can give each other." Interdependence is the underlying assumption, as is accepting people the way they are.

When asked whether she was changing, Anne identifies the emerging issues that would later challenge some of her values:

> New things are becoming important to me. It's like trying to become on an adult level . . . presenting my ideas and trying to make myself be as well as I possibly can, on an adult level, trying to get them up to standard. . . .

Table 7.1. Central Moral Issues of Care and Justice

Morality of Care	Morality of Justice
A. In What Becomes a Moral Problem	*A. In What Becomes a Moral Problem*
A morality of care rests on an understanding of relationships that entail response to others in their terms and contexts. What becomes a moral problem has to do with relationships or the activities of care.	A morality of justice as fairness rests on an understanding of relationships as reciprocity between separate individuals. What becomes a moral problem has to do with either mediating issues of conflicting claims in the relationships between people, or with how one is to resolve conflicts or how one can justify one's decisions and actions, considering fairness as a goal between individuals.
Conflicts of relationships are raised as issues surrounding the potential fractures between people; that is, with the breaking—not of trusts or obligations—but of ties between people; or conversely, with restoring or maintaining relationships.	The moral dilemmas of conflicting claims have to do with the conflicts of obligation, duty or commitment stemming from the different role-relationships one may have; that is, between self and others, self and society, or to one's own values and principles. The conflicts with respect to how one is to decide come from the need to have some impartial, and objective, measure of choice that insures fairness in arriving at a decision.
Conflicts surrounding the activities of care have to do with response itself, that is, how to respond or the capacity to respond to another within the particular situation one encounters: how to promote the welfare or well-being of another; or relieve the burdens, hurt, or suffering—physical or psychological—of another. Included in this construction can be particular concerns about care of the self; how to care for the self especially in considering care of others.	
B. In the Resolution of Moral Conflict	*B. In the Resolution of Moral Conflict*
In a morality of care, resolutions to moral conflict are sought:	In a morality of justice resolutions to moral conflicts are sought:
(1) in restoring relationships or the connections between people;	(1) in meeting one's obligations or commitments or performing one's duties;

(2) in carrying through the activities of care, ensuring that good will comes to others or that hurt and suffering will be stopped for others or oneself.

C. In Evaluation of the Resolution

In a morality of care the evaluation of moral choice is made considering:

(1) whether relationships were restored or maintained;

(2) how things worked out or will work out; and in some instances there is only the acknowledgment that there is no way to know or to evaluate resolutions.

Whether relationships are restored can be measured in several ways: simply if everyone is happy, if people talk to one another, or if everyone is comfortable with the solution. If people talk and everyone agrees with the solution, one knows relationships are maintained.

How things work out is a measure of resolution in that in seeking what happens to people over time, one then knows if the resolution worked. This marker also carries the notion that only over time can one know results, that is, know in the sense of seeing what actually happens.

(2) in holding to or not violating one's standards and principles, especially fairness.

C. In Evaluation of the Resolution

In a morality of justice the evaluation of moral choice is made considering:

(1) how the decision was justified and thought about;

(2) whether values, standards, or principles were maintained, especially fairness.

How the decision was justified or thought about is an important measure of how well one lives up to one's obligations (duty or commitments) or of fairness: whether values, standards or principles were maintained is a measure of both the self's ability to live up to one's obligations or principles and the standards used in decision making.

Commenting on this, she elaborates:

A child doesn't really take the world seriously, he doesn't see all the aspects of the world. And as an adult, you do. You see, you grasp what your world is about and . . . you take things seriously and start to bring them into reality, whereas [for] a child, it is kind of like a fairy world. I mean, you have your family . . . whereas as an adult you are brought into contact everyday to the different aspects of the world, be it starvation or poorness or the reality of having to get a job and have responsibility, whereas as a child you don't have any responsibilities really. Other people take care of those for you. . . .

Anne sees: "Now I've gotten to the point where I look outside myself . . . and look for things, even if it doesn't affect me directly. I look to see what's going on and what's happening and try to get some individualism, too. . . ." Thus, development for Anne is tied to one's connections to others and to seeing not just the realities of life around her but also those of a larger world.

Several years later, as a senior, Anne described herself, reflecting on her change over the three years of her high school: "I can look back on myself and. . . think about the decisions which I made or think about the way I felt about myself and that . . . I felt really responsible or really mature, and now it is not a question of, 'Oh, I feel mature,' because I am. It is there, and I know it." Calling herself "hardworking," "personable," "goal oriented," and "pretty well put together," Anne stated, "I enjoy interacting with people, getting to know them, seeing what they think about things." Although these statements of her self-description mark a sense of continuity and growth in her self-perception, it is clear there is a new assurance and confidence in her own strong point of view.

Each year over these three years of high school, Anne also described situations of conflicts that stood out for her, ones that she characterized as moral conflicts. In examining two of these conflicts, it is possible to see how and where chance events entered into them and to speculate on their effect on her developing sense of self.

As a sophomore, Anne described a seemingly everyday adolescent conflict that occurred when a "really good friend" wanted her to go to her house after school, but Anne couldn't reach her mother: "I think she wanted me to stay overnight or something because she had problems, and I couldn't get a hold of my mother, so I didn't know whether to go or not."

In that situation, Anne's concerns were: "My feeling of what I should do. And what my mother would want me to do. I didn't want to get in trouble." She went on: "It hurts, I guess, I mean it always hurts if you get in trouble. . . . I hate to have my mother upset with me for something. . . . It hurts both of us,

I think, you know, I don't think she likes to get mad at me either."

To Anne, trouble was not just an effect, some punishment, but involved hurt, both to her mother and herself. When trying to think about what to do, Anne introduced a second concern:

> Well, . . . it was something like I want to go for my own selfish reasons because I like to visit with my friend and I think she needs me there for her, too. I don't think it is just my own selfish reasons, but I think it would be good for my friend to have me there when she needs somebody to talk to or something, and then the other side is I just don't want to do something without mom's permission, I don't want to get in trouble . . . and that my friend wanted me to come, that also helped affect me and my decision. But the other side was very strong, I mean my mother's feelings on the subject were very strong, if she didn't like it, then I wouldn't do it, of course. . . .

In the end, Anne says, "I decided to go to my friend's, which was fine, because my mother wasn't mad anyway. She didn't mind at all." Anne felt she had made the right decision "because she would have let me do it and I wanted to do it and it was important to my friend that I do it. So, three ways in one direction is fine."

In the situation presented here, Anne grapples with the conflicts inherent in trying to be generous to all the people around her—not wanting to hurt her mother, being there for her friend—and doing what she wanted for her own "selfish reasons." She struggled to make her own decision, to be independent, and to consider what she wanted to do. But she was unable to grant her wishes parity with her concern for her mother; instead, she characterizes her own view as selfish. Although Anne did, in fact, go to her friend's—and thus did what she wanted to do—she did not find a way to deal with or legitimize her own point of view. Thus, she juggled her knowledge of her mother with her understanding of her friend's need. Although this situation presented Anne with a conflict, the situation was clearly one within her control. As she said, she did in fact decide to go to her friend's house. Giving priority to one thing, she acted on that. In contrast, a second conflict Anne reported a year later reveals different characteristics and different dynamics.

Acting When You Care Deeply About More Than One Thing   The second ethical conflict Anne reported occurred unexpectedly when her divorced father decided to get remarried and she had to decide whether to tell her mother: "It was really a hard decision on my part as to whether and when to tell my mother that, because on the one hand, I knew that it was really going to kill her to find that out, and on the other hand, I thought I had an obligation to tell her."

Anne's conflict centered on the fact that although her mother and father were divorced, she knew "my mother still loved my father a great deal" and "there was always hope there."

Asked by the interviewer to say why she termed this situation a moral problem, Anne indicated her own realization of life's contingencies, their interconnection with her values, and the difficulty of choosing between things equally valued. Moral problems usually occur for Anne when "I am struggling against myself to come to a solution to the problem because of values. I can't decide, and *they are both equally as important."* Anne describes the values that were conflicting:

> The fact that I had always been brought up to care a tremendous amount about my parents' feelings and the way they feel. On the one hand, that conflicted with itself because my mother's feelings were going to be really upset and my father's feelings were good, so that conflicted with itself, and, um, my (long pause) trying to figure out, I guess you would have to weigh *the love that I have for my mother, which is in effect my morals,* against if I love my mother enough to tell her something that she won't hear from other places and get upset. But then again, that's against mainly the feeling that I've been brought up with that I hate to see any member of my family hurt and that would conflict against that, so the two.

Thus caught in a dilemma between telling her mother what she knew and risking her mother's hurt or not telling her and risking the pain her mother would inevitably feel when she learned of the remarriage, Anne decided to reveal what she knew. In this calculation, she also considered consequences to herself: If she told, her mother would be really upset, and some of it would "fall back on me because I live with her" and "terrible things like that really bother her, but they hit me hard." But in the end, she also knew that she and her sister, who joined in the telling, could give their mother "our personal support so she could handle it."

In this dilemma, Anne confronted one of life's small but terrible chance contingencies. Having no control in the situation and facing the impossibility of preventing hurt to her mother yet desiring good for her father and understanding that she cared deeply for both of her parents, Anne saw, acknowledged, and dealt with the situation.

Three issues emerge in Anne's story: the value of her attachments to others, the elements of an ethic of care, and the intricate interaction of contingency in ethical choice. For Anne, connection to others had to be maintained as part of her growing independence. But independence comes within attachment to others and transforms both.

Significantly, Anne said that morality is her love for her mother. Thus, as Anne defined them, issues of morality do not solely concern fairness or rights, as traditional formulations of moral development suggest (Kohlberg, 1969, 1984), nor are they created by agreements between people (Haan, 1977; Youniss, 1980). Her concern was to sustain connections with others, not through a utilitarian calculus of "the greatest good for the greatest number of people," but rather through a dialectical process in which she weighed love, her "morals," against the realities of those involved and then considered their contexts as she decided how to act. "[Do] I love my mother enough to tell her something [so] that she won't hear [it] from other places and get upset? Or do I let her get upset at me?" Factored into this calculus of choice is the necessity to take into account when one cares deeply about more than one thing and cannot control the situation.

Although one cannot speak about girls in general without studying them in other situations, this connected mode of experiencing self and defining morality (previously identified within the Emma Willard sample of students as "interdependent in relation to others" [Gilligan, Lyons, & Hanmer, 1990]) reveals certain characteristics of adolescent development. These include a focus on attachment in at least two ways: in maintaining connections with others, either by renegotiating old attachments or forming new ones, and in dealing with issues of caring for the self while maintaining connections with others. Thus, the development of identity and morality takes place within the context of relationships with others (Grotevant & Cooper, 1983; Hartup & Rubin, 1986; Hinde, 1979).

But intricately interwoven in this outline of development can be the experience of contingency. Although further information is needed to understand more adequately how chance affects development, it does appear that an increased awareness of these experiences and the deliberations they trigger as one factors them into decision making may promote more complex social understanding. It may be that the shock and undeniability of such experiences generate ethical conflict and in turn facilitate ethical deliberation of the kind Anne revealed. Whereas not all conflicts Anne chose to discuss in her three years of high school contained such chance events, the situation of her father's marriage came unexpectedly, could not have been predicted, and did engage her in a broad consideration of the life circumstances of her mother, her father, and herself. Before elaborating on these speculations, it is useful to examine another characteristically different mode of ethical response found in the answers of Emma Willard students. Here, again, the interconnections of ideas of self, relationships, and chance are examined.

A Case Study: Choosing Between Two Values—Doing What the Rules Dictate or Maintaining a Friendship

In contrast to those Emma Willard students whose high school years seem to be a time to work on a new capacity to care for others and themselves, other students find a similar yet different configuration of these issues equally salient. Although issues of attachment, self, and relationships also emerge in their development, these students exhibit differences. For such girls (characterized as autonomous in relation to others), relationship concerns seem joined to issues of maintaining one's integrity, especially one's standards. In contrast to Anne's perspective, "standards" for these girls carry a different meaning, related more to personal integrity. A young sophomore, Rebecca, exemplifies this mode. As a member of the school judiciary committee, she had to confront her thinking about standards. In the contrasting conflicts she encountered during her three years of high school, it is possible to examine how her relations with others and her ideas about standards entered into her thinking and how chance played a role in the conflicts she describes.

Asked to describe herself, Rebecca, then a sophomore, began:

Oh, dear. I was thinking about that as I was getting dressed this morning. Um—to myself. I don't know, sometimes we have to do creative writing exercises, and who am I? I think of myself as a person who gets involved. I am doing a lot this year. In fact, I overextended myself this year, but no problem. I like to get involved in things. I think I am well known by a large part of the student body only because I am always sticking my fingers in a lot of business and stuff like that. My personality, I don't know. I have certain aspects of me, like I think I am a very warm person. I think I am very good at articulating how I feel, identifying parts of my life, like I've just done. But that's about it. I can't think of anything right now that I would describe myself as. I'd describe myself as a changed person, definitely.

Echoing a theme of her fellow student Anne, Rebecca continued, but her words emphasize characteristically different aspects of change:

I think I have changed a lot. I used to think when I was in the seventh and eighth grade that I was a liberated woman . . . but I don't know. I am at the stage now where I don't know if I'm liberated in the purest sense, simply because when in doubt, I always slip back into old traditions and old ways.

If I go to a mixer at a boys' school, I don't ask guys to dance simply because I'm afraid of what kind of reaction I'll get. So I don't know if I am liberated, if I'm completely, totally free about, you know, about being liberated in front of men because a lot of people . . . this girl was extremely, extremely liberated or whatever and she went to X [boys' school during exchange time], and she got nicknames like "Amazon" and these guys thought. . . . This school is like the way the world was in 1950, to give you a little background. But they called her the "Amazon,"

"Gloria Steinem," . . . and they saw her as some female castrating bitch. They just couldn't handle, they didn't understand what she was doing, so they tended to reject what she was saying. And I don't want to be rejected like that and I don't want people talking about me like that, so I don't know how liberated I am. So, I think I am a changed person is all I can say right now.

Although characterizing herself as "good at articulating how I feel, identifying parts of my life" yet saying, "I can't think of anything right now that I would describe myself as," Rebecca partly viewed herself in terms of her differences from others. In spite of her tentativeness, she did see that she had changed. Unlike Anne, who saw her change as becoming less childlike and more able to comprehend the world, Rebecca stressed a different set of issues. Rebecca saw herself as changed in relation to a marker—how "liberated" she was, liberated from the fear of being rejected by others. In a discussion of a moral conflict she had faced, she picked up this theme of difference and also identified the issues she would continue to deal with for the next three years: her integrity and the integrity of her standards, her relation to them, and how they mediated her relations with others.

In her sophomore year, Rebecca talked about a conflict in which "I was confronted with a situation where I could go out and get drunk with some friends." These friends, like Rebecca, sat on the Faculty Student Judiciary Committee, whose work included judging students who broke school rules. "This was at the time when I was saying, 'Well, . . . if this rule really isn't ethical or moral, then to hell with it.' They don't really expect us to follow these rules, they just don't want us to get caught." In the end, Rebecca refused to join her friends, as much, she said, "from an extreme fear of getting caught" as from any "great moral realization."

Reflecting on that situation, she elaborated on how her thinking was changing:

That was one of my extremist theories. . . . I just thought, I just went through a stage where I thought that anyone who came here and violated a rule should be kicked out of school because they couldn't handle it. They couldn't come here and totally stay within the rules, you know. And then I went through the thing: Is it possible to go through here four years without breaking a fundamental rule? And I asked someone, who said, "I don't think so." So, that is something I am going to have to deal with in the future.

In her construction of conflict and choice, Rebecca articulated a complex view of rules and their meaning in her life and in her relations with others.

But as she perceived the limits of her new perspective—that she might not be able to avoid breaking a rule—her thinking focused not on the situation and the others involved, but on her values and her integrity in maintaining them in dealings with others. Included in her calculations in a situation over which she did have control are her considerations in making a choice—of being able to rank one thing over others and to come to a decision in doing so. Three years later, she described a different conflict and revealed how some old issues were being reconstructed and how chance generates a new kind of deliberation.

Chance and Change   Talking about herself in her middle year of school, Rebecca articulated ideas about her relations with others that were important to her self-definition. Describing how she thought about herself in the past, she says:

> In that in the past I really had no notion of myself, of just me and not me in relation to my friends or me in relation to my parents or anything. I see myself I have a better notion of what I am and who I am and everything, and I didn't before because I was never, I never felt that I was really separate from my family or my friends, so that was a different behavior, a different person.

And now?

> Now, well, in friendships . . . before, I felt like I am just part of the group and I would mold myself to a group and what that group needed, I would be. I would change or act a certain way. If they needed an airhead, I would be an airhead, if they needed a jock, I would act like a jock, or whatever. And now I know that this is what I am like and the friendships that I find now, those are going to be people who are going to have to deal with me as I am and like me as I am.

Rebecca identified her separateness as giving her a "better notion of . . . who I am," and sought to maintain that identity, even if it might conflict with her friendships. People and friends, she believed, would have to deal with her as she "is." When asked about change and particularly about things that she would not want to change about herself, Rebecca said:

> Wouldn't want to change? I don't think I would like to change the way I look at life now and the way I see things. I don't really ever want to lose my perspective from the way I see things now. It's a perspective in that I don't totally divorce myself from the world, but I am not totally wrapped up in

the midst of. If somebody has a problem, usually, before, I'd get wrapped up in their problem and their problems would become my problem, you know, and I suppose that goes along with, like, molding into a group, you know. Now, I think the perspective I have is I can set myself apart from situations and I can see situations. I can see the humor, and I don't get too wrapped up, and I don't take everything too seriously and go overboard, which is what I used to do before.

Celebrating her perspective that sets her apart from situations and people and guards her from once more feeling lost, vulnerable, or "molded into a group," Rebecca emphasized her autonomy and her new sense of self in relation to others. This theme—continuous yet changing during her three years of high school—seems a central issue in her development. Manifest not only in her personal relationships but also in her schoolwide role as proctor, the themes of maintaining her separateness, maintaining her standards, and holding her perspective can be traced as her orientation toward others that evolved during the three years.

A conflict she faced in her second year of school may have introduced the new element that emerged in her thinking. The situation arose when her sister, who anticipated attending Emma Willard, wanted to visit Rebecca at school during Thanksgiving. Rebecca, however, wanted to go home for the holiday, and she knew that "the money for her to come here would be my money to go back home." Rebecca related how she thought about and acted on the situation—one in which she did not have total control. There was money for only one trip:

> I remember talking to my sister on the phone, saying, "you don't really want to come out here now, your grades are so bad." And it was pretty selfish and pretty low of me and so . . . I said to my mom, "I don't think she should come; her grades are bad." So she [did not come]. But I felt so guilty, I couldn't let myself go home!

When asked to describe the conflicts, Rebecca said:

> The right side was she has been talking, she has been planning on coming out here for a long time, and she wants to come. She should come. I promised that to her. My parents have made the arrangements. She should come—then the other side was I have never really gone home for Thanksgiving for several years. . . . I'd really like to see my friends.

Reflecting that "I think I hurt her feelings. . . . I was willing to walk all over her to get what I wanted. So, I guess that's what I mean by 'hurtful,'"

Rebecca had to wrestle with a new element in her moral code—not hurting somebody. Although she characteristically framed the conflict in terms of issues of fairness—of what had been promised to her sister and what was right—she weighed the conflict from both the perspective of fairness and the perspective of not hurting someone. Given the reality of her family not having enough money for airfare for both children, she saw that she had prevented her younger sister from visiting. And then she could not bring herself to go home.

Confronting one of life's unalterable choices, Rebecca saw that another person, her sister, had a context, goals, and aspirations of her own. And although she cared deeply about her trip home, Rebecca discovered that she cared as much about her sister and her sister's desires. Standards and integrity gave way to a new way of considering and maintaining relationships.

In sum, development for Rebecca seemed to center around issues of autonomy, individuation, and separateness—but only in relation to others. One feature of the developmental dynamic of this "autonomous" mode—identified and elaborated through the Emma Willard Study (Lyons, 1990)—is finding ways to hold onto one's integrity while dealing with one's relations with others. Coming to see others in their own terms and contexts may be the cutting edge of growth and change. Realistically, one does not necessarily lose control of one's integrity or standards through having relationships. This insight is mediated through one's relations with others and through the understanding that emerges from confronting life's contingencies.

In examining the conflicts that Anne and Rebecca reported, nuances can be perceived that suggest how certain themes will change over time. And although there are differences in the developmental tasks of students, as characterized by the two case studies, issues of contingency may function in a similar way for both. In confronting unalterable life situations, these individuals come—as did Jane Eyre—to some new, deeper understanding of others' values, feelings, hopes, and fears, as well as a deeper understanding of their own. Thus, in the themes of change and development shown by each of the two modes identified within the Emma Willard sample, it is possible to see how chance might affect development. Confronting an uncontrollable event seems to precipitate both ethical dilemmas and ethical reflection and deliberation. There is no way to generalize from these small examples, but it is interesting to speculate whether this kind of reflection fosters ethical considerations of a larger kind: How should one conduct one's own life and one's relations with others? What is fair or kind? How should one view the work one will do in the world? Simone Weil talked of the ethical as "attending to" others. Henry James argued, "The effort really to see and really to represent is no idle business in face of the constant force that makes for muddlement" (as cited in Nussbaum, 1990, p. 64).

Implications for Adolescent Development and for
Ethical and Intellectual Theory

When Martha Nussbaum (1986) took up her study "The Fragility of goodness," she was concerned with the following questions:

> To what extent can we distinguish between what is up to the world and what is up to us, when assessing a human life? How much can reason—our ability to deliberate and choose, to make a plan in which ends are ranked, to decide actively what is to have value and how much—control the happenings of our lives? (pp. 3–7)

She planned to examine these questions in light of Greek thought before the idea that luck can be checked by reason took precedence in ethical theory. Kantian ethics, for example, suggest that practical reason is the best guide to moral life, that two goods can never conflict with one another, and that there is always a way to rank and choose among one's deeply held values. But earlier Greek philosophers such as Aristotle argued differently.

Nussbaum joins this idea of conflicting goods with a fundamental question first presented by Aristotle: How should a human live? Nussbaum sees that in the stark experiences of Antigone or Agamemnon or Hecuba, the Greeks sought to portray the terrors of confronting what chance or luck has decreed. Such experiences, Nussbaum suggests, confront us with the inevitability of ethical deliberation and engage us in a dialectic that may contribute to our own answers to how to live a good human life.

The experiences of the students presented here have had this same effect. These interviews illustrate how chance contributes to ethical conflict and enters into ethical decision making. Choices may involve things one cares deeply about, and they may not always be susceptible to ranking—like the love for one's mother and one's father or the idea that one could value rules and principles but simultaneously find that one's relationships to one's sister and her life hopes were important, too. Indeed, recognizing that the value of these incommensurable goods cannot be ranked creates conflict. The girls at Emma Willard School confronted the existence of contingencies similar to those Nussbaum describes as precipitating ethical choices. These students described their experiences as they remembered them and shared their thinking about the ethical choices they made. But their ability to do so runs counter to traditional adolescent psychology, which characterizes coming of age as an advance in cognitive ability and abstract thinking; such a psychology is more often expressed in idealism and ideology (Erikson, 1968; Piaget, 1968) than in realism, in abstraction, and in the particular. As philosophers today recover this concept of contingency and the conflicts of incommensurable values, moral psychologists need to do the same. That Emma Willard students should reveal the role of contingency in their ethical dilemmas is not really surprising—luck is a clearly recognizable human phenomenon. What is surprising is how little this factor has been examined in moral psychology.

These studies with Emma Willard students suggest that future research should consider systematically how the realities and chance contingencies of life figure in adolescent ways of knowing and making ethical choices and in their development. A framework for the development of students' ways of knowing as articulated by Perry (1970) has been elaborated on in the work of Belenky, Clinchy, Goldberger, and Tarule (1986), who suggest that students move from the belief that knowledge is fixed and to the idea that knowledge is constructed. How contingencies fit into this type of epistemological development needs to be identified as well. Clearly, dealing with conflicts in which one must choose between two or more unrankable values could hasten the awareness that one acts on what oneself alone can know. It may be that confronting a conflict of incommensurable values precipitates this developmental shift toward an understanding of oneself as a constructivist.

In this chapter, students' moral decision making has been used to examine a dialectic of development and to discern the intricate relationship between self, one's relations with others, and the realities of the world. Who knows what may be at risk if one does not acknowledge at least to oneself what one knows?

A new research agenda, then, must consider the following:

- Chance events, those unalterable life happenings, are intertwined in adolescents' lives and can be experienced as ethical dilemmas they see and try to resolve.
- Confronting these chance occurrences over which one does not have control has the effect of setting up a kind of dialectic, an ethical deliberation. This is likely because the situation usually reveals deeply held values for people or things, values that cannot be ranked.
- The result of these deliberations can be a new awareness; a way of seeing oneself, one's values, and others in their concrete particularity with their hopes, fears, values, and ideals; and an expansion of one's moral imagination.
- The experience and recognition of life's unalterable contingencies and the resultant deliberations may be a significant part of adolescent ethical and intellectual development, especially of adolescents' ways of knowing.

These ethical deliberations may be part of the process of understanding oneself as a constructivist. If so, this work suggests that the traditional notions of idealism and ideology as the cornerstones of adolescent development need to be reconsidered. Awareness and understanding of the realities of chance in life contexts is not just a moral starting place, but one that may be an important part of healthy adolescent development. Researchers and practitioners need to understand this phenomenon in its particularity, especially in terms of how much adolescents themselves are aware of these issues.

Paying attention to how high school students act in their relations with others and perceive and deal with the ethical issues of their lives—considering what they can and cannot control—reveals the outline of an interconnected ethical and epistemological dialectic of development.

References

Adelson, J. (1971, Fall). The political imagination of the young adolescent. *Daedalus*, 1013–1050.

Adelson, J. (1980). *Handbook of adolescent psychology*. New York: Wiley.

Adelson, J., & Doehrman, M. J. (1980). The psychodynamic approach to adolescence. In J. Adelson (Ed.), *Handbook of adolescent psychology* (pp. 99–116). New York: Wiley.

Belenky, M. F., Clinchy, B., Goldberger, N., & Tarule, N. (1986). *Women's ways of knowing*. New York: Basic Books.

Bronte, C. (1960). *Jane Eyre*. New York: Washington Square Press. (Original work published 1846.)

Brown, L. (1989). *Narratives of relationship: The development of a care voice in girls ages 7 to 16*. Unpublished doctoral dissertation, Harvard University, Cambridge, MA.

Douvan, E., & Adelson, J. (1966). *The adolescent experience*. New York: Wiley.

Erikson, E. (1968). *Identity: Youth and crisis*. New York: Norton.

Fine, M. (1991). *Framing dropouts: Notes on the politics of an urban public high school*. Albany: SUNY Press.

Gilligan, C. (1977). In a different voice: Women's conceptions of the self and morality. *Harvard Educational Review, 47*, 481–517.

Gilligan, C. (1982). *In a different voice*. Cambridge, MA: Harvard University Press.

Gilligan, C. (1990, March). *Joining the resistance*. Tanner lecture presented at the University of Michigan, Ann Arbor, MI.

Gilligan, C., Lyons, N., & Hanmer, T. (1990). *Making connections: The relational world of adolescent girls at Emma Willard School*. Cambridge, MA: Harvard University Press.

Grotevant, H. D., & Cooper, C. R. (Eds). (1983). *Adolescent development in the family: New directions for child development*. San Francisco: Jossey-Bass.

Haan, N. (1977). *A manual for interpersonal morality*. Berkeley, CA: University of California, Institute for Human Development.

Hartup, W. W., & Rubin, Z. (1986). *Relationships and development*. Hillsdale, NJ: Lawrence Erlbaum.

Hinde, R. A. (1979). *Towards understanding relationships*. New York: Academic Press.

James, H. (1934). *The art of the novel*. New York: Charles Scribner's Sons.

Johnston, D. K. (1985). *Two moral orientations two problem solving strategies: Adolescents' solutions to dilemmas in fables.* Unpublished doctoral dissertation, Harvard University, Cambridge, MA.

Kohlberg, L. (1969). Stage and sequence: The cognitive developmental approach to socialization. In D. Goslin (Ed.), *The handbook of socialization theory and research* (pp. 90–125). Chicago: Rand McNally.

Kohlberg, L. (1984). *The psychology of moral development: Essays on moral development.* San Francisco: Harper & Row.

Lyons, N. (1982). *Conceptions of self and morality and modes of moral choice.* Unpublished doctoral dissertation, Harvard University, Cambridge, MA.

Lyons, N. (1983). Two perspectives: On self, relationships and morality. *Harvard Educational Review, 53,* 125–145.

Lyons, N. (1990). Listening to voices we have not heard. In C. Gilligan, N. Lyons, & T. Hanmer (Eds.), *Making connections* (pp. 30–72). Cambridge, MA: Harvard University Press.

Marcia, J. (1980). Identity in adolescence. In J. Adelson (Ed.), *Handbook of adolescent psychology* (pp. 125–136). New York: Wiley.

May, R. (1980). *Sex and fantasy: Patterns of male and female development.* New York: W.W. Norton.

Miller, J. B. (1976). *Towards a new psychology of women.* Boston: Beacon Press.

Nussbaum, M. (1986). *The fragility of goodness.* New York: Cambridge University Press.

Nussbaum, M. (1989, March). Tragic dilemmas: How difficult choices can lead to human progress. *Radcliffe Quarterly,* 7–9.

Nussbaum, M. (1990). *Love's knowledge.* New York: Oxford University Press.

Perry, W. (1970). *Forms of intellectual and ethical growth in the college years: A scheme.* New York: Holt, Rinehart, and Winston.

Piaget, J. (1965). *The moral judgment of the child.* New York: Free Press.

Piaget, J. (1968). *Six psychological studies.* New York: Vintage Books.

Piaget, J., & Inhelder, B. (1958). *The growth of logical thinking.* New York: Basic Books.

Weil, S. (1972). *Gravity and grace.* London: Routledge & Kegan Paul.

Williams, B. (1981). *Moral luck.* New York: Cambridge University Press.

Williams, B. (1985). *Ethics and the limits of philosophy.* Cambridge, MA: Harvard University Press.

Youniss, J. (1980). *Parents and peers in social development: A Sullivan-Piaget perspective.* Chicago: University of Chicago Press.

PART III

Young Adulthood

CHAPTER 8

Empathy, Social Cognition, and Moral Education

Martin L. Hoffman

New York University

Kohlberg's moral development theory assumes the primacy of cognition. It defines a moral act as one that follows a process of moral reasoning and judgment based on principles of justice or fairness. I define a moral act motivationally—that is, an act prompted by a disposition to do something on behalf of a person or group or to behave in accord with a moral norm or standard bearing on human welfare or justice. Moral reasoning or judgment *may* be involved, but not necessarily.

Where do moral motives come from? My answer, *empathy*, is suggested when we examine different moral encounters and look for the important things they have in common. Should we inform on someone who steals or cheats on his taxes? Should we lie to save someone's feelings, should we have or perform an abortion, and should we keep a promise to visit a sick friend or accept a last-minute invitation to a party? Should we terminate life-support systems for brain-dead patients? These and other—perhaps most—moral encounters have one thing in common: They involve potential victims or beneficiaries of someone's action.

Why should anyone be concerned about victims, or more generally, why should anyone feel an urge to go out of one's way to help other people and reduce their suffering or distress? An obvious answer is empathy, because if one empathized with a victim one would to some extent share the victim's distress. One would then be motivated to alleviate the victim's pain, if for no other reason than to reduce one's own empathic distress. There are other reasons as well, which I won't mention, except to note that a lot of research supports empathic distress as a motive for prosocial moral behavior (Hoffman, 1978).

My chapter has five parts. First, I summarize the latest version of my developmental scheme for empathy and related affects. Second, I point out how these empathic affects may be evoked in both simple and complex moral

157

encounters. Third, I suggest how empathic affects may contribute to the activation of certain moral principles. Fourth, I suggest implications for socialization and moral education. Fifth, I give hypothetical information-processing sequences that show how empathic affects may contribute to moral judgment and action.

Development of Empathy and Related Moral Affects

My scheme for empathic distress, which is an empathic affective response to another person's distress, starts with a simple innocent-bystander model in which one encounters someone in pain, danger, or deprivation and generates five empathic affects that are mediated by social cognitive development and various causal attributions or inferences (see Hoffman, 1987, for a detailed presentation of this schema).

Empathy Development

The developmental scheme includes five hypothesized modes of empathic affect arousal (see Table 8.1). The first three are largely automatic and involuntary. A, the primary circular reaction in which infants cry to the sound of another's cry, typically drops out after infancy owing to controls against crying, although even adults may feel sad when they hear a cry and some may feel like crying although they usually control it. The second and third automatic, involuntary modes (B and C)—conditioning and mimicry—may enter at various points in development and continue to operate through life. Mimicry, for those unfamiliar with the concept, pertains to a two-step process in which (1) the observer automatically imitates the model's facial and postural responses and (2) the muscle movements involved in this imitative response send messages to the brain that produce feelings corresponding to those of the model. Modes D and E involve language mediation, which enables one to empathize with another's verbal report of feelings, and putting oneself in the other's place. Both D and E call on higher-order cognitive processes that are far more subject to voluntary control than are A, B, and C modes. D and E presumably enter children's repertoires as soon as they develop verbal and role-taking capabilities.

The existence of five arousal modes suggests that empathy may be an overdetermined and hence reliable response. Thus, if the only cues present in a situation are expressive cues from the victim (i.e., his facial expression), then mimicry may be available to arouse empathic distress in observers. If the victim is not visible and only situational cues are provided, conditioning is available—that is, situational cues may serve as conditioned stimuli that evoke empathic distress. Even if the victim is absent and the only information about his or her distress is that communicated by someone else, empathy may still be aroused in an observer through the higher-level cognitive modes (see Table 8.1).

Although empathy may often be aroused by the simplest involuntary mechanisms, the subjective experience of empathy is complex. Mature empathizers know that the affect aroused in them is due to stimulus events impinging on someone else, and furthermore, they have an idea of what that person is feeling. Young children who lack the self-other distinction may be empathically aroused without this knowledge. This suggests that the development of empathic distress corresponds to the development of a cognitive sense of others, the four broad stages of which (listed under IIA–D) are as follows: (1) self-other fusion, in which the child does not yet experience a clear boundary between the self and others; (2) object permanence or, more specifically, person permanence, in which one is aware of others as physical entities distinct from the self; (3) perspective taking, in which one becomes aware that others have perceptions, feelings, and thoughts that are independent of one's own internal states; and (4) awareness of personal identity, in which one becomes increasingly aware that others have experiences beyond the immediate situation, as well as their own individual histories and identities.

Empathic affect is presumably experienced differently as the child progresses through these stages, and the resulting coalescence of empathic affect and social-cognitive development yields four levels of empathic distress (IIIA–D), which I now describe briefly.

1. *Global empathy.* Infants may experience empathic distress through the simplest arousal modes (IA, IB, or IC) long before they acquire a sense of others as physical entities distinct from the self. For most of the first year, then, witnessing someone in distress may result in a global empathic distress response. Distress cues from the dimly perceived other are confounded with unpleasant feelings empathically aroused in the self. Consequently, infants may at times act as though what happened to the other happened to themselves. An 11-month-old girl, on seeing a child fall and cry, looked as though she was about to cry herself and then put her thumb in her mouth and buried her head in her mother's lap, as she does when she, herself, is hurt.

2. *Egocentric empathy.* At about a year of age, when the child begins to be aware of other people as physically distinct from the self, the affective portion of the child's global empathic distress may be transferred to the separate image of self and image of other that emerge. The child may now be aware that another person and not the self is in distress, but the other's internal state remains unknown and may be assumed to be the same as the child's own internal state. An 18-month-old boy fetched his own mother to comfort a crying friend although the friend's mother was also present. This behavior indicates

Table 8.1. Development and Transformation of Empathic Distress

---

I. Modes of empathic affect arousal

Automatic—nonvoluntary

A. *Primary circular reaction:* Infant cries to the sound of another's cry

B. *Mimicry:* Automatic imitation plus afferent feedback

C. *Conditioning and direct association:* Cues in the immediate situation that resemble affectively charged events in the observer's past may now evoke the events' affect in the observer

Higher-order cognitive

D. *Language-mediated association:* Verbal cues in the immediate situation that are associated through their semantic meaning with affectively charged events in the observer's past may now evoke the events' affect in the observer

E. Putting self in other's place

   1. *Self-focused:* Imagine oneself in another's place, that is, imagine that stimuli impinging on the other are impinging on oneself

   2. *Other-focused:* Attend directly to other's internal states, that is, imagine how other feels in the situation

   3. Combination of 1 and 2

II. Development of a cognitive sense of others

A. *Self-other fusion:* Representations of self and of the other are not yet separate

B. *Object permanence:* Other is represented as physically distinct from the self

C. *Perspective taking:* Other is represented as having internal states independent of one's own internal states

D. *Personal identity:* Other is represented as having experiences beyond the immediate situation and as having his or her own history and identity

III. Developmental levels of empathy (coalescence of I and II)

A. Global empathy

B. "Egocentric" empathy

C. Empathy for another's feelings

D. Empathy for another's experiences beyond the immediate situation, including empathy for an entire group

IV. Partial transformation of empathic into sympathetic distress: Part of transition from IIIA to IIIB; one's response to another's distress may then have a pure empathic component and a sympathetic component

---

Table 8.1. *(Cont'd)*

V. Causal attribution and shaping of empathic distress into related moral affects

A. If victim is cause of own distress, he or she may no longer be viewed as a victim; this may remove the basis for the observer's empathy

B. *Sympathetic distress:* If victim appears to have no control over the cause of his or her distress (accident, illness, loss) or if victim's distress is highly salient although its cause is unclear, empathic distress may be transformed into sympathetic distress (as in IV)

C. *Guilt:* Observer is cause of victim's distress (e.g., accidentally or as the inadvertent result of competition); differs from Freudian, free-floating, or conditioned guilt

   Guilt over inaction: Observer, although not the cause, does nothing and therefore feels responsible for continuation of victim's distress; observer's relative advantage may increase this guilt

   Guilt by association: Observer's group is cause of victim's distress

D. *Empathic anger:* If someone else causes victim's distress, one's empathic distress may be transformed into empathic anger directed at the culprit

   1. Empathic anger may be reduced or even turned toward the victim in certain situations (e.g., if justified by the victim's past relationship with the culprit)

   2. If the culprit represents society, empathic anger may contribute to criticism of society and acceptance of relevant moral/political ideologies

E. *Empathic feeling of injustice:* Often implied in B, C, or D or may result from discrepancy between victim's character and his or her plight

---

that the child is responding with appropriate empathic affect, but it also illustrates the child's confusion about internal states.

3. *Empathy for another's feelings.* With the onset of perspective taking, at about two to three years, the child becomes aware that other people's feelings may differ from his or her own and are based on their own needs and interpretations of events. Consequently, the child becomes more responsive to cues about what the other person is actually feeling. Furthermore, as language is acquired, children become capable of empathizing with a wide range of increasingly complex emotions. Empathizing with a victim's distress, for example, children may also eventually be able to empathize with the victim's desire *not* to be helped. Finally, children can be empathically aroused by information about someone's distress even in that person's absence. This leads to the fourth, most advanced level.

4. *Empathy for another's life condition.* By late childhood, owing to the emerging conception of the self and others as continuing people with separate

histories and identities, the child becomes aware that others feel pleasure and pain, not only in the immediate situation but also in their larger life experience. Consequently, although the child still responds empathically to another's immediate distress, the empathic response may be intensified when he or she realizes that the other's distress is not transitory but chronic. Thus, the child's empathically aroused affect may now be combined with a mental representation of another person's general level of distress or deprivation. Furthermore, as the child acquires the ability to form social concepts, his or her empathic distress may be combined with a mental representation of the plight of an entire group or class of people (e.g., the poor, oppressed, outcast, or retarded).

To summarize, when one has advanced through these four levels and encounters someone in pain, danger, or distress, one is exposed to a network of information about the other's condition. The network may include verbal and nonverbal expressive cues from the victim, situational cues, and one's knowledge about the victim's life beyond the immediate situation. These sources of information are processed differently: Empathy aroused by nonverbal and situational cues can be mediated by the largely involuntary modes (mimicry and conditioning). Empathy aroused by verbal messages from the victim or by one's knowledge about the victim's life condition requires more complex processing, such as language-mediated association or putting oneself in the other's place.

The various cues, arousal modes, and processing levels usually contribute to the same affect, but contradictions may occur. For example, imagine someone who does not know that he has a terminal illness laughing and having a good time. Someone who knows nothing about the illness might respond with empathic joy. A young child who knows about the illness might also respond with empathic joy, because the knowledge is not activated or because it does not have the motivational power needed to override the impact of the child's immediate sensory experience. The knowledge of the illness might not be so readily dismissed, however, by a mature observer who realizes that it is a more compelling index of the other's welfare than is the other's behavior in the immediate situation. Such an observer might experience empathic sadness or at least a mingling of sadness and joy. Similarly, a mature observer's empathic distress might decrease if the other person is known to have a generally happy life and the immediate distress is a short-lived exception. Clearly, the most advanced empathic level involves some distancing—responding partly to one's mental image of the other rather than only to the other's immediate stimulus value. This fits my definition of empathy, not as an exact match of another's feelings but as an affective response that is more appropriate to the other's situation than to one's own situation.

Partial Transformation of Empathic Into Sympathetic Distress

The transition from global to egocentric empathy may involve an important qualitative shift in feeling. Once children are aware that others are distinct from themselves, their own empathic distress, which is a parallel response—a more or less exact replication of the victim's presumed feeling of distress—may be transformed, at least in part, into a reciprocal feeling of concern for the victim (see IV in Table 8.1). That is, children may continue to respond in a purely empathic manner—feeling uncomfortable and highly distressed themselves— but they may also experience a feeling of compassion, or "sympathetic distress," for the victim, along with a conscious desire to help because they feel sorry for the victim, not just to relieve their own empathic distress. In other words, the last three empathy levels (IIIB, IIIC, and IIID in Table 8.1) may describe the development of an affective response that has two components: a wish to terminate the other's distress—the sympathetic distress component— and a more purely empathic wish to terminate distress in oneself.

Causal Attributions, Empathy, and Related Moral Affects

Causal attributions of events that people always make are important cognitive input, and there is evidence that causal attributions are made spontaneously (Weiner, 1985). It therefore seems reasonable to suppose that when one encounters someone in distress, one will often make attributions about the cause. The particular attributions made, which are ordinarily derived from the network of situational cues and background information that I mentioned earlier, may be expected to determine how empathic affect is experienced. Consider now some causal attributions and the resulting affects.

Causal Attributions and Empathic Affects

Sympathetic Distress   I just discussed the transformation of empathic into sympathetic distress early in life, before causal attributions can serve as effective cognitive inputs. I assume that mature observers, too, will respond with sympathetic distress when the victim's plight is immediate and salient and when there are no causally relevant cues powerful enough to draw the observer's attention away from the victim's plight. Sympathetic distress may also be elicited when cues indicate that the victim has no choice or control over his plight, as in an illness or accidental injury.

Empathic Anger   If it is clear that someone else caused the victim's plight, one's attention may be diverted from the victim to the culprit. One may feel anger at the culprit, partly because one sympathizes with the victim and partly because one empathizes with the victim and feels oneself vicariously attacked. One's feelings may also alternate between empathic and sympathetic distress and empathic anger, or empathic anger may crowd out one's empathic and sympathetic distress entirely. A simple example of empathic anger is the 17-month-old boy in the doctor's office who, on seeing another child receive an injection and start to cry, responds by hitting the doctor.

Empathic anger is often complex and may shift from one target to another. For example, if one discovers that the victim had previously done harm to the culprit, one's empathic distress for the victim may decrease, and one may begin to empathize with the culprit. If one discovers the victim has a history of being mistreated in the relationship with the culprit, one might assume the victim had chosen to maintain the relationship (an abused spouse, for example) and is therefore responsible for his or her plight and is thus not a victim. This could reduce one's sympathetic distress for the victim and empathic anger at the culprit. Young children may miss these nuances, and they may respond with simple empathic anger directed toward the visible culprit. A final note on empathic anger: It must be distinguished from the type of self-righteous indignation that serves to tout one's own moral superiority and may be an excuse for aggressive behavior toward others.

Guilt Feeling   The observer thus far in my analysis is an innocent bystander. If the observer were not innocent but caused the other's distress, the conditions would be ripe for the observer to feel guilty—that is, to experience a combination of empathic and sympathetic distress and a self-blame attribution. It should be noted that this type of guilt differs from the early conception of guilt in the psychology literature as a conditioned anxiety response to anticipated punishment. Nor is it the same as Freudian guilt, which is a remnant of earlier fears of punishment or retaliation that resulted in repression of hostile and other impulses and which is triggered by the return of the repressed impulses to consciousness. It is, rather, a true, interpersonal guilt, which may be defined simply as the bad feeling one has about oneself because one is aware of actually doing harm to someone.

I have long suggested that this combination may originate in discipline encounters in which parents point up harmful consequences of the child's actions for others (Hoffman & Saltzstein, 1967), a point that may have implications for moral education, as I discuss later. In any case, even if totally innocent, one may feel guilty because one blames oneself for contributing to the *continuation* of the other's distress by not trying to help. This is guilt over inaction.

To summarize, the empathic reaction to someone's distress produces two basic affects: empathic distress and sympathetic distress. In addition—depending on the causal and other attributions made—empathic anger or guilt may be generated.

Empathic Affect Arousal Beyond the Bystander Model

Thus far, I have presented a scheme for empathic affects that may be aroused when the instigating stimulus is someone in distress. If this scheme is to provide the basis for a comprehensive moral theory, these empathic affects, although generated by a simple bystander model, must be arousable in other types of moral encounters. There are three reasons for expecting this to be true. First, humans can imagine themselves in different situations, and these imagined events can generate affect. Second, humans can imagine that stimuli that impinge on someone else are impinging on themselves, and this can generate empathic affect. Third, research has shown that the semantic meanings of events can become conditioned stimuli for arousal of affect. It follows from these facts that empathic affects can be aroused through the mediation of language and role taking (which were assumed in postulating arousal modes ID and IE in Table 8.1). This means that the victim does not have to be present for empathy to be aroused; the observer need only be informed about the victim's plight.

The essential features of my bystander model can thus be extended to include instances in which one hears about victims second- or thirdhand—from parents, teachers, newspapers, or television. The model's essential features may also obtain when one is talking, arguing, or thinking about contemporary moral issues such as racial integration, abortion, or how society's resources should be distributed. If in dealing with these issues victims come to mind, one is then cognitively placed in the bystander position of observing or imagining someone in distress, and the same empathic affects may be aroused.

Potential victims may also come to mind when one is more directly involved in action, such as when one is contemplating acting in a way that may have an effect on the welfare of others—for example, going back on a promise or satisfying some material need that seems at first to have no bearing on the welfare of others but on reflection clearly does have a bearing. Here again, once a victim or potential victim comes to mind, empathic affect may be aroused.

To summarize, I have argued that empathic affect may be aroused in response to another's plight not only when one is an actual bystander but also when one is in the cognitively extended bystander position and also when one is contemplating an action of one's own. Research that shows that empathic affect in bystanders motivates helping behavior (Hoffman, 1978) should also apply to these other situations.

Empathy and Moral Principles

The next step in broadening my scheme for empathic affect is to extend it into the domain of two of the major moral principles of Western society:

1. *The principle of benevolence,* associated mainly with writers in the utilitarian tradition, especially David Hume and Adam Smith, which states that a moral act is one that takes into account the happiness or well-being of all people likely to be affected by it. At the face-to-face level, this has become a principle of caring about and showing consideration for the needs of others, including their needs for self-respect, dignity, and avoidance of pain. This principle has been the focus of psychologists interested in empathy, for obvious reasons.

2. *The principle of justice or fairness,* essentially distributive justice, written about extensively by Immanuel Kant and his followers, which states that society's resources (rewards and punishments) should be allocated according to a standard equally applicable to all. Justice notions are at the heart of Kohlberg's theory, but I will try to show how some of them may relate to empathy.

A third major moral principle, that of maintaining the social order, is derived largely from Hobbes' view that without society the individual would be constantly embattled, hence nothing. This principle has been virtually ignored by psychologists, and I will say nothing more about it.

I do not view these principles as mutually exclusive but as potential components of all moral encounters. Consider a faculty vote on tenure for a candidate whose performance is not quite up to the standard. If one likes the candidate and knows that one of the candidate's children is very ill, the principle of caring may move one to vote in favor of tenure. The principle of justice, on the other hand, might argue for a negative vote because the candidate's performance does not warrant tenure and someone more deserving could be hired.

How does empathy relate to caring and justice principles? The link between empathy and the caring principle is obvious and direct, because any or all of the empathic affects (empathic distress, sympathetic distress, empathic anger, and guilt) may include a feeling of concern for victims and a disposition to act on their behalf, and the principle of caring operates in the same direction.

The link between empathy and the principle of distributive justice is less obvious and requires discussion. To begin, there are at least three justice principles:

1. *Need.* Society's resources should be allocated according to what people need: Those who need more should receive more; those who need less should receive less.

2. *Equality.* Each person has the same intrinsic worth in some larger religious or philosophical sense (e.g., in the sense of Bentham's principle, "Everyone to count for one and nobody for more than one"), and therefore society's resources should be divided equally.

3. *Equity.* People should be rewarded according to how much they produce (their output) or according to how much effort they expend.

Suppose one is deciding which type of distributive system is the best, most moral one. If one empathizes with poor people and imagines the consequences of different distributive systems for them, one is likely to advocate distributive systems based on the principle of need or perhaps on the principle of equality, because these principles have a clear caring component.

Something similar appears to be true, although less obviously, of the principle of equity of *effort* (one should be rewarded for hard work). One might end up affirming the principle of effort if one empathized not with poor people but with the needs and expectations of people who work hard and save for their families. Consider this response of a 13-year-old male research subject to the question, "Why is it wrong to steal from a store?" "Because the people who own the store work hard for their money and they deserve to be able to spend it for their family. It's not fair, they sacrifice a lot and they make plans and then they lost it all because somebody who didn't work for it goes in and takes it." In this response, the subject has transformed an abstract moral question about why it is wrong to steal into an empathy-relevant question by imagining a particular victim. The response has a clear empathic-identification component: One empathizes with the person's effort, sacrifice, plans, and expectations about enjoying the fruits of his or her labor and with his or her disappointment and loss if someone takes it all away. There also appears to be an empathic-anger component, as well as an empathic feeling of injustice. The response thus suggests that not only the need and equality principles but also the principle of effort may have a caring component, and this component may be activated when one empathizes with people who work hard but are not rewarded. Empathic affect may thus contribute to one's being receptive to the principle of equity based on effort.

The principle of equity based on *output* (e.g., paying more to those who make more profit for the company) is different. Distributing resources on the basis of output seems to imply that the individual's welfare and internal states are irrelevant, thus ruling out a direct link between empathy and the principle of output. There are two possible indirect links, however:

1. If output is assumed to reflect effort, then my argument about the contribution of empathy to effort may also apply to output. One may thus empathize with someone who produces a lot for little reward, because one assumes he or she worked hard and deserved more.

2. If distribution systems based on output motivate people to produce more, as many people believe, then there would be more resources to go around and everyone would benefit, including the poor (the trickle-down

idea). It may thus be possible for empathic identification with the poor to lead one to affirm equity of output as the moral principle of choice.

Both links are circuitous, especially the second one, and it seems more likely that people who empathize with poor or hardworking people will prefer the principles of need, equality, or effort. A recent study of adults in West Germany supports this expectation (Montada, Schmitt, & Dalbert, 1986). The researchers found a positive correlation between a questionnaire measure of empathy and a preference for need-based distribution and a negative correlation between empathy and output-based distribution. I found the same thing in an unpublished study of American college students.

To summarize, in contemplating how society's resources should be distributed, one might focus on the implications for oneself and on the implications for others. We would expect egoistic, nonempathic people to be receptive to distributive justice principles that coincide with their own condition: High producers would choose output; low producers would choose need or equality. For empathic people, the welfare of others may be important, and the task of choosing among abstract distributive justice principles may be transformed into an empathy-relevant task by imagining the consequences of distributive systems for certain (e.g., poor) people. Empathic people may thus end up selecting need or equality even if they are high producers themselves. Or their egoistic proclivities might prevail but be tempered by empathy. They might then choose a distributive system based on equity but regulated so that no one is extremely deprived (need) and vast discrepancies in wealth cannot occur (equality).

If empathy does relate to caring and most justice principles, as I suggest, how might these connections come about? One obvious possibility is that they occur in the normal course of development in empathic children. Most children have empathic capabilities, as I noted, and if their early socialization enhances these capabilities, the various empathic affects may become part of their affective and motivational structures long before they are expected to seriously consider society's moral principles. In late childhood or early adolescence, children may for the first time be exposed to various principles as principles, though usually in a loose, scattered fashion. Children who are empathic should be especially receptive to principles of caring, need-based justice, equality, and perhaps effort-based justice. In other words, children may be expected to select from the available moral principles, those that fit their empathic dispositions. Children may then internalize the principles with little external pressure because the principles are in keeping with their preexisting empathic leanings.

One's moral encounters through life may also contribute, because of the empathic affect they often arouse. It seems reasonable to assume that when one is in a moral encounter and wonders what to do, one may consider alternative actions and anticipate the consequences of each action. These thoughts may not only bring victims and potential victims to mind, thus arousing empathic affect but also activate the relevant moral principles that one has learned and stored in memory. The result is a co-occurrence of empathic affect and a moral principle, which may produce a bond between them. As a result, the principle may acquire an affective charge, and it may then be encoded and stored in memory as an affectively charged representation—or a "hot" cognition. Once this happens, whenever the principle is activated in the future, the person will also experience its associated empathic affect. This may be true even in emotionally cool situations. For example, in answering moral judgment research questions, an abstract principle's coming to mind may trigger empathic affect. The situation may then no longer be cool. This may explain the empathic, emotional tone of my young subject's explanation of why it is wrong to steal.

An important consequence of this hot-cognition concept of moral principles is that a person's empathic responses in moral encounters may be due not only to the immediate stimulus event (cues from the situation and from the victim), but also to the affectively charged moral principle that may be activated. In other words, the empathic affect elicited in moral encounters may have a stimulus- or cue-driven component and a component driven by the activated, affectively charged principle. If the stimulus-driven component is weak, say, because of a lack of expressive cues from the victim, activation of the principle may supply enough additional empathic affect to motivate the observer to help the victim. The opposite may also be true. The empathic affect elicited by the stimulus may be intense enough to produce the disruptive effects of "empathic overarousal," hence inaction (Hoffman, 1978). Here, activation of the principle may reduce the empathic affect intensity to a more manageable level. Thus, activation of an affectively charged moral principle may have a heightening or a leveling effect, and in general it might function to stabilize one's level of empathic affect arousal in different situations.

In sum, empathy may play a significant role in determining whether one becomes committed to a moral principle by giving the principle an affective base. But once the principle is in place, activating it in future moral encounters may increase or decrease the intensity of one's empathic-affective response. Moral principles may thus make it more likely that moral conflict will lead to moral action that is stable and reliable.

Implications for Socialization and Moral Education

An important thing about empathy as I define it is its amenability to cognitive influence. This gives a significant role to socialization and moral education. I first discuss the role of children's emotional experience, affection, and imitative modeling and then move on to more cognitive methods.

Contributions to Empathy of Experience, Affection, and Models

First, we would expect people to be more likely to empathize with someone else's emotion if they have had direct experience with that emotion themselves. It follows that socialization that allows children to experience a variety of emotions rather than protecting them from these emotions will increase the likelihood of their being able to empathize with different emotions. That is, it will expand their empathic range. The only evidence to date for this hypothesis is that preschool children who cry a lot appear to be more empathic than children who do not cry often (Lenrow, 1965). There is a theoretical limitation to this hypothesis: Certain extremely painful situations might be repressed, resulting in an inability to empathize with the emotions involved.

Second, we would expect that giving children a lot of affection would help keep them open to the needs of others and empathic rather than absorbed in their own needs. We would also expect that exposing the children to models who act altruistically and express their sympathetic feelings would contribute to the children's acting empathically rather than making counterempathic attributions about the cause of people's distress. Both these expectations have been borne out by the research (Hoffman, 1975).

A third expectation can be derived from the idea that empathy is a largely involuntary response. By involuntary, we mean that if a person pays attention to the victim, he or she will usually have an empathic response. It follows that socialization experiences that direct the child's attention to the internal states of other people should contribute to the development of empathy. We should therefore expect that in situations in which the child has harmed others, the parent's use of discipline techniques that call attention to the victim's pain or injury or that encourage the child to imagine him- or herself in the victim's place—inductive techniques—should help put the feelings of others into the child's consciousness and thus enhance the child's empathic potential. The positive correlation between inductive techniques and helping in older children has long been known (Hoffman, 1970), and the same correlation has more recently been reported in children under two years old (Zahn-Waxler, Radke-Yarrow, & King, 1979).

Fourth, we would expect role-taking opportunities to help sharpen the child's cognitive sense of others and increase the likelihood that he or she will pay attention to others, thus extending the child's empathic capability. We must remember, however, that role taking is an ego skill potentially useful in manipulating as well as helping others. Role-taking opportunities in positive social contexts should therefore be a more reliable contributor to empathy and helping than role-taking opportunities in competitive contexts. The research thus far seems to provide modest support for this expectation: Role-taking training in prosocial contexts has been found to increase helping behavior in children and adults; the research on role taking in competitive contexts, all of it correlational, unfortunately, appears to show a lack of relation between role taking and helping (Hoffman, 1983a).

Socialization and Empathy-Based Guilt Feeling

Socialization should be especially important in the development of guilt for the following reason. Guilt feelings are not only aversive, as is empathic distress, but they are also highly deprecatory and threatening to the child's emerging self-image. We may therefore expect children to be motivated to avoid guilt. And they can often succeed in this, because most situations in which children harm others are ambiguous in one way or another as regards who, if anyone, is to blame. That is, children rarely harm others intentionally and without provocation, in which case it would be easy to assign blame.

The ambiguity is most apparent when one has harmed another accidentally—whether in rough play or in independent pursuit of one's own interests. But ambiguity also exists in fights and arguments, where it may seem as reasonable to assign blame to the other as to blame the self. In competitive situations, one might conceivably feel guilt about wanting to be victorious over the other or about wanting the other to lose, but one knows that the other is similarly motivated and so there may appear to be little or no grounds for guilt. Besides blaming others or blaming no one, children can use perceptual guilt-avoiding strategies such as turning away from the victim. It seems to follow that even when children have the necessary cognitive and affective attributes for guilt, they often will not experience it unless an external agent is present who somehow compels them to attend to the harm done to the victim and to their own role in the victim's plight. This is exactly what parents often do when a child does harm to someone, and it seems reasonable to expect that the type of discipline used in these situations will have an effect on the development of a guilt disposition in children.

Parental Discipline and Guilt Feeling   Indeed, the discipline research does show fairly consistently that parents who frequently use discipline techniques in which the salient component is induction—that is, techniques in which the parent points up the harmful effects of the child's behavior on others—combined with a lot of affection outside the discipline encounter—have children who tend to experience guilt feelings when they have harmed others (Hoffman, 1970). Parents who frequently use power assertion—which includes force, deprivation of material objects or privileges, or the threat of these—are apt to have children who tend to respond with fear of retaliation or punishment rather than guilt. (The frequent use of love withdrawal, in which the parent simply gives direct but nonphysical expression to his anger or disapproval of the child for engaging in the undesirable behavior, does not seem to relate to guilt, although such a relationship might be expected from a psychoanalytic perspective.)

My theoretical explanation of these findings, presented elsewhere (especially Hoffman, 1983b) will be summarized briefly. First, although the research describes discipline techniques as fitting one or another category, when examined empirically most discipline techniques have power-assertive and love-withdrawing properties, and some also contain elements of induction. The first two comprise the motive-arousal component of discipline techniques that may be necessary to get the child to stop what he or she is doing and attend. Having attended, the child will often be influenced cognitively and affectively by the information contained in the inductive component, when it is present. Second, if there is too little arousal, the child may ignore the parent; too much arousal, and the resulting fear, anxiety, or resentment may prevent effective processing of the inductive content and may direct the child's attention to the consequences of his or her action for the self. Techniques with a salient inductive component ordinarily achieve the best balance and direct the child's attention to the consequences of his or her action for the victim. Third, the child may process the information in the inductive component, and the cognitive products of this processing constitute knowledge about the moral norm against harming others. Processing this information should also often enlist the capacity for empathy that the child brings to the discipline encounter. The child thus may feel badly due to the other's distress, rather than or in addition to anticipated punishment of the self. Fourth, as inductions also point up the fact that the child caused the victim's distress, these techniques may often result in the temporal conjunction of empathic distress and the attribution of one's own personal responsibility for the other's distress, which may be needed to transform empathic distress into guilt. (This analysis is most applicable to instances in which the victim of the child's act exhibits clear signs of being sad and downcast, hurt, or otherwise distressed. If the victim is angry and retaliates, the child may feel anger or fear rather than empathic distress and guilt.)

I also suggested that once guilty feelings are aroused in discipline encounters, the ideas about the harmful consequences of one's actions that gave rise to those guilty feelings may be suffused with guilty affect and may become hot cognitions whose affective and cognitive features are inseparable. These hot cognitions may then be encoded in memory and eventually experienced in temptation situations or moral encounters as an affective-cognitive unity. Another interesting possibility is that although the guilty feelings are derived from the ideas about harmful consequences, they may be encoded separately, through a special process or channel reserved for affects. If so, then in later temptation situations, the guilty feelings may be evoked without any conscious awareness of the ideas about consequences that gave rise to them. (This may sound like the Freudian notion of guilt, but it is different because it is not based on repression.) Stated most generally, this theory suggests that it is: (1) the appropriate mix of parental power, love, and information; (2) the child's processing of the information in discipline encounters and afterwards; and (3) the cognitive and affective products of that processing that determine the extent to which the child feels guilty when he or she has harmed another or contemplates acting in a way that might harm another. Thus, the child's empathic and cognitive capabilities that I described earlier may be mobilized for the first time in discipline encounters, with guilt feelings as the result, and the resulting guilt capability may then be generalized to other situations.

The blend of frequent inductions, occasional power assertions, and a lot of affection may also work well in the schools, provided discipline encounters do not arise too often and are not too emotionally loaded and disruptive. Teachers may be tempted to use power assertion because it gains compliance more quickly, and induction may seem a luxury they cannot often afford. Because there are many onlooking children, however, teachers may get a lot of mileage out of an occasional induction that is well worded and well timed. The reason is that the onlooking children are in the role of innocent bystanders, which is at the heart of my empathy scheme. This means that these children may have empathy aroused, engage in the causal attributional processes, and experience the various empathic affects I discussed—at least the children paying attention to what is going on. In formulating their inductions, teachers must, of course, consider the children's developmental levels, in particular their ability to comprehend complex explanations given in an emotional context.

To summarize, inductive discipline at home or in school may help train children to attend closely to the consequences of their actions for other people's feelings and their well-being in general. This should in turn increase the likelihood of empathy and guilt being aroused whenever one's action has a potential impact on others.

A problem I have not yet raised pertains to two kinds of empathic bias. One, for which there is research evidence (Hoffman, 1987), is the tendency to empathize more with people one likes or to whom one is similar than with strangers. The other is the tendency to empathize more with people who are present than with those who are absent. There is no research on this type of bias, but it seems obvious because the personal and situational cues required for the automatic, involuntary empathy-arousal modes discussed earlier are available only when the other is present. I call these the familiarity bias and the here-and-now bias.

To reduce the here-and-now bias, moral educators may need to teach children a simple rule of thumb: Look beyond the immediate situation and ask questions such as: How will my action affect the other person not only now but in the future? Are there still other people, present or absent, who might be affected by my actions? If children learn to ask these questions, this should enhance their awareness of potential victims of their actions who are not present and enhance their ability to empathize with them to at least some extent. To increase the motivational power of the empathic identification, children should also be encouraged to imagine how they would feel in the absent victim's place or to imagine how someone close to them would feel in that person's place. Furthermore, when children are prepared for complex moral encounters in which there may be two or more potential victims or beneficiaries of one's action—some who are present and some who are absent—it may be advisable to train children to engage in the difficult process of empathizing with more than one person in the situation. Children cannot be expected to engage in this laborious process of empathic identification with multiple others all the time (nor can adults), but training them to do this should at least make their empathic responses in many moral encounters less exclusively confined to the here and now and a closer approximation of the ideal of spatial and temporal impartiality.

As for the familiarity-similarity bias, it is interesting that over 200 years ago, David Hume (1751/1957) declared that it was perfectly natural for people to empathize more with their kin than with strangers and that doing this was not necessarily incompatible with being moral. But he also said that efforts must be made to minimize this bias and suggested that society can be organized so as to minimize it: People, each with his or her own bias and knowing about his or her own bias and the other's bias, can devise social rule systems that minimize bias and encourage impartiality. This still makes sense, but I would also say there is need for a moral education curriculum that stresses the common humanity all people share. This would include efforts to raise people's levels of empathy for people who are not members of one's own group, such as direct face-to-face cultural contact. It would also include training in role-taking and multiple empathizing procedures designed to produce images that are vivid enough to generate empathic feelings for people in vastly different circumstances than one's own. The combination of rule systems and empathy-enhancing moral education should expand the range of people to whom individuals can respond empathically. This should reduce familiarity-similarity bias.

Illustrations of Interaction of
Empathy, Moral Judgment, and Principle

My argument for the link between empathy, judgment, and principle is by no means foolproof, as the empirical research to test it has not been done. Consequently, to make the argument plausible, I must resort to anecdotal and literary examples that show that people's moral judgments often seem both to reflect moral principles and to have a quality of personal concern for others that reflects an underlying empathic responsiveness to them. In presenting these examples, I interpret them in a way that points up the information-processing sequences that may be involved. Consider first an example from the book *Uncle Tom's Cabin*, as reported by Kaplan (1989), in which an affluent, politically uninvolved housewife whose empathy for slaves she knew personally, who "have been abused and oppressed all their lives," leads her to oppose a newly passed law against giving food, clothes, or shelter to escaping slaves. Arguing with her husband, who supports the law on legal and economic grounds, she verbalizes what amounts to a general principle of caring—the Bible says we should feed the hungry, clothe the naked, and comfort the desolate, adding that "people don't run away when they're happy, but out of suffering." She becomes so intensely opposed to that "shameful, wicked, abominable" law that she vows to break it at the earliest opportunity. This episode may illustrate my claim that the empathic affects aroused in a particular situation, in relation to particular victims, may activate a general caring principle that transcends the particular victims. The principle may in turn serve as a premise for making the moral judgment that laws violating the principle are morally wrong.

Here is an example closer to home that illustrates several of the concepts I discussed. When writing a letter of recommendation for a former student, we may empathize with the student, to whom we feel close. When negative things about the student come to mind, we may feel tempted to exclude this information. Doing so, however, may activate our principle of being honest in relation to our peers (a variant of caring), which conflicts with our empathic concern for the student. We may resolve the conflict by withholding the negative information and simply tolerating the resulting guilt feeling. On the other hand, we may not only empathize with our student but also with our peer colleagues, who need an honest appraisal from us and have expectations that we will be truthful. This empathy with colleagues may activate our principle of not betraying a trust (another variant of caring). We may even go a step further and empathize with people whom we do not know at all and who will probably never see our letter but whose welfare may nevertheless be affected by it— namely, the other applicants for the job. This empathy for unknown applicants could activate not only caring but also justice principles, if these applicants were reviewed as possibly more deserving or needy than our student. Regardless of our final decision, the example shows how multiple empathizing can contribute to the complexity of moral judgment and conflict. It also shows how multiple empathizing may reduce the potency of our initial empathic bias in favor of a particular individual.

Here is an even more complex example adapted from an illustration used by Noddings (1984). In considering whether to sponsor a favorite graduate student's research proposal that requires deceiving subjects about the true purpose of the study, a professor might empathize with the student's pride in a well-written proposal and fear that months of work will be wasted if the proposal is rejected. This empathy may be strong enough to motivate the professor to approve the proposal. So far, there is no moral conflict. But the situation would be transformed into a moral conflict if deception in the research violated the professor's moral principles. An abstract, principled concern about deception might not be powerful enough motivationally to compete with the professor's empathy for the student, but the professor could penetrate the abstractness by thinking about subjects being harmed by the research—imagining, for example, how a hypothetical subject, perhaps someone he cares about, might respond to the experimental manipulation. If the danger perceived is great enough, the professor's anticipatory empathic distress might be more intense than his empathic concern for the graduate student. He might then make the moral judgment that to sponsor the student's research would be wrong and consequently refuse to do so. The anticipatory empathic distress might also activate the professor's principle that says one should care about others in general and the empathic affects associated with that principle. As a result, the professor may feel strongly motivated to propose guidelines for the control of all research that requires deception.

Finally, the professor might go yet a step further and empathize with other unseen, unknown groups whose welfare may be at stake—namely, other researchers whose careers could be jeopardized by excessive constraints on research or people in society who might ultimately benefit from the research. As a result of the multiple empathizing and the subsequent moral judgments, the professor might make any of a number of possible decisions. Whatever the outcome, the process illustrates, as does the letter-of-recommendation example, first, how one's initial empathic response may be biased toward individuals who are familiar and present and, second, how a more or less deliberate process of multiple empathizing may both reduce the bias and contribute to moral conflict complexity. This all sounds like traditional utilitarian moral reasoning: Consider the future as well as immediate consequences of one's action for people who are absent as well as present. But we should not lose sight of the role of empathy in providing both substantive input and motivation at various points in the reasoning process.

Summary

My aim in this chapter has been to demonstrate the possible role of empathy in a comprehensive moral theory and to point up the implications for socialization and moral education. To this end, I have argued as follows:

1. When one witnesses someone in distress, one may respond empathically—that is, with affect more appropriate to the other's situation than to one's own. More specifically, one is apt to respond with feelings of empathic or sympathetic distress, but depending on the available cues and one's prior knowledge about the victim, one may make certain causal attributions that transform these feelings into empathic anger or guilt.

2. The essential features of this bystander model, including the empathic affects it generates, do not require a victim to be physically present because humans have the capacity for representation and because represented events have the power to evoke empathic as well as direct affect. What is required is that a victim or a potential victim be imagined, as may occur when one is told or reads about someone's plight, is engaged in conversation or argument about moral issues, or makes moral judgments about other people's behavior in hypothetical situations. Occasions like these, although cognitively and motivationally more complex than most bystander situations, may arouse empathic affects in a similar way. In other situations, one's own actions are at issue, and when one acts or contemplates acting in a way that may affect other people's welfare, imagining the consequences for them may also arouse empathic affect. Many—perhaps most—moral encounters appear to involve victims and potential victims (and beneficiaries, although I focus on victims) and can be counted on to evoke empathic affects.

3. Empathic affects are by and large congruent with the principle of caring and with most forms of the principle of justice. Caring and justice are the prevailing moral principles in Western society and may be assumed to be the part of people's knowledge structures that are most often brought to bear in moral encounters. The content of these principles also makes them relevant, in varying degrees, to issues that involve victims. The moral principles may therefore be activated either directly because of the relevance of their content to the victim dimension of the moral encounter or they may be activated by the empathic affects initially aroused. Either way, the resulting co-occurrence of the empathic affect and moral principle creates a bond between them that is strengthened in subsequent co-occurrences. Moral principles, even when initially learned in cool didactic contexts, may in this way acquire an affective charge and take on the characteristics of a hot cognition.

4. An important implication of the hot cognition concept is that when a moral principle is subsequently activated even in cool, didactic contexts, empathic affect may be aroused. Another implication is that empathic affects aroused in moral encounters may have a stimulus-driven and a category-driven component. The category-driven component may have a heightening or leveling effect on the intensity of the stimulus-driven component in any given moral encounter. The overall result may be to help stabilize the individual's level of empathic affective reactions in different moral encounters over time.

5. Empathic affect may make important contributions to moral judgment and decision making. The contribution may be direct or it may be mediated by the moral principles that are activated by the empathic affects.

6. Although empathy may develop naturally in most humans, this development may be enhanced through socialization and moral education. Generalizing loosely from the research, I suggest that empathy is fostered by allowing children to experience a wide variety of emotions, by providing them with empathic models and with a lot of affection at home, by using inductive discipline in situations in which children harm others, and by giving children role-taking opportunities, especially in prosocial contexts.

Empathy's contribution to morality may be limited by empathic bias—bias in favor of familiar people and bias in favor of people who are present. These biases may be reduced to a tolerable level by socialization and by moral education that highlights the commonalities among human groups, places high value on impartiality, and trains people in the techniques of multiple empathizing—that is, empathizing not only with familiar people and people in the vicinity but also with strangers and others who may be affected by one's actions, although they are absent.

References

Hoffman, M. L. (1970). Moral development. In P. Mussen (Ed.), *Handbook of child psychology* (pp. 261–361). New York: Wiley.

Hoffman, M. L. (1975). Altruistic behavior and the parent-child relationship. *Journal of Personality and Social Psychology, 31,* 937–943.

Hoffman, M. L. (1978). Empathy, its development and prosocial implications. In C. B. Keasey (Ed.), *Nebraska symposium on motivation* (Vol. 25, pp. 169–218). Lincoln, NE: University of Nebraska Press.

Hoffman, M. L. (1983a). Affective and cognitive processes in moral internalization: An information processing approach. In E. T. Higgins, D. Ruble, & W. Hartup (Eds.), *Social cognition and social development: A socio-cultural perspective* (pp. 236–274). New York: Cambridge University Press.

Hoffman, M. L. (1983b). Empathy, guilt, and social cognition. In W. F. Overton (Ed.), *The relationship between social and cognitive development* (pp. 1–51). Hillsdale, NJ: Lawrence Erlbaum.

Hoffman, M. L. (1987). The contribution of empathy to justice and moral judgment. In N. Eisenberg & J. Strayer (Eds.), *Empathy and its development* (pp. 47–80). New York: Cambridge University Press.

Hoffman, M. L., & Saltzstein, H. D. (1967). Parent discipline and child's moral development. *Journal of Personality and Social Psychology, 5,* 45–57.

Hume, D. (1957). *An inquiry concerning the principle of morals* (Vol. 4). New York: Liberal Arts Press. (Original work published 1751.)

Kaplan, E. A. (1989). Women, morality, and social change: A historical perspective. In N. Eisenberg, J. Reykowski, & E. Staub (Eds.), *Social and moral values* (pp. 347–361). Hillsdale, NJ: Lawrence Erlbaum.

Lenrow, P. B. (1965). Studies in sympathy. In S. S. Tomkins & C. E. Izard (Eds.), *Affect, cognition, and personality.* New York: Springer.

Montada, L., Schmitt, M., & Dalbert, C. (1986). Thinking about justice and dealing with one's privileges: A study of existential guilt. In H. W. Bierhoff, R. L. Cohen, & J. Greenberg (Eds.), *Justice in social relations* (pp. 125–143). New York: Plenum Press.

Noddings, N. (1984). *Caring.* Berkeley: University of California Press.

Weiner, B. (1985). "Spontaneous" causal thinking. *Psychological Bulletin, 97,* 74–84.

Zahn-Waxler, C., Radke-Yarrow, M., & King, R. A. (1979). Childrearing and children's prosocial initiations towards victims of distress. *Child Development, 50,* 319–330.

CHAPTER 9

Ways of Knowing and Ways of Being: Epistemological and Moral Development in Undergraduate Women

Blythe McVicker Clinchy

Wellesley College

In Henry James' novel, *The Ambassadors,* a middle-aged man named Strether goes to Paris to convince the errant young son of a friend to return to the bosom of his conventional family in Massachusetts, but instead of performing his mission as instructed, Strether finds something admirable in the young man, struggles to understand him, and ultimately undergoes an alteration in his own vision. As the philosopher John Kekes (1984) points out, this is a story of moral development. It is similar to stories told by young women in interviews that my colleagues and I have conducted in an effort to understand women's conceptions of truth and value.

In this chapter, I will explore the relationship between epistemological and moral development among undergraduate women. My thoughts on these matters have been formed largely by two separate but related research projects: a longitudinal study in which Claire Zimmerman and I interviewed students annually during their four years at a women's college (Clinchy & Zimmerman, 1982, 1985a, 1985b), and a study involving extensive interviews with women from a wide variety of ethnic, social, and educational backgrounds, carried out with my colleagues in the Women's Research Collaborative (Belenky, Clinchy, Goldberger, & Tarule, 1986).

The research this chapter draws upon has been supported by the Andrew W. Mellon Foundation, the Spencer Foundation, the U.S. Department of Education Fund for the Improvement of Post-Secondary Education, the Carnegie Foundation, and Wellesley College.

Both of these studies owe much to Perry's (1970) scheme, which traces changes in conceptions of knowledge, truth, and value among Harvard students (mostly male) during the college years. The Clinchy-Zimmerman study was originally designed to test the applicability of Perry's scheme to a female sample, and questions devised to tap positions on the scheme were also included in the Women's Research Collaborative interview. Perry has been criticized for confusing two distinct lines of development—epistemology and commitment—within a single scheme, but my colleagues and I saw this as one of his many deep insights: that one's ability to venture upon new ways of being is intimately connected with one's ways of knowing.

And so, although epistemology remained at the heart of our inquiry, we also tried to explore our informants' ethical positions through the use of the following: (1) Lawrence Kohlberg's standard "Heinz Dilemma" interview (Kohlberg, Colby, Gibbs, & Speicher, 1978), in which the informant is asked to reason about a hypothetical situation involving a man whose dying wife might possibly be saved by a drug that costs more than he can pay (see Appendix, Chapter 10); (2) Carol Gilligan's standard interview exploring an actual moral conflict (Brown, 1988) in the informant's life; and (3) questions of our own design.

All three approaches produced some puzzling responses. Like other researchers, we found that many women disliked the Kohlberg task. Being "hypothetical," it seemed remote from their experience ("unreal, "academic," "just a game," as some women said), and it lacked the contextual detail they felt they needed to make a thoughtful judgment. I believe, too, that women dislike the task because it forces them to make a moral judgment about another person, and as has been noted before (Clinchy & Zimmerman, 1982; Gilligan, 1982), women are often reluctant to make such judgments. Many of the women we interviewed refused even to call Hitler wrong.

Most of our informants preferred Gilligan's actual moral conflict to questions about Heinz or Hitler. As this task requires them to describe a situation from their own experience, they possess the necessary contextual detail, and they need not make a judgment of anyone other than themselves. But asked to "describe a situation when you faced a moral conflict and you had to make a decision but weren't sure what you should do" (Brown, 1988), many women said they had never faced such a conflict or made such a significant decision. Some produced stories that did not seem to involve decisions. For example:

> I think a big moral dilemma for me would be if I ever got raped. . . . A lot of things would come rushing upon me. I would know that I myself was unchanged, that I am still the person I am. And yet it would be a big change. It would be an outside action coming in upon me, and it would be hard for me not to hate the individual who had raped me.

Responses of this sort both puzzled and disturbed us. These women seemed to have no sense of themselves as moral agents. They appeared to be incapable of exercising moral judgment or making moral choices, and they perceived themselves as powerless to affect others' convictions while attributing considerable power to others (for example, socializers and rapists) in shaping their own values.

I now see these responses in a different light. It is not that these women are deficient in moral understanding, but that the sort of moral understanding they have is not easily elicited by questions asking for choices and judgments such as "What did you decide to do?" and "Was it the right thing to do?" (Brown, 1988). Their moral understanding has to do not with "rightness" but with "goodness" or "virtue," in Iris Murdoch's (1970/1985) terms. "This alternative view," as Lawrence Hinman (1985) writes,

> is concerned with understanding virtues, with the cultivation of moral sensitivity rather than the development of a foolproof decision procedure for dealing with moral problems, and with the quality of an individual's entire life rather than with the assessment of isolated choices. (p. 64)

Choice is rarely at issue. As the philosopher John Kekes (1984) writes, "Most actions most of the time follow from the character of the agent. People normally do just the sort of thing they would do. Choosing an action is rarely and only exceptionally a conscious active process of deliberation" (p. 7). We do not usually make a choice so much as do what our present state of consciousness dictates. As one student said, describing her "decision" to marry, "I don't remember deliberating about that being right or wrong, because by the time I decided, I knew it was right. The other [options] didn't have any reality for me." Similarly, Ann Colby (1990) reports that the "living moral exemplars" whom she and William Damon have studied describe themselves as rarely making choices; rather, they did what they knew to be right and thus had to do. In Murdoch's (1970/1985) terms, we act out of a kind of "necessity," in "obedience" to the vision of reality we hold (p. 39).

Using this conception, responses that seemed baffling now make a kind of sense. For instance, if actions follow from character, then it is futile to make judgments about Hitler's actions, but it may be instructive to try to understand the nature and origins of his character and his vision of reality. And it is reasonable to worry about the way in which the experience of being raped might alter one's vision of reality and compromise one's virtue by instilling hatred.

I think that the notion of "contextual morality" (Tronto, 1987) put forth by Murdoch, Kekes, Hinman, and other contemporary philosophers is close to the implicit conception held by many of the women we have interviewed. These women find it hard to respond to our standard questions about morality because the notion of moral life as a series of choices does not fit their experience. An artful interviewer can coax these women into producing codable conflicts in response to standard questions, but these responses seem to tell us less about the women's moral development than do the "growth stories" they spontaneously generate in the course of an interview. These stories usually have to do not with critical decisions but with the discovery of new ways of being, usually embodied in people they care about.

These narratives can be seen as modest versions of the kind of growth story James tells in *The Ambassadors*. As Kekes (1984) says, the alteration in Strether is not in the particular values he holds. Moral development here does not consist in the substitution of new values for old. "Strether makes no significant choices; he decides very little. . . . His decision is not about choosing to do this or that, but about being the kind of person who is alive to moral possibilities" (p. 6). Strether becomes "the kind of person who is alive to moral possibilities," and this "aliveness" is what Kekes means by "moral sensitivity" (p. 6).

To become alive to moral possibilities, one must encounter a way of being that is both attractive and strange—different (but perhaps not too different) from the realities one has known. But the encounter alone is not enough. The way in which one deals with difference depends on one's epistemological position. In *Women's Ways of Knowing* (Belenky, Clinchy, Goldberger, & Tarule, 1986), we describe a series of epistemological positions that are built on Perry's positions although diverging in certain respects, especially in emphasizing people's conceptions of the source rather than the nature of knowledge and truth. In the rest of this chapter, I want to share some speculations about the ways in which each of these "ways of knowing" both allows and constrains the development of moral sensitivity and thus of new ways of being.

Received Knowledge and the Denial of Difference

Some of the students we interviewed arrived at college equipped with an unexamined set of values inherited, usually, from their parents. Students at this position take, as Perry (1970) says, a "dualistic" view of the world. Actions are absolutely right or wrong, and people are absolutely good or bad. The world is divided into two camps: "we-right-good" and "other-wrong-bad."

At first, these *received knowers* cling fiercely to their values. The theme of *resistance to change* was one of the most frequent themes that appeared in interviews that Zimmerman and I conducted with first-semester students and in weekly journals that the students kept during the same period. The friendships that students form at this point serve not to introduce the students to new possibilities but to affirm their old ways of being. Received knowers tend to assume that anyone who is part of their "we" is exactly like them, morally and in every other way. They assume that "they and their friends share exactly the same thoughts and experience. Young women who hold this perspective celebrate and magnify the experiences of similarities and intimacies with others" (Belenky, Clinchy, Goldberger, & Tarule, 1986, p. 38).

Initially, this denial of difference prevents the exploration of divergent realities; friends construct and solidify their relationships by sharing commonalities. Eventually, however, in the course of endless conversations, friends become aware of divergences in values. At first, they may maintain the relationship by agreeing to ignore the conflict. For example, a student we call Terry, who strongly disapproved of smoking, drinking, and taking drugs, discovered that her best friend was guilty of all these sins:

> We just never mention them. We have a ground rule: she will not smoke in my presence or drink or take drugs, nor will she discuss them with me. I know she does it; she knows I know, but that's it.

Terry can preserve the relationship only by excluding from it those aspects of her friend's behavior that are alien to her. She is not "alive" to her friend's divergent reality. But by insisting on maintaining the friendship rather than terminating it, as she says she would once have done, and by sustaining the awareness of moral discrepancy rather than denying it, Terry has, perhaps, taken a step toward moral sensitivity.

Ultimately, the security of these affectionate relationships makes it possible for the received knower to listen without anxiety and with respect to a friend's dissenting voice. For example, Valerie, a senior, recounted a conversation during her first year in college that stood out as a "turning point" in her thinking. At the time, Valerie believed, as her parents and teachers had taught her, that "abortion was a terrible sin," and she assumed that her friend agreed:

> I was pressing on about how wrong I thought abortion was and then my friend revealed that she had, in fact, had an abortion. Well, this was quite a revelation to me because she didn't look "abnormal" or "different." She was a good person whom I liked a lot. She seemed to function in life and was not obviously impaired by her past experience.

Unlike Terry, Valerie accepts the divergent view as a part of the loved person. She does not adopt it for herself, but she does hold it in consciousness, refusing to dismiss it or deny it. Valerie's story, like Strether's, is not about making a choice or coming to a decision; it is about an enlargement of vision: "I began to see that everything isn't black and white, right or wrong. Perceptions and values were suddenly different for different people, and their experience was not good or bad but simply was their particular experience." In our terms, Valerie was moving out of the *received knowledge* position and into a *subjectivist* perspective.

Subjectivism and the Two Enemies of Love

The subjectivist resolves conflicts between love and goodness by redefining goodness as "purely personal." Subjectivists see firsthand experience as the only reliable source of knowledge and value. Moral values are intuitions that are formed as the residue of experience; they are determined by one's particular circumstances.

Subjectivists refuse to make moral judgments. It is senseless to criticize someone else's moral standards because she did not choose them and cannot change them and because they are not, after all, a matter of reason but of experience. By reconstructing values as individual rather than as absolute, subjectivists manage to preserve both their values and their attachments. The core notion here is *subjective validity:* "I think that everyone's opinion is right for her." There is no universal wrong (except, perhaps, that it is wrong to call someone wrong); there is only disagreement. There are only multiple realities grounded in individual life histories.

Although subjectivists preach "openness," they actually practice a sort of aloof tolerance toward other points of view: They listen politely, but they do not really hear. In Murdoch's terms, they are unable to love. "Love," Murdoch (1970/1985) says, "is the extremely difficult realization that something other than oneself is real. Love . . . is the discovery of reality" (p. 51).

Subjectivists are prey to the two "enemies of love" that Murdoch describes. The first of these is social convention. Murdoch (1959) writes, "One may fail to see the individual . . . because we are ourselves sunk in a social whole which we allow uncritically to determine our reactions, or because we see each other exclusively as so determined" (p. 52). Although superficially individualistic, subjectivists are often quite conventional: Moral intuitions are based on personal experience, but personal experience is constrained by the standards of one's society. "I just kind of feel whether things are right or wrong," an undergraduate said, adding, "I think that my ideas about it are mostly like the norms." The subjectivist assumes that other people's values, like hers, are shaped by the standards of their societies, and so she fails to see what is unique to their moral vision and to hers.

The second of love's enemies is what Murdoch (1959) calls "neurosis" (p. 52). In using this rather harsh label, Murdoch does not mean to imply that the condition she has in mind is abnormal or unusual—indeed, she considers it all too typical. Psychologists might call the condition "egocentrism," and it is typical of subjectivism. Kohlberg and Gilligan (1971) report that when they asked an adolescent what was most real to her, she replied, "Myself." The subjectivist lives inside her own head. Although she acknowledges in theory the existence of other realities, only her own is real to her. She can only look out through this subjective reality; she cannot transcend it or detach herself from it.

Subjectivists perceive others in terms of themselves, "autocentrically," as the psychoanalyst Ernst Schachtel (1959) might say. This being so, other people's worlds seem to them either inscrutably foreign or identical to their own. In the first case, they remain aloof, fundamentally untouched by the other person's vision. Their conversations are like parallel play. In the second case, they intersect with the other only when the other's reality appears to match their own. The psychotherapist Maurice Friedman (1985) calls this latter process *identification,* giving as an illustration the inept therapist who "resonates with the experiences related by the client only to the extent that they resemble his or her own." He writes, "[Identification] says, in effect, 'I am thou,' but misses the Thou precisely at the point where its otherness and uniqueness takes it out of the purview of one's own life stance and life experience" (p. 197).

Sometimes, as in this case, subjectivism causes the person to see only a fraction of the other's reality. At other times, subjectivism results in *distortion* of the other's reality. The subjectivist may project herself into the other, seeing resemblances between her views and the other's views that would not be apparent to a detached observer. It is this distorting tendency that Murdoch (1959) calls "neurosis":

> We may fail to see the individual because we are completely enclosed in a fantasy world of our own into which we try to draw things from outside, not grasping their reality and independence, making them into dream objects of our own. (p. 52)

"Fantasy," she continues, "is the enemy of true imagination," and love— the discovery of reality—is "an exercise of the imagination." Love requires "the expulsion of fantasy" (Murdoch, 1959, p. 52). Many of the women we interviewed whom we saw as moving out of subjectivism were engaged in the expulsion of fantasy. They described themselves as awakening from a dream. For example, Minna, a deserted wife and mother of an 8-year-old daughter, had recently enrolled in a community college and was studying to be an occupational therapist. She told us that she had finally taken charge of her life after years of living "in a fantasy world." She said, "I was confused about everything. I was unrealistic about things. . . . You have to see things for what they are, not for what you want to see them. I don't want to live in a dream world" (Belenky, Clinchy, Goldberger, & Tarule, 1986, p. 99).

Procedural Knowledge and the Attainment of Moral Breadth

At the next step in development, the person turns toward the real world and so, in Murdoch's terms, moves toward "goodness." She undergoes a process Murdoch (1970/1985) calls "unselfing" (p. 84), achieving in Simone Weil's (1951) words "a way of looking" that is "first of all attentive. The soul empties itself of all its own contents in order to receive into itself the being it is looking at, just as he is, in all his truth" (p. 115). She learns procedures—in some cases, procedures prescribed by the disciplines she is studying—for "looking carefully" and "really listening." Naomi, for example, learned in an introductory art history course that although she "preferred to explain her responses to paintings in terms of herself—her background, moods, feelings and tastes— . . . the teacher deflected her attention from herself to the painting," insisting that she analyze it in terms of its characteristics—its composition, texture, and so on (Belenky, Clinchy, Goldberger, & Tarule, 1986, p. 89). Murdoch (1970/1985) quotes Rilke's comment that Cezanne "did not paint 'I like it,' he painted 'There it is'" (p. 58). Naomi learns to look at paintings as Cezanne looked at the objects he painted. With this new objectivity, the procedural knower is open for the first time to alternative visions of reality.

We identified two types of procedures—*separate* and *connected* knowing (Belenky, Clinchy, Goldberger, & Tarule, 1986; Clinchy & Zimmerman, 1985a, 1985b). Most of the procedural knowers we have interviewed seem to use both procedures, although they are often tipped more toward one method than the other, and at this point in development, they do not integrate the two.

Separate Knowing

At the heart of separate knowing is the *detachment* characteristic of critical thinking and scientific method. The separate knower keeps herself at a distance from the object she is examining. To avoid personal bias, she uses objective techniques of analysis and objective criteria of evaluation. Her approach is impersonal: She analyzes and evaluates a position—a moral position, for example—in its own terms, without regard to its creator.

Separate knowing often takes the form of an adversarial proceeding. Its primary mode of discourse is the argument. Separate knowers play what the writer Peter Elbow (1973) calls the "doubting game," which involves "putting something on trial to see whether it is wanting or not" (p. 173). They look for what is wrong with the position they are examining; they imagine opposing positions. For example, one young woman said, "As soon as someone tells me his point of view, I immediately start arguing in my head the opposite point of view. When someone is saying something, I can't help turning it upside down." And another said,

I never take anything someone says for granted. I just tend to see the contrary. I like playing devil's advocate, arguing the opposite of what somebody's saying, thinking of exceptions to what the person has said or thinking of a different train of logic.

Separate knowing seems especially relevant to the kind of moral development traced by Kohlberg and his associates (Kohlberg, 1984), which stresses rational justification and entails increasing abstraction, impersonality, and impartiality. Separate knowers, unlike subjectivists, believe that it is legitimate to make moral judgments of another person's behavior (and of their own). They do not think that "it's all relative." Some arguments are better than others, measured in terms of objective criteria. To judge the argument is not to judge the person. Because separate knowers distinguish between persons and their behavior (their arguments or their actions), they understand what Kohlberg means when he says that his coding scheme is to be used to score arguments, not persons.

Separate knowing has some of the characteristics required for moral sensitivity: It is selfless, objective, and attentive. Separate knowers scrupulously avoid projection—and, thus, Friedman's "identification"; they have succeeded in "the exercise of overcoming one's self" (Murdoch, 1959, p. 52) and in "weeding out the self" (Elbow, 1973). Although the separate knower's soul may "empty itself of all its own contents," it does not "receive into itself the being it is looking at"; it keeps its distance. The separate knower's attention is not the kind required for moral sensitivity. It is "just," but it is not "loving" (Murdoch, 1959, 1970/1985); it is primarily critical rather than receptive.

Connected Knowing

In our research, Zimmerman and I asked undergraduate women to read one of the quotations I used earlier to illustrate separate knowing ("I immediately start arguing the opposite point of view. . . . "), which we had excerpted from an interview done the year before, and we asked the women to tell us what they thought about it. Most of them said they didn't like it much and they didn't do it much. For instance, a woman we call Grace said that when she disagreed with someone she didn't start arguing in her head; she started trying to imagine herself in the other person's situation. She said, "I sort of fit myself into it in my mind and then I say, 'I see what you mean.'" She said, "There's this initial point where I kind of go into the story, you know? And become like Alice in Wonderland falling down the hole."

It took us a long time to hear what Grace was saying. At the time, her comment indicated to us not the presence of a particular way of thinking but the absence of any kind of thinking—not a difference but a deficiency. Now, we see it as an instance of connected knowing. As we go back over the interviews we have done with women over the years, we see it everywhere, and it is clear to us that many women have a proclivity toward connected knowing.

Here is an especially clear illustration of connected knowing from a college student named Priscilla:

> When I have an idea about something and it differs from the way another person's thinking about it, I'll usually try to look at it from that person's point of view, see how they could say that, why they think they're right, why it makes sense.

Now contrast this quotation with the ones illustrating separate knowing. When you play devil's advocate, you take a position contrary to the other person's, even when you agree with it, even when it seems intuitively right. Priscilla turns this upside down. She allies herself with the other person's position even when she disagrees with it. Priscilla is playing a version of what Elbow (1973) calls the "believing game." Instead of looking for what's wrong with the other person's idea, she looks for why it makes sense and how it might be right. As another student, Cecily, says, "If you listen to people and listen to what they have to say, maybe you can understand why they believe the way they do. There are reasons. They're not just being irrational." Cecily takes this approach not only to people but to philosophical texts:

> When I read a philosopher I try to think as the author does. It's hard, but I try not to bias the train of thought with my own impressions. I try to just pretend that I'm the author. I try to really just put myself in that person's place and feel why is it that they believe this way.

Connected knowing, like separate knowing, requires imagination, but the connected knower tries to "imagine the real"—to "make present," in Martin Buber's terms, the other's reality rather than to invent alternative realities (Friedman, 1985, p. 4).

Connected knowing is based on attachment rather than on detachment. One must treat the text, as another student put it, "as if it were a friend"—form an intimate relationship with it. In Buber's (1966) terms, the text is a "Thou," a subject, rather than an "It," an object of analysis. The heart of connected knowing is empathy, and empathy entails acceptance. While the separate knower doubts everything, the connected knower doubts nothing. She does not try to assess the validity of the perspective she is examining; she tries to understand it. The question is not "Is it right?" but "What does it mean?" The philosopher Richard Rorty notes that Anglo-American philosophy has been preoccupied with the question of validity–of how to determine the truth of a

proposition (Bruner, 1986, p. 12). He contrasts this with the equally important—and to him more interesting—question of how we make meaning of
experience. Connected knowers, like novelists and poets, are more concerned
with meaning than validity.

Connected knowers, although accepting, do not take things at face value.
Like separate knowers, they look beneath the surface. Cecily, for instance, says
she looks for "reasons" behind the other person's view. Priscilla wants to
know, she says, how the person's position "makes sense" and "why they think
they're right." But the reasons that these women search for are different from
the reasons that separate knowers seek. Cecily does not demand that the other
person support or justify her position; she asks only that the person explain,
articulate, or make her position clear. In many cases, when a woman says she
wants to know why someone thinks as she does, she means: What is the history of the idea? What in this person's experience has led to the idea? She
wants to share that experience and to know the story behind the idea. "The
focus," as Elbow (1986) writes, "is not on propositions and validity of inferences but on experiences or ways of seeing" (p. 261). In the psychologist
Jerome Bruner's (1986) terms, connected knowing often makes use of the narrative mode, while separate knowing makes use of the paradigmatic or analytic
mode. Although the development of concepts of justice or "moral rightness"
seems to be helped by argument, the development of moral sensitivity or
"goodness" seems to depend on the sharing of stories that reveal new ways of
seeing and of being. To appreciate the texture of moral life, Kekes (1984) says,
"one must start with how a person sees the situation in which he is to act. Sensitive perception is the heart of the matter" (p. 7). This is where the connected
knower starts. She believes that to understand what a person is saying, one
must adopt the person's own terms. One must not judge others in terms of
one's own beliefs.

Connected knowing, like separate knowing, is selfless and, in this sense,
objective. When we asked college women the question "Why be objective?"
they often replied that to help a friend, one had to be objective. Suppose,
Priscilla said, that your friend is considering an abortion:

> You might find that extremely horrifying, but you have to be objective in
> the sense of looking at it in terms of the relationship of the problem to her
> and not to you. . . . I think you have to really look at it in terms of her
> situation and in terms of what *she* really wants to do. I mean, help her fig-
> ure out what *she* wants, rather than tell her what *you* want for her.

This is a peculiar definition of objectivity, entailing the adoption of
another person's subjectivity rather than the disinterested stance of an impartial observer "from no position in particular" (Shweder, 1986, p. 172). Like

Gilligan's (1982) "care" orientation, in contrast to Kohlberg's (1984) "justice" orientation, connected knowing is partial and biased. Connected knowing builds on the subjectivist's doctrine of subjective validity—the notion that beliefs are determined by personal experience and that "experience can't be wrong." But the connected knower's approach is drastically different from the subjectivist's; far from being mired in her own subjectivity, she can to a degree float right up out of it and into other people's heads.

Connected knowers, like subjectivists, cannot make moral judgments, but for different reasons. It is sometimes difficult to distinguish between subjectivists and connected knowers on this point, but it is important. The connected knower has crawled right inside the perspective she is attempting to understand. To make a judgment about that perspective, she would have to climb outside it and, in the opinion of many women, above it, because judgment implies superiority. She would have to break the connection.

Among the quotations Zimmerman and I asked undergraduates to consider was one taken from an interview with the writer Frances Fitzgerald that appeared in *Vogue* several years ago. In the quotation, Fitzgerald lists some of the behaviors she finds intolerable (such as failing to do what you say you will do) and ends by remarking that she cannot help but feel "morally alienated" from people who exhibit such behaviors. On the whole, we agreed with Fitzgerald's statement, but very few of the students did. Most of them virtually ignored the list of behaviors, fastened on the phrase "morally alienated," and indignantly denied that they ever felt this way. They seemed to think that it was immoral to feel morally alienated from one's fellow humans. For example, Fran said:

> I think I'm a good empathizer in that if I were to sit there with someone in his or her jail cell and have a discussion—who knows? Maybe I would be able to see their point of view. I might not be able to agree, but I might be able to see that this person's background or parents or environment had been particularly stressful, and I could understand that. And I would not feel superior. I don't think I could give you many examples of when I would feel morally above or separate from someone else to the extent that I wouldn't make the attempt to understand.

Fran's reluctance to judge is not based on the subjectivist's hands-off policy of relativistic tolerance. Subjectivists tolerate other people's visions; connected knowers explore them. Subjectivists want to leave other people alone. Fran does not want to leave the person alone in his or her jail cell; she wants to enter his or her mind. Judgment is to be avoided not because—or not merely because—it involves inflicting one's own standards on others, but because it interferes with the process of understanding.

Perhaps we can sympathize with Fran and even endorse her attempt to understand the hypothetical prisoner, but what if she were sitting in that jail cell with one of the white adults who threw rocks at black schoolchildren during the integration of the Boston schools? Would she feel empathy with them? Would we? Perhaps we would not, but the comments of several of Fran's classmates suggest that she might. For example, Jacqueline said that although she thought that "it was wrong to beat a child just because he's black," she felt "uncomfortable" judging the person who committed the act. "I don't like to say he was morally right," she said, "but—let's say I'm entering the guy's mind. Now he probably thinks that what he is doing is okay." Jacqueline invokes the doctrine of subjective validity, but something more seems to be involved; subjectivists do not speak of entering other people's minds.

This brings us to what Zimmerman and I came to call the "convince Hitler problem." Whenever our interviewees asserted the standard of subjective validity, we tried to test the limits of their reluctance to judge by asking whether they believed Hitler was "right." Often they said that although they thought he was wrong, this was just their opinion; they would not be able to convince him that he was wrong. We found this response not only puzzling, but irritating. Who cares, we asked each other, whether you can convince Hitler he is wrong?

Why do these women care? What is it they are trying to say? Cecily tries to explain:

> Ninety-nine percent of the "civilized" world doesn't look upon what he did as right, and I myself do not. But, trying to judge it as objectively as possible, it was what he considered to be the right thing, so for him it was morally right. Whether it is for me or not isn't—I don't know if that's the question. . . . My judgment is colored by my culture. . . . You can't just say, "Well, I'm right and he's wrong." You're making a judgment that's not really yours to make. You can have an opinion, but you can't just have such prejudice that you can't change your mind about anything. If that's the way it was, nobody would be able to change their minds about anything.

Cecily seems to be saying that moral judgment is beside the point: "I don't know if that's the question." Connected knowers believe that Hitler's actions proceeded from his consciousness. Like Kekes (1984), they believe that a person's behavior depends on his perceptions, or as Murdoch (1970/1985) says, "true vision occasions right conduct" (p. 64). One cannot change Hitler's consciousness—cannot convince him that he is wrong—because his consciousness is a product not of reason, but of life history. In this context, moral judgment becomes pointless name-calling.

But moral judgments are not merely futile: They are dangerous, not so much to the person who is the object of judgment, but to the person who makes the judgment. An "opinion" can easily become a "prejudice." If you look at a friend's problems from the friend's point of view, Priscilla said, "it makes you more sensitive. You're not always just thinking of your way, but letting your mind open up to other points of view and considering other things, rather than just assuming your way is absolute." What is at stake is the connected knower's newfound "objectivity," her capacity to enter into new realities, her habit of "just and loving attention" (Murdoch, 1970/1985), and her "moral breadth" (Kekes, 1984). In refusing to judge Hitler, Cecily awkwardly but firmly holds the two enemies of love at bay: She resists defining his behavior in terms of her own or her society's norms, and she insists on trying to discover his "reality." In so doing, she protects her own developing capacity for transformation and her ability to "change her mind." If we play the believing game, we can see that there is something right about Cecily's refusal to judge Hitler.

But surely there is also something wrong with it. Hitler *was* wrong. If we switch to the doubting game, putting Cecily's response on trial, we can see that something is wanting in it. For instance, where are the Jews? They do not figure in Cecily's ruminations. And where, for that matter, is Cecily? She has no "opinions"; opinions are prejudices.

The constriction of Cecily's vision is a consequence of the limitations of *empathy* as a means of understanding. The sort of empathy practiced at the procedural level is the sort described by Friedman (1985), involving "transposing oneself into the other":

> One brackets or suspends one's awareness of oneself . . . in order better to understand the other . . . . Empathy (in the narrower sense) and identification are both very limited means of understanding . . . and for the same reason; both rely on only one side of the relationship. Empathy attempts to get over to the other while leaving oneself; identification tries to tune in to the other through focusing on oneself. (pp. 197, 201)

The very empathy that allows Cecily to enter Hitler's reality imprisons her within that reality. She cannot examine Hitler from her own perspective. Trapped behind his eyes, she sees only what he sees, and from this vantage point the Jews are invisible. The psychologist Robert Hogan (1973) identified a group of people who scored relatively high on a measure of empathy and relatively low on a measure of autonomy. The behavior of these "overempathizers" suggests, Hogan says, that "unleavened role-taking can produce an equivocating jellyfish as well as a compassionate person with a broad moral perspective" (p. 224). Connected knowers sometimes look like equivocating jellyfish, clones, or chameleons, even to themselves. For example, Adrienne, in her first year at college, laments:

> It's easy for me to take other people's points of view. It's hard for me to argue, sometimes, because I feel like I can understand the other person's argument. It's easy for me to see a whole lot of different points of view on things and to understand why people think those things. The hard thing is sitting down and saying, "Okay, what do *I* think, and why do *I* think it?"

In psychology it has been customary, at least until recently, to see empathy as the enemy of autonomy. And, indeed, when one listens to procedural connected knowers like Adrienne, this supposition seems reasonable. But our longitudinal observations suggest a different hypothesis. Consider Adrienne's comment in her second-year interview:

> All through high school I had one or maybe two close friends, and even they didn't know me very well. Here at Wellesley I have really, really close friends who know me very well. They know the way I feel, 'cause I make my feelings felt to them. And at first I felt, "My God, I'm becoming—I'm not me anymore. I'm not thinking my own ideas anymore." I was becoming very affected by other people's opinions and ideas. And at first that really bothered me. But I've come to realize that the only way you can become a person with real ideas that are independent is when you've seen as many as you possibly can, and then make a decision, your own decision, based on those that you've seen. And the only way you can really do that is through experiencing numerous people.

Hogan himself suggests that overempathizing is in some cases a transitory developmental phenomenon, which dissipates when excessive empathy is balanced by a subsequent growth in autonomy. Adrienne's development might look like this from the outside; it does not look like this to her. She sees her autonomy as emerging out of empathy, not in spite of it; she sees empathy as prerequisite to autonomy. As the philosopher Sheila Mullett (1987) says, "What is paradoxical . . . is that we acquire a truer sense of self only when we forget about the self and focus upon others with this particular attitude of interest and care for them apart from ourselves" (p. 319). "Overempathizing," from this point of view, can be seen as a kind of "growth error" (Bruner, Olver, & Greenfield, 1966), necessary although not sufficient for the development of the capacity to construct one's own knowledge and beliefs. But the procedural knower has not yet developed this capacity. She has achieved Kekes's "moral breadth," an appreciation of the diversity of ways of being, but she has not yet achieved "moral depth." Immersed in the reconstruction of other people's realities, she is not yet able, as Adrienne finally is, to use other people's visions to construct her own. At the next developmental position, other people's realities will become genuine possibilities for her.

Constructed Knowledge and the Attainment of Moral Depth

Our understanding of this developmental position is still sketchy, partly because of its complexity and partly because of the paucity of data; few of the women we interviewed had reached it. Rita, whom we saw annually from her first through her final year in college, is one of the few. Like many of the students we interviewed, she began her college career with a subjectivist conception of truth and then moved into procedural knowledge, with a bent toward connected knowing. However, by her senior year, she made it clear, as few did, that she could construct her own opinions, using and even integrating both separate and connected procedures. To paraphrase the psychologist Robert Kegan (1982), although once Rita had "been" her procedures, now she "had" procedures.

In her final interview, Rita, like Cecily, tries to understand Hitler's reality, but she also stands outside it. She holds it up for judgment and finds it wanting. Rita includes the Jews in her construction of the Hitler issue, and she includes herself. She thinks—indeed, she knows—that Hitler was wrong:

Hitler didn't realize that the people he was killing were real people. I don't think Hitler realized that other people existed that were as real as he was. They were just pawns in his imagination. He did not accept the fact that they were real.

Procedural knowers use connected procedures in attempting to understand a position; they turn to separate knowing to evaluate the position. Rita integrates the two procedures. She constructs her own understanding of Hitler's behavior and uses it as the basis for her judgment. She attributes Hitler's actions, in part, to a deficiency in connected knowing: If Hitler had been a connected knower, the Holocaust might never have happened. Hitler's flaw is a lack of moral imagination. Rita sees it as a lack of objectivity. "Goodness," Murdoch (1970/1985) says, "is a form of realism" (p. 58). It is this kind of goodness that Rita thinks Hitler lacks.

In our interviews with Rita over the years, we can trace her own struggle to achieve this kind of goodness—to become, as she puts it in senior year, more "objective," more capable of "seeing the realities." In an interview two years earlier, she had said that interpretations of poems were "purely subjective." Now, although recognizing that an interpretation is inevitably influenced by "the interpreter's way of looking at things," she is scornful of critics who use their interpretations "as an excuse to get their own ideas off the ground," and she measures the quality of an interpretation in terms of "how closely it accepts the text for what it is, how much the critic has really accepted the author's opinions as real."

Rita remembers a time when the only thing that was really real to her was herself. As she says, "I was so caught up in my own identity crisis that I didn't really realize [my friends] were real people and were just as present as I was." She has learned that you must treat a friend as you should treat a text: "Accept the person as very real, very independent of your existence. You're not using him for your convenience or your reinforcement."

Through a process of "unselfing," Rita transcended the "neurosis" of identification—Elbow (1973) calls it "projection in the bad sense"—and achieved empathy with her friends and even, to a degree, with Hitler. But now she has gone beyond empathy to practice "projection in the good sense" (Elbow, 1973, p. 171): Instead of suppressing the self and ignoring her own experience, she uses her own experience to construct her understanding of other people's realities. She uses her understanding of herself, for example, to construct an understanding of Hitler. And she judges him not by his own standards or by conventional norms, but by standards she has induced from her own experience. Although Rita now feels able, as she did not in earlier years, to stand outside Hitler and judge him, she does not totally detach herself from him. He is not utterly alien to her because she has felt in herself what she sees in him: For her, as for Hitler, other people were once pawns of the imagination. Rita thus avoids both the danger of blindness to the other's reality, inherent in separate knowing, and the danger of "self-denial" (Ruddick, 1980) inherent in connected knowing.

Rita's insistence on realistic perception—on the expulsion of fantasy from judgment—makes it clear that her interpretation and evaluation of Hitler's behavior are based on projection in the good sense, not the bad sense. Friedman (1985) calls it "inclusion." Unlike identification and empathy, inclusion embraces both self and other:

> In contrast to both empathy and identification, inclusion means a bold imaginative swinging "with the intensest stirring of one's being" [Buber] into the life of the other so that one can, to some extent, concretely imagine what the other person is thinking, willing, and feeling and so that one adds something of one's own will to what is thus apprehended. (p. 198)

Inclusion preserves identity and facilitates its development:

> A person finds himself as person through going out to meet the other, through responding to the address of the other. He does not lose his center, his per-

sonal core, in an amorphous meeting with the other. If he sees through the eyes of the other and experiences the other's side, he does not cease to experience the relationship from his own side. (p. 199)

It is this active experiencing of both sides of the relationship that Adrienne seems to be trying to describe: While "experiencing numerous people," she also "makes her feelings felt."

I think that it is only when one becomes capable of inclusion that one attains genuine moral sensitivity. Through empathy, one can achieve Kekes' (1984) "breadth of moral understanding," the understanding of realities that are unique and distinct from one's own, but these realities do not become possibilities for one's self until one brings one's own unique self into active engagement with them. This is what Kekes calls "depth" of moral sensitivity and Mullett (1987) calls "edification":

> The capacity to be moved, to be inspired or to receive strength from the qualities we discern in people with whom we are in relation. We become aware of qualities in others which we can develop in ourselves. . . . Appreciation of forms of goodness becomes a form of personal practice. The varieties of goodness which such a person cares for are seen not as something "out there" separate from self, but as genuine possibilities for the self. (p. 320)

In this passage, Mullett seems to portray moral development as occurring through a series of one-sided encounters between solitary individuals actively contemplating essentially passive objects of beauty, truth, and virtue. Similarly, most of Murdoch's (1970/1985) illustrations involve the contemplation of art and of nature, which are less likely than people to talk back to the observer. In one extended illustration involving a woman's struggle to achieve a more generous and accurate perception of her daughter-in-law, Murdoch, to simplify the exposition of her point, asks us to assume that the daughter-in-law does not change over time. But both Mullett and Murdoch are aware that in real life, relationships are reciprocal rather than unilateral and dynamic rather than static.

For our constructed knowers, moral development evolves in this more interactive fashion, through a type of dialogue that we have called "connected conversation" and our informants call "real talk" (Belenky, Clinchy, Goldberger, & Tarule, 1986). In real talk, each participant is an active subject; each speaks as well as listens, trying to articulate her own perspective as well as eliciting others' perspectives. Together, the participants construct new perspectives. As the psychologist James Youniss (1983) says, "One person does not come to understand another by mentally imagining what it might be like to be in the other's shoes," for, as the philosopher Elizabeth Spelman (1988) puts it, "if I only rely on my imagination to think about you and your world, I'll never come to know you and it" (p. 179). "Rather," Youniss says, "common perspectives are co-constructed through discussion" (p. 39). Perhaps the development of moral sensitivity is more accurately described as taking place between individuals, rather than within them.

Participants in real talk offer each other "confirmation" rather than mere acceptance:

> Neither empathy, in the strict sense, nor identification can really confirm another person, since true confirmation means precisely that I confirm *you* in your uniqueness and that I do it from the ground of my uniqueness as a really other person. Only inclusion, or imagining the real, can confirm another; for only it really grasps the other in his or her otherness and brings that other into relationship to oneself. (Friedman, 1985, p. 201)

The confirmation is mutual, with each participant "making the other present" (p. 4). Confirmation can promote growth in a way that mere acceptance cannot. Confirmation, like acceptance, involves what Carl Rogers (1951) calls "unconditional positive regard": There are no strings attached. But confirmation means "accepting the whole potentiality" of "what you are meant to become" (Buber, 1966, p. 181). One confirms the other not only in her present reality but also in her possibility.

For the constructed knower, judgment and understanding are no longer incompatible: "Often the most direct confirmation is to take a stand in opposition to the disclosures of the other" (Friedman, 1985, p. 136). Arguments are admissible—indeed, essential—in the context of real talk, and disagreement signifies not condescension but genuine respect.

> The beginning of all human relationships . . . is "I accept you as you are." But that does not mean I confirm everything you do just because you do it. That would be putting aside the reality of the relationship, the reality of myself as a person confronting you. It is not that I judge you from above or that I moralize at you. Yet our very relationship is a demand on you as on me. I have to come to you from where I am in my uniqueness. I cannot make myself a cipher in order to help you. To confirm the other is only possible within the relationship itself, insofar as the other can communicate his self or her self to you and you can experience both his and your own side of the relationship. (Friedman, 1985, p. 137)

Mutual confirmation takes place over time in the context of evolving relationships. These relationships both promote and require moral sensitivity. Each participant becomes increasingly "alive" to the possibilities for herself and for the other in an "infinitely extensible work of imaginative understanding of two irreducibly dissimilar individuals" (Murdoch, 1959, p. 52). Each participant feels obliged to explore her own potentiality through the "intro-spection" that Mullett (1987) defines as "a caring attention to self-in-relation," which "can only be attained by reflection upon ourselves within specific rela-tionships" (p. 321). An observer may mistake the constructed knower's pro-clivity toward introspection as subjectivist self-absorption, but it is quite dif-ferent. The subjectivist cannot look at herself; she can only look through herself. She cannot see herself in relation to others.

Constructed knowers see themselves not only in relation to friends but in relation to the larger community, and this relationship, too, places demands on them. Constructed knowers, more than any other group we studied, feel obliged to act on the moral visions they have constructed and to help establish in the wider world the sort of community they have helped to create in micro-cosm in their personal relationships. They are, as we say in *Women's ways of knowing*, "a refreshing blend of idealism and realism" (Belenky, Clinchy, Gold-berger, & Tarule, 1986, p. 152). "Seeing the realities," they know what the world is like, but they also dream of a more livable world, and they will work to make the dream come true.

Acknowledgments

Many friends and colleagues, in innumerable "connected conversations," have helped me to think about the issues explored in this chapter. I thank especially Claire Zim-merman, Mary Belenky, Nancy Goldberger, Jill Tarule, and Annick Mansfield.

References

Belenky, M. F., Clinchy, B. M., Goldberger, N. R., & Tarule, J. M. (1986). *Women's ways of knowing: The development of self, voice, and mind.* New York: Basic Books.

Brown, L. M. (Ed.). (1988). *A guide to reading narratives of conflict and choice for self and moral voice.* Cambridge, MA: Harvard University Graduate School of Education, Center for the Study of Gender, Education, and Human Development.

Bruner, J. S. (1986). *Actual minds, possible worlds.* Cambridge, MA: Harvard University Press.

Bruner, J. S., Olver, R. R., & Greenfield, P. M. (1966). *Studies in cognitive growth.* New York: Wiley.

Buber, M. (1966). *The knowledge of man: A philosophy of the interhuman.* New York: Harper & Row, Torchbooks.

Clinchy, B., & Zimmerman, C. (1982). Epistemology and agency in the development of undergraduate women. In P. Perun (Ed.), *The undergraduate woman: Issues in edu-cational equity* (pp.161–181). Lexington, MA: D. C. Heath.

Clinchy, B., & Zimmerman, C. (1985a, July). *Connected and separate knowing.* Paper presented at the eighth biennial meeting of the International Society for the Study of Behavioural Development, Tours, France.

Clinchy, B., & Zimmerman, C. (1985b). Growing up intellectually: Issues for college women. *Work in Progress, 19.*

Colby, A. (1990, November). *Case studies of living moral exemplars.* Paper presented at the Murray Center Colloquium Series, Cambridge, MA.

Elbow, P. (1973). *Writing without teachers.* London: Oxford University Press.

Elbow, P. (1986). *Embracing contraries.* New York: Oxford University Press.

Friedman, M. (1985). *The healing dialogue in psychotherapy.* New York: Jason Aronson.

Gilligan, C. (1982). *In a different voice: Psychological theory and women's development.* Cambridge, MA: Harvard University Press.

Hinman, L. (1985). Emotion, morality, and understanding. In C. G. Harding (Ed.), *Moral dilemmas* (pp. 57–70). Chicago: Precedent.

Hogan, R. (1973). Moral conduct and moral character: A psychological perspective. *Psychological Bulletin, 70,* 217–232.

Kegan, R. (1982). *The evolving self.* Cambridge, MA: Harvard University Press.

Kekes, J. (1984). Moral sensitivity. *Philosophy, 59,* 3–19.

Kohlberg, L. (1984). *Essays in moral development: Vol. 2. The psychology of moral development.* San Francisco: Harper & Row.

Kohlberg, L., Colby, A., Gibbs, J., & Speicher, B. (1978). *Standard form scoring manual.* Cambridge, MA: Harvard Graduate School of Education, Center for Moral Education.

Kohlberg, L., & Gilligan, C. (1971). The adolescent as philosopher: The discovery of self in a postconventional world. *Daedalus, 100,* 1051–1086.

Mullett, S. (1987). Only connect: The place of self-knowledge in ethics. In M. Hanen & K. Nielsen (Eds.), *Science, morality and feminist theory* (pp. 309–338). Calgary, Alberta, Canada: University of Calgary Press.

Murdoch, I. (1959). The sublime and the good. *Chicago Review, 13,* 42–55.

Murdoch, I. (1985). *The sovereignty of good.* London: Routledge & Kegan Paul. (Original work published 1970.)

Perry, W. G. (1970). *Forms of intellectual and ethical development in the college years.* New York: Holt, Rinehart, & Winston.

Rogers, C. (1951). *Client-centered therapy.* Boston: Houghton Mifflin.

Ruddick, S. (1980). Maternal thinking. *Feminist Studies, 6,* 70–96.

Schachtel, E. G. (1959). On two basic perceptual modes. In *Metamorphosis* (pp. 81–84). New York: Basic Books.

Shweder, R. A. (1986). Divergent rationalities. In D. W. Fiske & R. A. Shweder (Eds.), *Metatheory in social science: Pluralisms and subjectivities* (pp. 163–196). Chicago: University of Chicago Press.

Spelman, E. V. (1988). *Inessential woman: Problems of exclusion in feminist thought.* Boston: Beacon Press.

Tronto, J. C. (1987). Beyond gender difference to a theory of care. *Signs, 12,* 644–663.

Weil, S. (1951). Reflections on the right use of school studies with a view to the love of God. In S. Weil (Ed.), *Waiting for God* (pp. 105–116). New York: Harper Colophon Books.

Youniss, J. (1983). Beyond ideology to the universals of development. *Contributions to Human Development: On the Development of Developmental Psychology, 8,* 31–52.

CHAPTER 10

Research on Moral Judgment in College Students

James R. Rest

University of Minnesota

Research on moral judgment has been active for decades, and several thousand studies have been published. This chapter summarizes the research findings that are particularly relevant to college students and points out the implications for moral education.

Six conclusions are especially noteworthy from this literature:

1. Dramatic and extensive changes occur in young adulthood (the 20s and 30s) in the basic problem-solving strategies used to deal with ethical issues. That is, the basic assumptions and perspectives by which people define what is morally right or wrong change in this period, and the change is just as dramatic and fundamental as change in the years before puberty.

2. These changes are linked to fundamental reconceptualizations in how the person understands society and his or her stake in it. The changes are not merely attitudinal fluctuations that vary with passing fads and fancies.

3. Formal education (years in college or professional school) is a powerful and consistent correlate with this change. Development continues as long as a person is in a formal educational setting but plateaus when the person leaves school. In short, college is tremendously powerful in promoting development of moral judgment.

4. Deliberate educational attempts (formal curriculum) to influence awareness of moral problems and to influence the reasoning or judgment process can be demonstrated to be effective. Students in moral education courses show more gain than students in control groups. Furthermore, some of the largest gains in moral education programs have come with participants in their 20s and 30s, showing more gains in these older students than in school-age students.

5. We are beginning to understand the impact of cocurricular and extracurricular activities. In fact, in most students, cocurricular and extracur-

201

ricular activities may be more important than the formal curriculum. Most students do not take explicitly moral education or moral philosophy courses. Yet most students show a dramatic gain in moral judgment over their college years.

6. Studies link moral judgment with actual, real-life behavior. Scores on psychological tests of moral judgment are significantly and consistently correlated with behavior.

Methods of Assessing Moral Judgment

The defining issues test (DIT) is the instrument of moral judgment most extensively used with college and adult populations. The DIT is a multiple-choice instrument. It can be handed out in large groups in which people mark little circles with #2 pencils on printed answer sheets, and then the answers can be fed to an optical scanner for reading and scored by computer. Currently, the DIT is being used in about 50 colleges and universities for assessing the impact of higher education. The DIT has six stories; each story presents a moral problem. Following each problem, 12 issues are presented. The subject is asked to consider each issue and pick the issues that are most important in deciding what ought to be done in the story. The Appendix shows one story and one set of items of the DIT.

Changes with Age and Education

In the chapter introduction, I assert that important changes in ethical development are occurring in young adults in their 20s and 30s and that these are linked to formal education and to increasing cognitive complexity. A number of different studies are relevant here. One line of evidence comes from cross-sectional studies. Here, comparisons are made, say, between college freshmen and advanced graduate students (Pascarella & Terenzini, 1991). The assumption is made that differences between such younger groups and older groups indicate developmental change. A number of recent large-scale secondary analyses of several thousand subjects each indicate that age-educational differences account for about 40% to 50% of the variance in moral judgment scores (Rest, 1986). Change in adulthood is dramatic; although sex is a trivial variable, accounting for less than 0.5% of the variance, education is 250 times more powerful (Thoma, Rest, & Barnett, 1986).

A second line of evidence comes from longitudinal studies. Here, the same subjects are followed over the years and are retested at periodic intervals. In a 20-year longitudinal study by the Harvard group (Colby, Kohlberg, Gibbs, & Lieberman, 1983) and a 10-year longitudinal study by the Minnesota group (Rest, 1986), significant changes are seen from high school into adulthood.

Figure 10.1 plots data from the 10-year longitudinal study on 102 subjects from the Minnesota group. DIT scores are indicated on the vertical axis, and time of testing is on the horizontal axis. The three lines, "high," "moderate," and "low," represent groupings by the amount of college education the subjects received. The P-score is a measure of the relative importance a subject gives to principled considerations. Subjects with 4 years or more of college are grouped as high. Subjects with 2 to 4 years of college are grouped as moderate. Those with no college or less than 2 years of college are grouped as low. As can be seen, the high group continues to gain over testings, and the other groups either plateau or drop over time. Although the high education group had higher DIT scores in high school, over time with differences in education, the groups become increasingly different. If we adjust for initial differences in high school, education accounts for 12.3% of the variance of DIT scores in young adulthood. Therefore, comparisons of subjects attending college with those not attending college show divergent paths of development over time: Gains in moral judgment are related to attending college. These data show that people are changing the way they make moral judgments long into adulthood. Moral development does not stop with the onset of puberty or before then. The college years are a time of dramatic change.

Figure 10.1. Results of the Minnesota group study.

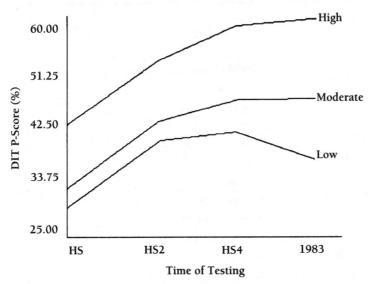

HS, high school; HS2, 2 years beyond high school; HS4, 4 years beyond high school; 1983, 10–11 years beyond high school.

Source: Rest, J. *Moral Development: Advances in Theory and Research.* New York: Praeger, 1986.

Changes in Moral Judgment and Conceptual Capacity

The typical college student is not thinking like a moral philosopher. As Table 10.1 indicates, the average college student has a DIT score in the 40s, but moral philosophers have DIT scores in the 60s. There is about as much difference in scores between college students and moral philosophers as there is between junior high school students and college students. This means that the concepts that are operational for college students in making moral judgments are not inevitably like those of moral philosophers. A lecture on ethics that does not take into account the level of conceptualization of the students in the class is not likely to be understood or appreciated by them. Ethical instruction that disregards the conceptual frameworks of students and that assumes either too much or too little cognitive sophistication is likely to seem artificial or irrelevant to the student.

Are the changes merely superficial fluctuations in attitudes and styles of talk or do they reflect more fundamental reconceptualizations of the social world and one's understanding of one's place in society? Is thinking like a

Table 10.1. Average P-Scores on the DIT for Various Groups

P-Score (%)	Group
65.2	Moral philosophy and political science grad students
59.3	Liberal Protestant seminarians
52.2	Law students
50.2	Medical students
49.2	Practicing physicians
47.6	First-year dental students
46.3	Staff nurses
42.8	Grad students in business
42.3	College students in general
41.6	Navy enlisted men
40.0	Adults in general
31.8	Senior high school students
23.5	Prison inmates
21.9	Junior high school students
18.9	Institutionalized delinquents

philosopher any better or any more advanced than not thinking like a philosopher? Two lines of evidence bear on this issue: one that involves a correlational strategy and a second that involves experimental manipulation. The correlational strategy is to determine if people with so-called higher development on psychological tests of moral thinking such as the DIT or Kohlberg's (1984) moral judgment interview also have higher scores on other measures of problem solving and cognitive complexity. Presumably, if only people who are developmentally advanced on other measures are the ones who have high scores on moral thinking, then it seems reasonable to assume that high scores on moral thinking indicate developmental advance. It turns out that this is the case (Rest, 1983). A more focused version of this correlational strategy is to test the capacity to comprehend specific kinds of moral argumentation and then to ask whether the ideas that a person uses in deciding among moral choices are related to the cognitive capacity to understand more complicated moral ideas. A series of replicated studies show that people who do not use "high stage" moral reasoning in making moral decisions tend not to understand those ideas; people who do understand higher stage ideas tend to use them in decision making (Rest, 1983).

The second strategy used to address the question of the meaning of changes in developmental scores involves experimental manipulation. Here, the assumption is that if change in developmental scores is superficial and attitudinal only, then scores on these tests should be easy to manipulate (both upward and downward). But if change in developmental scores is not superficial but reflects deep-seated, fundamental reconceptualizations of the social world, then test scores should not be so easily manipulatable (that is, not manipulatable *upward* according to the cognitive developmentalist's view, although if development is cumulative, then scores can always be faked *downward*, because presumably one has the capacity to recognize "childish" thinking—old forms of thinking that have been discarded). A series of studies shows that it is difficult to fake upward but easy to fake downward (Rest, 1983, 1986). The evidence is that upward movement is slow and difficult, which is consonant with the view that the test scores are reflecting fundamental reconceptualizations of one's social world.

Moral Education Programs

Recently, we published a meta-analysis of over 50 moral education studies using the DIT (Schlaefli, Rest, & Thoma, 1985). The studies involved pretesting and posttesting the treatment groups on the DIT and comparing the gains of the treatment groups with the gains of the control groups. Several questions

are of interest here: What about deliberate attempts to influence moral judgment development? Can you speed it up with moral education programs?
More specifically, what works with whom?

    Treatments can be divided into four groups:

1. *Dilemma discussion* involves a case approach; controversial cases are discussed by groups. People get lots of practice in moral problem solving here.
This is an inductive approach, not a didactic approach.

2. A second kind of intervention is called *personality development:* This
kind of intervention includes deliberate psychological education programs
developed here by Norm Sprinthall and Lois Erikson and elsewhere by Ralph
Mosher. The activity here involves some sort of experiential learning project
coupled with a reflective seminar. "Learning by doing" is a phrase often used.
What one learns about oneself in doing these activities is blended with what
one learns generally about psychological theories in the seminars.

3. A third kind of intervention is called *academic.* These are the traditional,
didactic courses in church history, humanities, social studies, history, and eco-
nomics.

4. The fourth kind, called *short term,* is simply interventions that last less
than 2 weeks and have only a few hours of intervention.

The results show that the first group, dilemma discussion, produced the
greatest effects, followed by the personality development treatment. Academic
and short-term treatments did not have significant effects. Furthermore, we
found that the older groups (adults postcollege) gained more than the younger
groups (junior high school students).

    We also looked to see how the effectiveness of the programs related to how
long the program lasted. As mentioned before, if the treatment was very short
term (that is, 2 weeks or less), there were no gains on the DIT. But we wanted
also to look at whether really long programs produced more gains than
medium-length programs. If we grouped programs that last from 2 to 12 weeks
into a medium group and programs that last more than 12 weeks into another
group, we could find no advantage in having a program longer than 12 weeks.
Somewhat to our surprise, we found that the longer programs were no more
effective than the medium-duration programs. Perhaps subjects grow tired of
moral education past 12 weeks. Perhaps interventions need to shift gears after
10 to 12 weeks and attempt something very different from what goes on in the
first part of the program. Perhaps artificial stimulation is effective for just limited periods of time and a subject needs to rest and consolidate after intensive
stimulation and growth.

Influences Beyond the Formal Curriculum

One line of research is focused on finding out what—in ordinary life (outside deliberate moral education programs)—seems to be promoting development in moral judgment. After all, not everyone in college takes a moral education course or a moral philosophy course, yet students in general show big gains in college. To study this, we conducted intensive interviews with subjects about their life experiences and their interests and attitudes. After gathering this interview material, we tried many different ways to characterize and code this material. Variables important to moral judgment are called academic or career orientation, continued intellectual stimulation, career fulfillment, political awareness, and civic responsibility. To give you some idea of what kinds of things these variables are, some excerpts follow.

Academic Orientation

The first variable is coded as academic orientation, and the following are examples of high and low codes.

Examples of High Codes
1. I really enjoyed the academic support groups and the professors. I liked many of my classes. I liked to be in the academic atmosphere. You would go and you would talk to interesting people about interesting things. Life just seems higher pitched. I like that atmosphere.
2. I was in the honors program. That was really good training. I had good grades, about a 3.7 approximately. I studied real hard especially right before a test. I enjoyed living on campus because there were always people around to do something with, something to talk about.

Examples of Low Codes
1. I was always undecided. I never had a major. Somebody would tell me, "Hey, this is an easy course," and I'd take it. I took a little of everything, mostly entry-level classes. I never applied towards anything. [*Interviewer:* How did you spend your time?] I didn't do much. I worked a little. I was living at home and probably worked half the week. I was doing a lot of drugs at the time. And I did a lot of partying. Hence the effect on my GPA. They weren't particularly happy or productive years. There isn't anything that sticks out in my mind that was really enjoyable.
2. I went to college right after high school. I was sort of forced to by my folks. I didn't particularly want to, but parental pressure dictated. I

went to a college close by my home. I figured that's as good a place as any. I never had a major. I eventually dropped out. I'd go for a quarter or two, then take a quarter off, and then go back the next quarter. All the time I was going to college, I didn't really have any interest in it, and I was just more or less buying time, and I didn't study.

Career Orientation

Of course, not all people who graduate from high school go to college. In our longitudinal study, we found college students' academic orientation paralleled the way that noncollege subjects oriented toward their work. We called this code career orientation, with the following examples representative.

Example of High Codes
My first responsibility was just to make sure the electrical jobs got installed. Then I got into computer programming. I really blossomed there. I got a good understanding of electricity. I guess I learned a lot about computers and about electronics, and it got to a point where I was actually doing, like, engineering training. I started putting in a lot of hours again. . . . I'm fairly intelligent and can use my brain, and I wanted to do something that I could use my brain and physically do something for people.

Example of Low Codes
At first when I got out of high school, I worked in an office and thought that being in an office would be all right, but it was just a bore anyway. Then I went into factory work because I knew there was money in that. You get paid nothing unless you really had a good education, which I didn't have. Where I am working now is a real drag, but it is good money. That is what I'm after. I just want my paycheck, and the rest of my life is my time and I'll do with it what I want. I enjoy what is *after* work. Work is not my highlight in life. I don't want to stay where I am. I'll let my husband do the work. That's the way I see it.

Continued Intellectual Stimulation

Another code, continued intellectual stimulation, characterizes the extent of intellectual stimulation provided by one's environment. For instance, a person who goes to college and secures a professional job that involves many challenges would be coded high. A person who went to college but then worked in a stifling job would be coded lower. A person who worked in a routine job in a factory would be coded very low. Examples of high codes are not difficult to imagine. These include people in both academic settings and work settings.

Examples of Low Codes
1. I get bored easy. Most of the jobs that I had were for a couple of months here, a couple of months there. I get bored real easy with what I'm doing. I don't like to get stuck in a rut. All those places I worked until I couldn't go no higher.
2. All I do is stay home with the baby. With a small baby, you don't get a chance to meet people. I don't go out except to the grocery store.

From this interview material, we have tried to find out what kinds of life experiences are related to gains on the DIT. We have found that the experience code academic orientation correlates highly ($r = 0.50$) with later DIT scores in young adulthood even after controlling for differences in DIT scores in high school. Similarly, continued intellectual stimulation and the other codes are highly predictive of who gains in moral judgment and who does not. These experience codes together produce a multiple regression r of 0.70 predicting to moral judgment scores in young adulthood (late 20s). The experience codes account for 26% of the variance of DIT scores in young adulthood above and beyond that accounted for by high school DIT scores (Deemer, 1986).

The picture that emerges from interviews with 102 subjects in our 10-year longitudinal study is the following: The people who develop in moral judgment are those who love to learn, who seek new challenges, who enjoy intellectually stimulating environments, who are reflective, who make plans and set goals, who take risks, who see themselves in the larger social contexts of history and institutions, and who take responsibility for themselves and their environs. The high gainers receive support and encouragement to continue their education and their development. They are stimulated by their social milieu, are asked to do interesting things, and are rewarded for their accomplishments.

What is striking about this analysis is the general and diffuse level at which we found it necessary to characterize experience. When we looked at many specific experiences (e.g., particular course work, specific travel, specific living arrangements, specific work experiences), we could find no consistent patterns of experiences related to moral judgment gains. Likewise, we found no evidence that moral judgment development was triggered by specifically moral leaders, moral crises, or moral causes. Moral judgment seems to be part of general social development on a wide, broad base. And broad-spectrum aspects of the social environment, such as atmosphere, general intellectual stimulation, and supportive social milieu, seem to be critical.

It would seem, therefore, that for colleges to facilitate the moral judgment development of students, colleges need to be concerned with these aspects of the student experience. It is not sufficient for students to read books, to attend formal course offerings, or to be aware of the achievements of their professors. What is important to moral judgment development is the social interrelationships of students, the general atmosphere of the institutions they attend, and their involvement in college activities.

Behavior

This point deals with the relationship of internal psychological processes as assessed through various tests to real-world, actual behavior. Several hundred studies have now been reported on this relationship; however, the matter is complex and subject to various interpretations. In general, two basic facts seem reasonably well established:

1. There seems to be a consistent link between the tests of moral judgment and behavior beyond the test setting.
2. The strength of the association is not high, implicating the interplay with other as yet unmeasured factors.

Behavior has been assessed in various ways. Some of the different kinds of behavior assessed in these studies include delinquency/nondelinquency, school problems, ratings of medical interns on clinical performance, promise keeping, compliance and conformity, distribution of rewards, cheating on school tests, voting in the 1976 presidential election, and public policy issues. Consistent and significant relations with DIT scores have been found in all these variables.

See Blasi (1980) for a review of about 100 studies and Thoma, Rest, and Barnett (1986) for a review of more recent studies. One of the most provocative studies has been done by Sheehan, Husted, Candee, Cook, and Bargen (1980). The researchers found that test scores from the DIT predicts to clinical ratings of medical interns in their overall performance as doctors. Whereas course grades and aptitude tests for medicine do not predict clinical performance, moral judgment does.

It should be pointed out that the strength of the correlations of moral judgment with behavior are consistently significant but are not usually very high (typically in the 0.3 to 0.5 range). The point of view of the group at Minnesota is that the production of moral behavior involves the interplay of at least four major kinds of processes. Some recent studies have pursued this assumption by simultaneously assessing more than one process at a time (one at a time has been the usual kind of study), and this has resulted in significant increases in the predictability to behavior (Rest, 1986). The major point, however, is that moral judgment as studied in the Piaget and Kohlberg traditions seems to be an important component in determining ethical behavior—and worthy of focus for educational programs in professional schools—yet there are other components to address in research and in educational programming.

The educational relevance of the research that links the DIT with behavior is that if an educational experience can show that it has produced gains in moral judgment, then those changes are worthwhile and the program can claim to have had an effect on life beyond the classroom itself. In contrast, we note that there is hardly any empirical evidence that course exams predict to anything outside the course. So much of school life has a dubious connection to anything beyond the school. But as DIT scores do demonstrate this link, educators have a way to claim the worthwhileness of their educational experiences for students.

References

Blasi, A. (1980). Bridging moral cognition and moral action: A critical review of the literature. *Psychological Bulletin, 88,* 1–45.

Colby, A., Kohlberg, L., Gibbs, J., & Lieberman, M. (1983). A longitudinal study of moral judgment. *SRCD Monograph 48*(4).

Deemer, D. (1969). *Life experiences and moral judgment development.* Unpublished Ph.D. dissertation. University of Minnesota, Minneapolis.

Kohlberg, L. (1984). *Essays on moral development: Vol. 2. The psychology of moral development.* San Francisco: Harper & Row.

Pascarella, E., & Terenzini, P. (1991). *How college affects students.* San Francisco: Jossey-Bass.

Rest, J. (1983). Morality. In P. Mussen (Ed.), *Manual of child psychology* (Vol. 3, pp. 556–629). New York: Wiley.

Rest, J. (Ed.). (1986). *Moral development: Advances in research and theory.* New York: Praeger.

Schlaefli, A., Rest, J., & Thoma, S. (1985). Does moral education improve moral judgment? A meta-analysis of intervention studies using the Defining Issues Test. *Review of Educational Research, 55,* 319–352.

Sheehan, T., Husted, S., Candee, D., Cook, C., & Bargen, M. (1980). Moral judgment as a predictor of clinical performance. *Evaluation in the Health Professions, 3,* 393–404.

Thoma, S., Rest, J., & Barnett, R. (1986). Moral judgment, behavior, decision making, and attitudes. In J. Rest (Ed.), *Moral development: Advances in research and theory* (pp. 133–175). New York: Praeger.

Appendix: Defining Issues Test

Heinz and the Drug

In Europe a woman was near death from a special kind of a cancer. There was one drug that doctors thought might save her. It was a form of radium that a druggist in the same town had recently discovered. The drug was expensive to make, but the druggist was charging ten times what the drug cost to make. He paid $200 for the radium and charged $2,000 for a small dose of the drug. The sick woman's husband, Heinz, went to everyone he knew to borrow the money, but he could only get together about $1,000, which is half of what it cost. He told the druggist that his wife was dying and asked him to sell it cheaper or let him pay later. But the druggist said, "No, I discovered the drug and I'm going to make money from it." So Heinz got desperate and began to think about breaking into the man's store to steal the drug for his wife.

Should Heinz steal the drug? (Check one.)

_____ Should steal it   _____ Can't decide   _____ Should not steal it

IMPORTANCE:

Great	Much	Some	Little	No	
					1. Whether a community's laws are going to be upheld.
					2. Isn't it only natural for a loving husband to care so much for his wife that he'd steal?
					3. Is Heinz willing to risk getting shot as a burglar or going to jail for the chance that stealing the drug might help?
					4. Whether Heinz is a professional wrestler or has considerable influence with professional wrestlers.
					5. Whether Heinz is stealing for himself or doing this solely to help someone else.

Great	Much	Some	Little	No	
					6. Whether the druggist's rights to his invention have to be respected.
					7. Whether the essence of living is more encompassing than the termination of dying, socially and individually.
					8. What values are going to be the basis for governing how people act toward each other.
					9. Whether the druggist is going to be allowed to hide behind a worthless law that only protects the rich anyhow.
					10. Whether the law in this case is getting the way of the most basic claim of any member of society.
					11. Whether the druggist deserves to be robbed for being so greedy and cruel.
					12. Would stealing in such a case bring about more total good for the whole society or not?

From the list of questions above, select the four most important:
Most important _____   Second most important _____
Third most important _____   Fourth most important _____

_____

Source: Rest, J. Development in Judging Moral Issues. Minneapolis: University of Minnesota Press, 1979.

CHAPTER 11

Young Adults, Mentoring Communities, and the Conditions of Moral Choice

Sharon Daloz Parks

Harvard University

Becoming an adult in the modern world is a complicated affair. A challenging, hazardous path awaits the young man or woman who seeks to contribute responsibly to society, to pursue a good livelihood, and to build emotionally satisfying relationships anchored in a meaningful sense of self and the world. Maps offered earlier by psychological theory and other sources of cultural lore and wisdom are insufficient in the face of the chasms that have now yawned open on the path toward mature adulthood.

Today's young adult must cope with a series of gaps: the gap between the limited preparation provided by a bachelor's degree and the educational demands of a global and technological age; the gap between the relatively simple set of life-style choices offered to earlier generations and a dizzying array of possibilities opened up by ease of travel, a global economy, and a reexamination of gender roles; the gap between the desire for meaningful work (and adventure) and the difficulty of finding work of any sort that offers more than a chance to be a mere cog in someone else's machine; and the gap between the erosion of the expectations of upward mobility previously assumed by anyone with "a good education" and the wildly lucrative options now open to an elite few. Meanwhile, vocations that directly serve the public good lose ground in their capacity to promise a stable and rewarding future (Bok, 1988), and an increasing number of lower-class young adults seem to face a forced choice between poverty and the criminal economy.[1]

If the "work" side of the passage into adulthood seems overwhelming, the "love" side offers bleak promise of an easy alternative. As a consequence of the profound historical-cultural upheavals now upon us, the young adult faces a host of barriers that inhibit movement toward adult intimacy and belonging.

214

Although one may wonder if it hasn't always been this way, I suggest it has not. Issues of relational identity may now be more difficult to resolve, and composing a supportive intimacy with another may be more difficult to achieve and maintain. Family, kinship, and neighborhood bonds are less easily presumed. Even ethnic and national identities become more complex in an increasingly global culture. The path toward adulthood becomes for many a labyrinth of relational dead ends, vocational wanderings, moral bewilderments, and philosophical-faith gropings as the social structures, values, myths, and moral assumptions that served as guiding wisdom in an earlier age are now under review or have been jettisoned altogether.

These broad descriptions of the dynamics of self and culture are embodied in young adult lives. As I write, I see, for example, the faces of "Jeff," a young man of 29, and "Lisa," a young woman of 25. Lisa was raised on the Eastern seaboard of the United States, and Jeff was raised on the West Coast. Both Jeff and Lisa are notably attractive, bright, likable, and socially sophisticated. Both have professionally successful parents who care about their children. Jeff attended college and hoped to play professional sports. Lisa graduated from a prestigious university and hoped to work abroad. Each has been thwarted in their vocational hope, and neither seems to have found their niche.

Both Jeff and Lisa suffered the divorce of their parents before they were 15, and neither has had positive, significant, and sustained relationships with adults other than their parents. Although Lisa and Jeff functioned well through their early 20s, Jeff is now an alcoholic and Lisa flirts with both alcoholism and anorexia. Jeff's girlfriend just abandoned him, and Lisa recently left her boyfriend after he beat her. Both continue to receive emotional and economic support from their parents (who agonize over whether they are "doing the right thing" in continuing to provide financial resources), but neither Jeff nor Lisa has a stable, positive social network beyond their families—although each has lived outside the family home for several years. Both of them seem to be floundering at sea, resentful of their dependence on their parents but unable to sight any alternative mooring.

The stories of Jeff and Lisa bear unique features, but their underlying dynamics are not atypical. Jeff and Lisa represent a host of other young adults who share their dissatisfactions: jobs that are only marginally satisfactory and relationships (or a series of relationships) that lead to a sense of routine dullness or stalemated stress rather than delight.

Reflecting on these young adult lives, I am haunted by the awareness that not only young adult lives are at stake: The ongoing viability of a culture is tested by its capacity to nurture and receive its young into adulthood. Young adulthood is the locus of the renewal of culture in every generation (Erikson, 1964, p. 126). Building on constructive-developmental perspectives and my own empirical observation and research, I contend, therefore, that although attention to any single dynamic cannot account for the loss of meaning and vibrancy in a particular human life or society, nevertheless, there is a dynamic that is insufficiently recognized when we try to discern the needs, treatment, and/or education of young adults or assess the strength of the fiber of our social fabric. This crucial and underrecognized dynamic is the young adult's appropriate dependence on mentors and on a mentoring community.[2]

A mentoring community is a form of social belonging that is grounded in a shared understanding of self and the world and that beckons and anchors the future promise of a young adult life, particularly in terms of his or her vocation—his or her potential relationship with and contribution to the larger society. Typically, a mentoring community is wider and often other than the family of origin and is centered and nourished by at least somewhat older adults (or an adult) who by the character of their lives and action provide confirmation of the young adult self as well as direction toward the future. Such a mentoring community can play an essential and vitalizing role in the young adult life.

Young Adulthood

Elsewhere, I have described young adulthood as a new era in the human life span (Parks, 1986). Following Kenneth Keniston (1960), I have likewise argued that the phenomena of ambivalence, indecision, wariness, and a consequent "inability to settle down" that we observe in the lives of many who are in their 20s and perhaps early 30s cannot be adequately understood in terms of prolonged adolescence, moratorium, or mere transition. Rather, just as cultural developments in an earlier period gave rise to what we now term "adolescence," another reordering of culture has given rise to "young adulthood." Young adulthood is a postadolescent period. One becomes a young adult when the primary task of adolescence has been achieved: the composing of a self-consciously reflective self. The young adult has gained a self-reflective identity and a capacity for critical thought and is prepared to take responsibility for the relationship of self and the world.

In his definition of identity, Erik Erikson (1963) linked identity and vocation—a correspondence between a sense of self and a place in society. Indeed, forming a self and securing a role in adult society were once perceived as a single task, but for many young adults this is no longer the case. Lisa and Jeff and a host of others like them have achieved a self-reflective identity and the capacity for critical thought, but that does not mean that they can envision that self as a related and contributing member of the adult world. Lisa, for example, can reflect critically on who she is, who she is not, and who she does and does not want to be. Yet the task of finding a fitting connection between that self and the roles and relationships accessible in the adult world as it is presented to her still remains. Thus, for Lisa and for most of her generation, finding a place where one can responsibly contribute as an adult to society has become a separate, second task—the task of young adulthood.

Vocation

This task is best described as the formation of vocation. The word vocation connotes the *relation* of self and the world. To have a vocation is to have more than a position, a job, a role, or even a career that one arbitrarily chooses on the basis of personal preference or inclination because one is forced to answer the perennial questions posed to the self: What are you going to do when you grow up? How are you going to earn a living or otherwise secure a livelihood?

Vocation depends on relationship. Rooted in the Latin, *vocare,* to call, it connotes a sense of being beckoned or invited, and it requires a response. Vocation conveys the sense of a meeting. It has been said that the deepest sense of vocation is found when "the heart's deep gladness meets the world's deep hunger" (Buechner, 1973, p. 95). Thus, the question of vocation is larger than the question of self-fulfillment. Vocation is a profoundly moral question; embedded in the issue of vocation is a question of the good: What is good for myself and for my world? Any response to this question affects both the self and others. Thus, the question of vocation can be neither posed nor answered by the self alone. Vocation conveys a sense of being called to a relationship and to an interdependence that is larger than the self. Saying yes (or no) to a beckoning vocation is an act of moral choice.

Potential and Vulnerability

When a readiness for vocation initially emerges, the young adult stands in a place of extraordinary potential and extraordinary vulnerability. This paradox becomes particularly vivid when we set the young adult's search for vocation within the larger activity of making meaning, an activity that lies at the core of human being. It has been said that what an organism does is organize and what the human organism organizes is meaning (William G. Perry, quoted in Kegan, 1982, p. 11). We are beings who require a sense of the connections between things; we seek to make sense out of the disparate, discrete features of our every day, and still not satisfied, we continuously compose meanings by which we may understand the whole of our environment—the cosmos—in which we dwell. We are inveterate seekers of patterns of order and significance, and our survival is threatened when these patterns of meaning are too seriously disturbed. Indeed, when our patterns of meaning are disrupted, we become dismayed and disoriented; unless we are able to recompose a sense of meaning, we become finally dysfunctional.

When educators and others who work with young adults prepare to teach moral understanding and the capacity for moral choice, they often presume that what is needed is exposure to moral philosophy and ethical thinking. I contend that it is equally if not more important to ask: How is this young adult, who is daily facing moral choices and seeking a sense of vocation, composing his or her sense of self and the world? How is this young adult making sense of life? How is this young adult making meaning?

Meaning, Faith, and Moral Choice

Constructive-developmental psychology, rooted in the genius of Jean Piaget, traces this pattern-making activity across the life span. Contending that "knowledge" is located neither in the person nor in the environment but rather in a composition arising from the interaction between them, Piaget attended to the underlying logic of thought as it develops in children. His insights are being extended into the study of adolescents and adults by theorists such as Kohlberg, Selman, Fowler, Perry, Gilligan, Kegan, Belenky, Clinchy, Goldberger, and Tarule. Each of these theorists takes seriously the nature of the composing mind (or better, the composing person) and the character of the environment with which the person is composing his or her sense of self and the world. James Fowler (1981) and his associates were the first constructive developmentalists to call attention to the full scope and significance of this meaning-making interaction. Linking this understanding of the composing of self and the world to a dynamic understanding of "faith," we are beginning to see that human beings not only seek to make sense of self and the world but also of the most comprehensive domain we can imagine: the cosmos and all of its component parts—the material, physical, emotional, and spiritual dimensions of life intuited as a whole.

It is this sort of meaning making—the composing of meaning in its most comprehensive dimensions—that we refer to when we speak of faith. Faith (when it is not confounded with a narrow understanding of belief) is the activity of composing a sense of or a conviction about all that is most ultimate and intimate. Faith is formed by one's deepest sense of what is true, trustworthy, and dependable—whether it is named in secular or religious terms. Human beings must compose, for better or for worse, some sort of a faith to live by. In this sense, faith is not something that only religious folk have; faith is something that all human beings do. Thus, as Kegan (1980) also has recognized, when we speak of a faith or a religious dimension of the Piagetian paradigm, we are not adding something to its periphery; rather, we are recognizing something at the heart of the paradigm—the interaction, the relation, the motion—that is the ongoing creation of life itself (p. 409).

The composing of meaning in these most comprehensive dimensions—this activity of faith—is intimately linked with the conditions of moral action.

Kohlberg was the first to explore deeply the implications of Piagetian thought for moral reasoning. He did not claim that a given capacity for moral reasoning would determine moral action. It can be argued from a faith development perspective, however, that the composition of a person's faith will determine his or her moral behavior. Human beings do act in a manner that is consistent with what we ultimately know, trust, and depend on, irrespective of what we may merely espouse.

Now, remembering that faith as we are using it here is the composing of meaning in its most comprehensive dimensions, we can begin to understand better that the one question we want to ask in relation to young adults as they search for the ground of moral choice and a sense of vocation is: What is the faith that conditions their moral, life choices, and how is it composed? The latter part of this question directs our attention to a new strength in the young adult—a strength that is also a new vulnerability.

Critical Thought

The young adult who has developed a self-reflective identity and the capacity for critical thought has undergone a shift in the "locus of authority" (Fowler, 1981, pp. 244–245). In adolescence, authority is located outside the self in the conventions of one's environment (note that in this sense, a punk hairdo may be regarded as conventional). As one moves through adolescence toward young adulthood, however, one may begin to recognize competing and conflicting claims to truth and find that it is no longer possible simply to adhere to the truth of an assumed authority (whether parent, peer, or "priest"). One may begin to recognize that everyone is composing a sense of "reality," conditioned by time, place, and circumstance. If so, one will begin to seek a way of making meaning that is not merely received from others but is a composing of truth more closely aligned with one's own experience of things (Belenky, Clinchy, Goldberger, & Tarule, 1986). Authority is no longer simply located outside the self. The self begins to be included in the arena of authority—the self thus develops a new strength. This move constitutes the emergence of critical thought and signifies the onset of young adulthood.

In contrast to reflective thought, which can emerge in early adolescence, critical thought is the capacity to stand outside one's own thinking and to critique the presuppositions of one's conventional world. This capacity, essential to a fully responsible adulthood, may be manifest in the young adult as wariness and ambivalence. For the young adult now has the strength to critique both self and the world, can doubt the self, and can if necessary stand over and against the conventional world. The corresponding development is a capacity to envision and to dream—to imagine the world as it could be and the self as it could become.

Herein lies the potential of young adulthood: a new capacity to see the world as it is, as it is not, and as it might become. This is the capacity to compose a critical and potentially positive, prophetic faith. Every movement for social reform depends, in part, on young adult souls and their capacity to critique and to dream. Such critical passion is often evident in the chronicles of world events and is celebrated, for example, in the stage production of *Les miserables*. This story portrays the young adults in France who, as faithful harbingers of the ideals of the French revolution, sing of "a world about to dawn" and a "night that ends at last." It is a young woman who is the first to die in the crossfire between established forces of oppression and the yet naive but valiant, inspired hope of a new generation. As poignant and more contemporary are the young adult martyrs of Tienanmen Square.

Vulnerability, Authority, and Mentorship

Within this capacity to be inspired also dwells, however, the vulnerability of the young adult. When we look carefully at the dynamics of young adult lives, we discover that the shift in the locus of authority from without to within is a two-step process. It is not a simple shift from dependence on others "out there" to an equilibrated sense of a trustworthy self "within." (This is especially true when one must begin to take responsibility for composing a faith to live by—a sense of what is ultimately true and dependable.) Instead of a simple shift from dependence to inner dependence, it appears that there is a shift from dependence on an assumed, conventional authority outside the self to a new form of authority—one still located outside the self but different in an important way. Rather than simply giving unreflective allegiance to a source of authority outside the self, one now *depends on an authority that one has "chosen"*—because that authority makes more sense than other possible candidates. Authority is now centered in a new relationship between choice and dependence. Thus, young adulthood is the appropriate time for dependence on and thus vulnerability to a mentor, guru, or guide.

This means that the potential of the young adult capacity to compose meaning, faith, and vocation depends in part on accessibility to an appropriate mentor. An appropriate mentor is one who recognizes and honors the potential of the young adult, while pointing the way and providing trustworthy support toward the fulfillment of that potential (Daloz, 1986).

It is significant that neither Jeff nor Lisa has a mentor. Both of them are critical thinkers; both of them are, as best they can, confronting the limits of their conventional world. And both of them are increasingly alone. They are like the caterpillar which makes its way to the end of a branch and then reaches out, out, in every direction but cannot find anything to support its further travel. With great resentment, both Lisa and Jeff are going back whence they came, going back to their families in which they function as adolescent children. Imagine their anger, frustration, sense of failure, and despair! Lisa drifts from her room at home to visits with friends, from one semisatisfactory job to another. Jeff now drifts from a treatment center to the streets, from bar to apartment to an uninspired job. Neither of them has connected with a mentoring adult "out there" who recognizes their potential and beckons them into a viable pattern of meaning, faith, and vocation.

Each of them does have a counselor, someone who provides regular contact with an adult outside the family (albeit someone they have to pay to listen to them). Some counselors serve a mentoring function, holding the hope of a young adult's life as it unravels and helping it to be rewoven in a stronger form. However, for both Jeff and Lisa, their counselors—who do serve important, even crucial functions—are nevertheless limited in their ability to mentor. Both of them represent the past rather than the future. Lisa has sought out her former high school counselor in her home town. Jeff's counselors at the treatment center and the leadership at the halfway house he resists consulting are all oriented to his alcoholism—his past and his failed present—rather than to vibrant images of a viable future.

Where do young adults in our culture find mentors? In graduate school, once you have committed yourself to a program, a professor may become a mentoring figure. In industry, a master craftsperson or supervisor might see your potential and initiate you into the refinements of the trade. If you are an athlete, a coach may link his or her life with yours. In the corporate business world, a senior manager may spot you and give you the support and cues you need to make your way up the ladder. But what if you are not yet committed to studies, to a trade, or to a particular business or profession? What if no one appears? Or, what if, like Jeff, a crucial injury blocks your path into professional athletics? Where and how is the yet uncommitted young adult mentored into the promise of his or her life? Who will confirm, hold, and beckon the promise of a young adult life, while not yet knowing its potential form? Who conveys the message: "There is a world that needs you"? Who enables young adults to fulfill their potential to serve as a renewing force in the ongoing transformation of culture?

Mentoring Communities

Each of these questions—and especially the last—points toward the importance of our recognizing the power of mentoring communities. Indeed, like all other human beings, young adults are social creatures. To be sure, human beings need the autonomy and agency so salient and celebrated in American culture as a mark of adulthood, but we never outgrow our need to belong, to be connected, and to be in relation. Each of us needs a "network of belonging" (Parks, 1986, pp. 61–62). Constructive-developmental psychology assists us in recognizing that this ongoing motion of interaction between self and other—the interaction that we are—requires an "other."

Robert Kegan (1982) describes this truth by appropriating the metaphor of a "holding environment" (p. 116). In the journey of human becoming, we always require a "home," a context in which the self may continue to become (Parks, 1989). I have discussed elsewhere the implications of Fowler's attention to the evolving "bounds of social awareness" and the insight that as we grow and develop the forms of our belonging also undergo transformation (Parks, 1986, pp. 61–69, 89–96). This recognition of a fundamental need for belonging whose forms change over time suggests that just as the young child requires the presence of a parenting other and the adolescent requires a peer group that serves as an enlargement of both family and self, the young adult requires a particular sort of sociality, belonging, and community. The young adult requires a mentoring community. What I mean by this is that the young adult requires a sociality that by its very character confirms and beckons the promise of the young adult life. Such a network of belonging is constituted not only by other young adults but also by a mentor or mentors—older adults who, less by admonition than by example and encouragement, offer images of the future that attract and anchor the emerging potential of young adults.

Jeff and Lisa still reach out for company with a larger world in whatever contexts are accessible to them. For Lisa, this means staying in touch with a couple of friends from her university days and then going out to join the "club scene" after work or in her free evenings—a practice that meets her need for connection but unfortunately also fosters an alcoholic dependence, particularly when she is lonely and seeking solace and when the community that the club scene offers is generally superficial at best. If Jeff and Lisa had more viable access to social contexts in which there was a positive mixture of generations engaged together in activity that was both enjoyable and significant, each might have better access to the meaningful adulthood for which they most deeply long. These individual young adult lives might then be able to compose a fitting relationship between self and the world—in more adult and satisfying terms.

But, again, more is at stake in the notion of mentoring communities than only the individual lives of all the Lisas and Jeffs. As recognized earlier, young adulthood is the location of the renewal of a culture in every generation. Indeed, the young adult's capacity to critique, to dream, and to stand over and against his or her conventional world sets in place a readiness to speak prophetically to the culture and to build transforming alternatives. What we are beginning to discover, however, is that as important as mentors are in this process, mentors are not enough. A mentor is sufficient if one is to serve the company, the trade, the profession, or the team in conventional terms—in a manner that is contiguous with the past.

But if one is to help transform the structures of society in the direction of more truth, justice, and love, one will have to compose a new faith—a conviction of a more truthful, trustworthy, and dependable pattern of meaning in which one can invest one's life. That sort of reordering of conventional meanings requires the promise that if I go out on this limb, I will have more than a guide pointing the way; I want to see also the promise of a new home, a new network of belonging, a new community, and a new communion. If I am going to sustain a stance that places me over and against my conventional world to potentially serve the quality of its future, I cannot sustain it alone; I cannot stand all alone for very long. If a young adult is to fulfill his or her potential to contribute to the ongoing, positive transformation of society, a mentoring community grounded in a worthy vision is crucial.

Our society has structures that recognize these dynamics. For example, some graduate programs, the military, the Peace Corps, and traditional forms of religious orders all understand the power of mentors and mentoring communities in the lives of young adults. Each offers the promise of a community with one's peers, older adults to point the way, a faith to live by, a cause to live for, and a future as an adult who is needed in the world. Likewise, the world of technology and commerce may also, at times, offer these dynamics. In the creation of the Macintosh® computer, for example, those at the heart of the project were bright young adults in their early 20s. Their relatively young mentor was 28-year-old Steve Jobs. One participant, who described the project as a "pirate operation" conducted by the "bad kids in the company" (note the over-against-ness), said that the group had a "vision we could believe in" of "how we want the world to be" and we "wanted to attract converts." Each member's signature was imprinted inside every Macintosh case, testimony to the group's solidarity and pride in their "mentoring community" (Public Broadcasting System, 1985).

Not every young adult will be disposed to explore the microchip path. Many will not find their dream in graduate academia or in a military that makes less and less sense to critically aware young adults coming of age within a global family. Neither Peace Corps nor traditional religious orders can be options for everyone, particularly when most of the latter require the promise never to marry. Innumerable young adults will find themselves having to search elsewhere.

Images of the Future

To speak simultaneously of the military and the Peace Corps, of religious orders and commercial corporations, may appropriately direct our attention to another crucial aspect of the conditions of moral choice. Our meaning making—our faith—is shaped not only by the dynamics of mentoring communities but also by the particular value content such communities hold. Piagetian insights suggest that the underlying cognitive and social structures (stages) by which our world is composed are significant only because they hold and interpret the images, symbols, and myths we live by. Our meaning making—our faith—is not shaped only by the capacity for critical thought, by the capacity to envision and dream, and by mentors and mentoring communities. The formal properties of thought and the forms of necessary relationships they foster are both relativized by the imagination they serve. Whatever faith we live by, it is formed and held by means of the *images* and the contents that these capacities and structures hold (Parks, 1986). Each mentor and mentoring community holds differing images of the self, the world, and the human future. Different images may have dramatically differing moral valence. To state the case most sharply, one can be mentored into organized crime as well as into a life of altruistic service on behalf of humankind. Both the Ku Klux Klan and the NAACP may serve as mentoring communities. We are accountable for the images and ideologies we do or do not make accessible to young adults. Are the forms we offer for the ordering of life strong enough and true enough to hold and convey the vision of justice and compassion on which the potential of the young adult imagination depends? Do we believe that the image of personal economic success is sufficient to order the path of an adult life? Can we hand on the myth that individual freedom is all that we seek and protect? Do we want another generation to seek a "new frontier" at the price of our planet home?

In light of these concerns, we must recognize that the mentoring structures and images offered to most young adults in our culture exercise their moral power in less dramatic but effectively subtle forms (Parks, 1990). In a portrayal of the current moral climate of the corporate business world, Louis Auchincloss (1986) writes:

> It's all a game, but a game with very strict rules. You have to stay meticulously within the law; the least misstep, if caught, involves an instant penalty. But there is no particular moral opprobrium in incurring a penalty, any more than there is [in] being offside in football. A man who is found to have bought or sold stock on inside information, or misrepresented his assets in a loan application, or put his girl friend on the company payroll, is not "looked down on," except by sentimentalists. He's simply been caught, that's all. Even the public understands that. Watergate showed it. You break the rules, pay the penalty and go back to the game. (pp. 27–28)

Auchincloss helps us to recognize that for a great host of young adults, mentorship, mentoring community, and the images of the future that serve to ground moral choice are mediated through the conventional cultural fabric of the time. The culture itself is, for better or worse, a mentoring community that offers in both explicit and diffused forms the meanings and finally the faiths by which young adults will be initiated into full adulthood. Consider the growing phenomena of many young adults who seem increasingly dependent on "name brand" consumer goods. While they are groping for direction, they mark time on a Gucci watch and head out in a BMW. These images, crafted so as to be resonant with aspirations for excellence and success, are central among the primary "dreams" that our culture—a mentoring community—offers to this generation of young adults.

This means that in every place where young adults dwell, we must ask: Do they have mentors, and if so, who are they? Do they have a mentoring network of belonging? Do their mentors and mentoring communities offer images of the future that are worthy of the potential of the young adult soul? What are we nurturing or neglecting in the lives that hold the power of our own cultural renewal—as we stand on a new frontier in human history when we must build a global sociopolitical community, renew our relationship with the environment, and for the first time have the power to eradicate systemic poverty?

It is tempting to limit our address of these questions about young adults to only the Jeffs and Lisas and their more successful peers—upper-middle-class, urban young adults. However, if the future of our culture and of the wider human family is at stake, it must be recognized that young adults seek to compose the meaning of their lives under a very broad range of social conditions. It must be remembered, for example, that our prisons house predominantly persons of young adult age, increasing numbers of them caught in the quick-fix dream economy of cocaine. Young adults represent also the future of rural, working-class populations (William T. Grant Foundation Commission on Work, Family, and Citizenship, 1988, pp. 113–116). For example, during the writing of this chapter, the windshield of our family car was shattered by a rock as we traveled one warm afternoon along a scenic country highway; the rock was thrown by an unknown strong, attractive young adult with the encouragement of his beer-drinking friends. These young men represent the rural form of young adult anger, frustration, and moral vacuousness as, in the absence of any accessible image of a productive and vibrant future, the potential power of their lives can find only adolescent and increasingly dangerous forms of expression. Two generations now estranged from the farm and its meaning as a way of life, they flounder in the backwaters of rural society, living in barely adequate trailers, experimenting with drugs, working as and where they must, spinning the wheels of the junk cars they manage to piece together so as to create a roar of rage and protest that declares: "I am." But they have no viable place to become and thrive—and no support for finding one. No mentors. No mentoring communities.

Conclusion

We live at a time of extraordinary historical transition, and the moral challenge to all of us who potentially serve a new, young adult generation is clear. If we desire to reorder our personal, public, national, and global life so as to move us into a more just and vibrant future, do we have the will to create and sustain mentoring communities centered in worthy and compelling images of the future? Are we willing both to honor the vulnerability of young adult lives and to mentor the promise of a potentially more faithful generation? As young adults seek to compose the meaning and faith by which they may stake a claim on a vision of adult self and vocation, how will we who are older adults shape the conditions that will ground their moral choice?

Notes

[1]"The forgotten half: Pathways to success for America's youth and young families" (William T. Grant Foundation Commission on Work, Family, and Citizenship, 1988), portrays today's youth as struggling very hard to find their place in a rapidly changing economy. Most work for youth and young adults today is in low-paying service and retail jobs that offer half the earning that many young workers received in manufacturing in the early 1970s. The real median income of young males aged 20 to 24 has plummeted by 25.8% in the past decade. Black high school graduates are substantially more likely to be unemployed than are white dropouts. Between 1973 and 1986, the earnings of black high school graduate males plunged 43.8% (p. 27).

[2]For the concept of a mentoring community, I am indebted, in part, to a conversation with Sr. Mary Hennessey, r.c.

References

Auchincloss, L. (1986). *Diary of a yuppie*. New York: Houghton Mifflin.

Belenky, M., Clinchy, B., Goldberger, N., & Tarule, J. (1986). *Women's ways of knowing: The development of self, mind, and voice*. New York: Basic Books.

Bok, D. (1988). America's crises: Matching talents with public challenges. *Harvard Alumni Gazette, 83*, 13–14.

Buechner, F. (1973). *Wishful thinking: A theological ABC*. New York: Harper & Row.

Daloz, L. A. (1986). *Effective teaching and mentoring: Realizing the transformational power of adult learning experiences*. San Francisco: Jossey-Bass.

Erikson, E. (1963). *Childhood and society* (2nd ed.). New York: W.W. Norton.

Erikson, E. (1964). Human strength and the cycle of generations. In E. Erikson, *Insight and responsibility* (pp. 111–157). New York: W.W. Norton.

Fowler, J. W. (1981). *Stages of faith: The psychology of human development and the quest for meaning*. San Francisco: Harper Collins.

Kegan, R. (1980). There the dance is: Religious dimensions of a developmental framework. In Brusselmans, C. (Ed.), *Toward moral and religious maturity*. Morristown, NJ: Silver Burdette.

Kegan, R. (1982). *The evolving self*. Cambridge, MA: Harvard University Press.

Keniston, K. (1960). *Youth and dissent: The rise of a new opposition*. New York: Harcourt Brace Jovanovich.

Parks, S. (1986). *The critical years: Young adults and the search for meaning, faith, and commitment*. San Francisco: Harper Collins.

Parks, S. D. (1989). Home and pilgrimage: Metaphors for personal and social transformation. *Soundings, 72*, 297–315.

Parks, S. D. (1990). Social vision and moral courage: Mentoring a new generation of educators. *Cross Currents, 40*, 350–367.

Public Broadcasting System. (1985). *In search of excellence* [Film]. Boston: WGBH Television.

William T. Grant Foundation Commission on Work, Family, and Citizenship. (1988). *The forgotten half: Pathways to success for America's youth and young families* (Final report on Youth and America's Future). Washington, D.C.: Author

Index

About the Contributors

Carole R. Beale, who earned her Ph.D. in psychology at Stanford University in 1983, is currently an associate professor of psychology at the University of Massachusetts at Amherst. Her grants, journal publications, and conference presentations focus primarily on children's cognitive monitoring. Specifically, her scholarship deals with children's developing understanding of communication and comprehension processes and their recognition of ambiguity in text. Forthcoming are two coauthored books regarding the development of text interpretation and the recognition of conceptual inconsistencies. Also due to be published by McGraw Hill is *Girls and Boys: The Development of Sex Roles.*

Blythe McVicker Clinchy is professor of psychology at Wellesley College, where she holds the Class of 1949 Chair in Ethics and teaches courses in research methodology and human development. She received her A.B. from Smith College, her M.A. from the New School for Social Research, and her Ph.D. from Harvard University. She is a coauthor of *Women's Ways of Knowing,* published by Basic Books in 1986. She has also published papers on the evolution of conceptions of knowledge, truth, and value in males and females from early childhood through adulthood and on the implications of this development for the practice of education from nursery school through college.

William Damon is chairman of the Education Department at Brown University. He is the author of *The Social World of the Child* and *The Moral Child* and is editor-in-chief of *New Directions for Child Development,* a Jossey-Bass series. His most recent work, coauthored with Anne Colby, his wife, is *Some Do Care: Contemporary Lives of Moral Commitment,* a study of how moral commitment develops throughout life in some extraordinarily dedicated people. He teaches courses on moral education at Brown and has recently been active creating new after-school environments for child development in a project supported by the MacArthur Foundation and Pew Charitable Trusts.

Andrew Garrod is associate professor of education at Dartmouth College in Hanover, New Hampshire, where he teaches courses in adolescence, moral development, and moral education. His recent publications include an essay review, "Making Moral Youth," written with Robert Howard in the *Harvard Educational Review;* an edited book entitled *Learning for Life: Moral Education Theory and Practice;* a two-volume anthology edited with Janet Webster, *Worlds Unrealized: Short Stories of Adolescence in Canadian Fiction;* and a casebook coedited with L. Smulyan, S. Powers, and R. Kilkenny entitled *Adolescent Portraits*. His research interests include adolescence, moral development, and moral education. In 1991, he was awarded Dartmouth College's Distinguished Teaching Award.

Carol Gilligan is the author of *In a Different Voice: Psychological Theory and Women's Development* published by Harvard University Press, and is the director—as well as a founding member—of the Harvard Project on the Psychology of Women and Development of Girls. As professor of human development and psychology at the Harvard Graduate School of Education, she works collaboratively with students, colleagues, clinicians, and teachers. The work of this collaboration appears in *Making Connections*, edited with Nona Lyons and Trudy Hanmer and published by Harvard University Press; *Mapping the Moral Domain*, edited with Janie Ward and Jill Taylor and published by Harvard University Press; *Women, Girls, and Psychotherapy: Reframing Resistance* published by Haworth Press; and a series of working papers.

Martin L. Hoffman is currently chair of the Department of Psychology at New York University. Hoffman, whose Ph.D. is in social psychology from the University of Michigan, has been editor of both the *Merrill-Palmer Quarterly* and the *Psychological Review* and associate editor of *Developmental Psychology*. His most recent publications include articles discussing empathy, justice, and society and have appeared in *Psychological Inquiry, Human Development, Motivation and Emotion* and *Social Justice Research*. He has also contributed numerous chapters to collected works on aspects of moral development.

Robert Kegan is on the senior faculty of the Harvard Graduate School of Education and the Massachusetts School of Professional Psychology. He is a fellow of the Clinical-Developmental Institute. Author of *The Evolving Self: Problems and Process in Human Development* and the forthcoming *Over Our Heads: The Mental Burden of Modern Life*, both published by Harvard University Press, he has been a classroom teacher of junior high, high school, undergraduate, and graduate students. In 1992, the Massachusetts Psychological Association named him Teacher of the Year.

Sharon Lamb, currently an assistant professor at Bryn Mawr College, graduated from Harvard with an Ed.D. in human development in 1988. Her current research centers on the beginnings of moral development in the child and includes early empathy, childhood sexual play and games, responses to distress in a daycare setting, and the moral development of toddlers of adolescent mothers. She coedited *The Emergence of Morality in Young Children* with Jerome Kagan in 1987.

Sharry Langdale is currently assistant professor of psychology and transfer student coordinator at Wheelock College in Boston. Since entering the field of moral development, she has contributed to its body of scholarship. Her publications on moral orientations and development have appeared in various journals, among them *Currents* and *Merrill-Palmer Quarterly*. A graduate of Harvard's doctoral program in education, she has gone on to teach psychology, human development, and education at a number of universities, including the University of New Hampshire, Wheaton College, and the California Institute of Technology.

Nona P. Lyons is the director of teacher education at Brown University. She is coeditor of the book *Making Connections: The Relational World of Adolescent Girls at Emma Willard School*. Before going to Brown University, Lyons taught at the Harvard Graduate School of Education, where she had completed her doctorate in human development. Her research interests have focused on adolescent development and on ethical decision making and conflict resolution with both adolescents and adult men and women managers. Her current work includes a project exploring the ethical and intellectual dimensions of teachers' work, for which she received a Spencer Fellowship, and more recently, a project exploring the use of portfolio narratives in teacher assessment and development.

Sharon Daloz Parks is the author of *The Critical Years: Young Adults and the Search for Meaning, Faith, and Commitment*. She is a senior research fellow in leadership and ethics at Harvard Business School and at the Kennedy School of Government. She is a fellow at the Clinical Developmental Institute in Belmont, Massachusetts. Her current research is focused on the formation of leadership, ethics, and the common good in the face of global complexity. She has served widely as a lecturer and consultant for institutions of higher education, campus ministry associations, and other professional organizations.

Joseph Reimer is an associate professor at Brandeis University working in the Hornstein Program in Jewish Communal Service. After earning his Ed.D. in human development from the Harvard Graduate School of Education, he coordinated the program in human development and education at Boston University. A coauthor of *Promoting Moral Growth: From Piaget to Kohlberg*, his recent contributions to developmental psychology include longitudinal studies concerning moral education and reasoning within communal models. In 1988, he was given the Human Development Research Award along with his coauthors Snarey and Kohlberg.

James R. Rest worked with Lawrence Kohlberg in the early 1970s in the Center for Moral Education at Harvard's Graduate School of Education. Since then, he has authored *Judging Moral Issues* and *Moral Development: Advances in Theory and Research.* A professor in the Department of Education and Psychology at the University of Minnesota and research director of the Center for the Study of Ethical Development, he is also well known for his development of the defining issues test (DIT). The most prominent recognition measure derived from Kohlberg's moral judgment interview, the DIT assesses the evaluation of moral reasoning.